Wild Hokkaidō

*A Guidebook to the National Parks
and other Wild Places
of Eastern Hokkaidō*

JN122163

Mark Brazil

Other Books by Mark Brazil include:

A Birdwatcher's Guide to Japan (1987)
The Birds of Japan (1991)
Wild Asia: Spirit of a Continent (2000)
The Whooper Swan (2003)
Helm Field Guides: Birds of East Asia (2009)
The Nature of Japan: From Dancing Cranes to Flying Fish (2013)
Helm Field Guides: Birds of Japan (2018)
Birds of East Asia (Chinese Edition 2020)
Japan: The Natural History of an Asian Archipelago (2021)

Wild Hokkaidō
A Guidebook to the National Parks and other Wild Places of Eastern Hokkaidō

First published 8 June 2021
Copyright © Mark Brazil 2021

Published by The Hokkaido Shimbun Press,
6 Ōdōri Nishi 3, Chūō-ku, Sapporo, Hokkaidō 060-8711
Tel: +81-11-210-5744

Issued by Hokkaido Shimbun Hot Media

ISBN 978-4-86721-027-7

In cooperation with the Ministry of the Environment

Designed, printed and bound by
iWORD Co. Ltd., Sapporo, Japan

CONTENTS

Preface ⸻ 4

Acknowledgements ⸻ 7

Introduction ⸻ 8

Chapter 1: Eastern Hokkaidō: An Overview ⸻ 16

Chapter 2: Kushiro Shitsugen National Park ⸻ 28

Chapter 3: Akan–Mashū National Park ⸻ 54

Chapter 4: Abashiri Quasi National Park and the Sea of Okhotsk
Coast ⸻ 80

Chapter 5: Shiretoko National Park and World Heritage Site ⸻ 96

Chapter 6: Hokkaidō's Eastern Coast ⸻ 122

Chapter 7: Southeast Hokkaidō and Akkeshi–Kiritappu–
Kombumori Quasi National Park ⸻ 138

Chapter 8: Many Ways to Enjoy Eastern Hokkaidō ⸻ 158

Recommended Hiking Routes ⸻ 162

Bibliography ⸻ 164

Directory ⸻ 166

Index ⸻ 178

The sound of bugling cranes displaying and dancing in falling snow. The noise of sea ice being forced onshore by the wind and tide. The buzz of insect wings over summer flower meadows. The music of swans as they rest and refuel during their long migrations. To the naturalist, east Hokkaidō is a kind of paradise, where all these sights and sounds — and many more besides — can be experienced through the seasons on Japan's northernmost main island.

Iramkarapte! — Irasshaimase! — Welcome!
Ainu greet their guests with the delightful
Iramkarapte —
'Let me gently touch your heart.'
Japanese greet their guests with *Irasshaimase —*
'You are Welcome.'

The people of Hokkaidō have been welcoming visitors for centuries and as a resident of Japan's northernmost prefecture for over 20 years I now feel part of that tradition. You too will find a warm welcome when you visit.

The impetus for creating this guidebook stems from my first visit to Japan in February 1980. I was fortunate to spend time in Hokkaidō and fell in love at first sight. The landscape, the winter season, the wildlife — all were magical to me. I was a postgraduate student then and had hardly stepped outside Britain before so everything about Hokkaidō seemed exotic and exciting.

The only drawback for me during that first and subsequent visits during the 1980s and 1990s was the lack of books in English covering the natural history of the region that was eventually to become my home. Over the intervening decades I have done my best to fill that gap by writing the books[1] I wished had been available when I first visited.

My writing has been inspired by a guide book I found on the shelves of a secondhand book shop in the central English county of Staffordshire in the 1970s, during my studies at Keele University. That serendipitous find was the excellent *Handbook to the Japanese Empire* dated 1891[2], itself incor-

Flocks of Red-crowned Cranes gather at feeding sites in Tsurui Village during winter

1 Brazil (1987, 1991, 2009, 2018a, 2018b).   2 Chamberlain & Mason (1891).

porating an earlier volume *Handbook for Central and Northern Japan* published a decade earlier. Now, 130 years later, I turn to it frequently — it still makes for fascinating reading. As a student, my fascination with Japan was long-range, and all those years ago I had no reason whatsoever to suspect I might one day visit or even live here in the Land of the Rising Sun.

My aim in writing this guidebook to the national parks and other wild places of Eastern Hokkaidō is to introduce you to the lesser-known side of Japan — the wild side — and to lead you to some of my all-time favourite places. In Eastern Hokkaidō you may experience an exciting array of marine and terrestrial mammals such as Northern Minke Whale *Balaenoptera acutorostrata*, Brown Bear *Ursus arctos*, Tanuki *Nyctereutes procyonoides* and Sable *Martes zibellina*. You may also encounter

An adult Red-crowned Crane at Tsurui

dramatic resident birds such as the Red-crowned Crane *Grus japonensis*, which is the prefectural bird of Hokkaidō, and the White-tailed Eagle *Haliaeetus albicilla*[3], as well as numerous delightful summer and winter migrants such as Siberian Rubythroat *Calliope calliope* and Dusky Thrush *Turdus eunomus*.

Kushiro Shitsugen National Park

3 Hereafter referred to as eagles.

The Sable is one of Hokkaidō's top predators

ology of other parts of Japan, then you may enjoy *Japan: The Natural History of an Asian Archipelago*[5]. Then, if you become more interested in the birds of the country, I recommend my field guide *Birds of Japan*[6] which fills that niche. If mammals are your main interest, then there are two excellent books available in English — you need look no further than *A Guide to the Mammals of Japan*, or *The Wild Mammals of Japan*[7]. Other excellent resources are photographic guides to the *Wild Flowers of Hokkaidō*[8] and the *Trees and Shrubs of Hokkaidō*[9]; both are in Japanese but include scientific names.

The majority of the key species of Hokkaidō can be found in the eastern quarter of the island in its three outstanding national parks and many other natural areas — hence my title: *Wild Hokkaidō*.

The maps included will make it possible for you to find most main locations mentioned. In addition, I have provided GPS co-ordinates for all visitor sites to make it easy to locate them. In transliterating local place names I have relied on the long-established and most widely used Hepburn romanisation system[4] for ease of pronunciation.

The structure of this book follows a circuitous journey around the eastern quarter of Hokkaidō — the portion richest in wildlife with its three superb national parks — providing details of when and where to go and how to get there. It also contains information about the sights you might encounter along the way. Short accounts and 'boxes' explore various aspects of the landscape, natural history and wildlife in more detail.

Should you wish to read further to understand more about the natural history, geography, and ge-

This book is the culmination of years of exploration around my favourite region of my favourite Japanese island. It should provide you with sufficient information and insights to enhance your own visit by facilitating a range of rich experiences while drawing you, I hope, into the grip of Hokkaidō's fascinating natural history, natural heritage, and wildlife.

The language of Hokkaidō's indigenous Ainu people is said to have no word for 'Nature', because for them the natural world is divine, to be respected for supporting life, not an object to be exploited. We can and should emulate them. I hope that this book will help you to visit Hokkaidō with a new found sense of respect for this beautiful land.

Should you have suggestions for additional information to include in future editions I would be delighted to hear from you.

Mark Brazil, Teshikaga, Hokkaidō, April 2021

4 Japanese is written without spaces between words rendering transliteration and the interpretation of road signs difficult at times. I have provided names using hyphens to indicate separate words in Japanese to aid in pronunciation. The invaluable Hepburn romanisation system dates back to 1886. Unfortunately, government ministries and agencies often use different systems including the less easily understood (to the non-Japanese ear) Kunrei-shiki form of romanisation. As Hepburn romanisation pronunciation charts including macrons are readily found on the internet I have not included one here. I recommend starting with: https://en.wikipedia.org/wiki/Hepburn_romanization. 5 Brazil (2021). 6 Brazil (2018b). 7 Abe *et al.* (2008) and Ohdachi *et al.* (2015). 8 Umezawa (2007 & 2018). 9 Sato (1990).

Acknowledgements

I have long wanted to write a guidebook to Hokkaidō, so I was delighted when Sasabuchi Kōhei and Kobayashi Yukiko of the Ministry of the Environment, National Parks of Japan, raised the possibility with me. Then they kindly brokered all the many necessary arrangements to make it possible. I give them my greatest thanks.

I thank my colleagues Shinshō Hisashi, curator of Natural History, Kushiro International Wetland Center[10], a specialist on the Kushiro Shitsugen National Park (NP), Dr Wakana Isamu previously curator of Algology at Akankohan Eco-museum Center and a specialist on the Akan–Mashū NP, Kawasaki Yasuhiro, an environmental consultant with considerable experience of the Abashiri Quasi NP, Terayama Gen previously of Shiretoko Nature Foundation, a nature guide, backcountry skier and conservationist specialising on the Shiretoko NP, and Lan Pingfang founder and editor of *It's Hokkaidō!* and a winter ice guide, each of whom gave so generously of their time during interviews and shared so much information on their favourite subjects and sites in Eastern Hokkaidō.

I give special thanks to my friends who have supported me by reading and commenting on early drafts of this book, in particular Chris Cook, Chris Harbard, Brian Haycox, Lois Gray, Kobayashi Yukiko, Kurosawa Nobumichi, Kurosawa Yūko, Angus Macindoe, Ohno Mitsuko, Shinshō Hisashi, Bob Quaccia, and Saga Ayami. I also thank Shiraishi Kai, Takahashi Sumire, Takiguchi Akira, Takiguchi Sayaka, and Yamada Akina, park rangers of the Ministry of the Environment, for kindly fact-checking the manuscript.

I thank Ōtsuka Tamaki at Hokkaido Shimbun Press for promoting this project and bringing it to fruition.

While most of the photographs are from my own collection, taken over a period of nearly 40

Birch woodland supports many insects and birds

years travelling and exploring Eastern Hokkaidō, I am delighted that others graciously gave me permission to use their work for this project. In particular I would like to thank: Akan Ainu Craft Union, Fukuda Toshiji, Gojira-iwa Kanko, Itō Akihiro, Kamada Sachiko, Koshimizu Tourist Association, Kurita Masateru, Ministry of the Environment, Peter Porazzo, Stuart Price, Shiretoko Nature Foundation, Sobue Kenichi, Sugimura Wataru, Nick Szasz, Terasawa Takaki, The Hokkaido Shimbun Press, Wakasa Masanobu, Wada Masahiro, Wakana Isamu and John Williams.

Finally, I thank my wife, Mayumi, for her help and support during the process of writing this book and for her inspirational statement:

'It's not about what you see, it's about being in nature — and Hokkaidō has lots of wild places and wonderful nature. Each season here has its own enticements to make it enjoyable.'

---

10 Although this book is written in English, various organisations have adopted American spelling and used it in their names and signs. I have retained their chosen names regardless of spelling.

Introduction

The Geography of Japan

The elongated Japanese archipelago extends for more than 3,000 km, and lies just east of the margin of the Eurasian continent. It stretches roughly northeast–southwest, spans subtropical to subarctic, and has a topography dominated by mountain ranges and narrow valleys. The multiple islands spanning several climatic zones, with differences in elevations and terrain, combined with the varied seasonal climate in each region of the country, provide conditions suited to a large range of environments and wildlife habitats. More than two-thirds of Japan's landscape is forested and mountainous and, given the ancient sanctity of the mountains, and hence the taboo against building and living there, the majority of the country's 126 million population occupy, in somewhat crowded fashion, the coastal areas, lowlands and inland plains. The majority of Japan's major cities from Okinawa to Hokkaidō, are coastal.

An adult Steller's Eagle rests on sea ice off Rausu

Japan consists of four main islands — in order of size they are Honshū, Hokkaidō, Kyūshū and Shikoku — and thousands of lesser islands. Island chains such as the Izu and Ogasawara islands, that stretch south more than 1,000 km into the Pacific south of Tōkyō, and the long chain of the Nansei Shotō (literally southwest islands) stretching between Kyūshū and Taiwan, add yet further dimensions to the biodiversity of the archipelago, supporting high numbers of endemic species.

The geology, geography, and biodiversity of Japan's islands each make for fascinating subjects, which I have described in some detail in *Japan: The Natural History of an Asian Archipelago*[11]. Japan's culture is equally fascinating, adding intrigue and pleasure to any exploration of the islands; as background reading I recommend *Japanese Culture*[12] and *The Japanese Mind*[13] and the 1946 classic by Ruth Benedict *The Chrysanthemum and the Sword*[14].

Hokkaidō, as Japan's northern main island, offers a wide range of opportunities for adventure travellers and travelling naturalists. Much of the landscape is recognised as having significant conservation and cultural value, as does the wildlife that shares the island with the human population. In the region of this book you will find three very special national parks and many other sites worth visiting.

Japan's Noteworthy National Park System

Japan's first national parks, Setonaikai, Unzen and Kirishima, were nominated in March 1934, and to date a total of 34 national parks have been designated. A little under six percent of the total land area of Japan is currently categorized as national park land. However, as land ownership in Japan follows an ancient and complex system, the land within the national parks is not owned exclusively by the nation; in fact, much of it remains within pri-

11 Brazil (2021).   12 Varley (2000).   13 Davies & Ikeno (2002).   14 Benedict (1989).

vate hands. Consequently, Japan's park system is a co-operative one between public and private entities, making it more similar to the national park system of the UK than that of the USA or Canada. Regardless of land ownership, designation attests to a desire by Japan to protect scenery representative of the country's natural beauty. Today, the national park system in Japan combines that goal of sustaining natural beauty with further aims of conserving Japan's rich biodiversity and educating the public about Japan's environment.

Three of Hokkaidō's six national parks are in the eastern quarter of the prefecture. The three, Kushiro Shitsugen[15] NP, Akan–Mashū NP, and Shiretoko NP, rightly form the major part of this book. These three are joined by numerous other sites of interest, including the Abashiri Quasi NP, the Akkeshi–Kiritappu–Kombumori Quasi NP, and various prefectural parks (designated and managed at the prefectural level) that include the coastal wetlands of the east and southeast coasts. All may be visited readily while travelling around Eastern Hokkaidō.

Hokkaidō, the second largest, and northernmost, of Japan's main islands, differs dramatically from the remainder of Japan to the south. Its climate, habitats and biodiversity, not to mention its history, all differ from mainland Japan. Eastern Hokkaidō in particular is a region beloved of naturalists and is widely considered to provide the richest year-round wildlife-watching opportunities in Japan.

The three national parks of Eastern Hokkaidō may seem like geographically isolated entities, but, as discussions with Wakana Isamu and Shinsho Hisashi revealed, they are in fact intimately connected geologically and hydrologically. The volcanoes of the Shiretoko NP and Akan–Mashū NP actually belong to the same volcanic arc, while the numerous freshwater springs that well up in the Kushiro Shitsugen NP are derived ultimately from the Akan volcanoes. They also share many features of their natural history in common and with other

Aerial view of Hokkaidō's mountainous terrain and boreal forest

areas described in detail in this book.

Under Japan's Natural Parks Law, the Ministry of the Environment makes a distinction between those places of greatest natural scenic beauty with landscapes of national importance, which are designated as national parks, and protected directly by the ministry, and those recognised at the national level but considered to be of a secondary rank (perhaps because of their lesser beauty, size, diversity, or state of preservation), that are also designated by the ministry but as quasi national parks and which are managed by local prefectures.

Japanese law recognises three types of natural parks: national parks, of which there are currently 34, quasi-national parks of which there are currently 58, and more than 300 prefectural natural parks (designated and maintained at the prefectural level). Japan's natural parks provide the framework for conserving landscapes, natural environments and the nation's considerable and unique biodiversity. Together with the national parks, natural

15 Shitsugen means wetland

The Jōmon and the Ainu

This northern island has been known as Hokkaidō only since the beginning of the Meiji Period in 1869 (the name, the characters for which mean north, sea, road, was only formally adopted in 1910). Hokkaidō was previously called Ezo-chi and Yezo and has been home to the indigenous Ainu people for centuries, and their only remaining homeland from the 12th century onwards. Ainu people outnumbered the Japanese in Yezo until the 1800s, though now in Hokkaidō they are a very small minority.

The majority of topographical and place names (mountains, rivers, capes, settlements) in Hokkaidō reflect the cultural heritage of the Ainu. As the Ainu had an oral tradition without a written language and, as the Ainu language was overwhelmed by Japanese following the colonisation of Hokkaidō and the consolidation of modern Japan, the transliteration and pronunciation of Ainu place names today is 'Japanised', nevertheless the Ainu linguistic origins are clear.

The key wildlife species, that so excite visitors to eastern parts of Hokkaidō, are not merely well-known to the Ainu, they are revered by them as deities. For the Ainu, the wild animals that they encountered, hunted and depended on for their livelihoods were deeply significant and recognised as a pantheon of beneficent gods. They believed in them as deities and communed with them in dreams. Some, such as the salmon and bear, were particularly significant because they provided important food at different times of the year, and for the Ainu wild areas were the homes of the gods.

The animistic Ainu traditionally revere physical locations, mountains, rocks and rivers, and living entities such as bears, cranes, eagles, and fish owls. The bear is known as *Kim-un-kamuy*, the deity of the mountains, while the Red-crowned Crane[16] is *Sarurun-kamuy*, the deity of the marshes. The Killer Whale *Orcinus orca* is recognised as *Rep-un-kamuy*, the god of the sea, while somewhat less romantically Steller's Sea Lion *Eume-*

topias jubatus is known as *Etaspe* — the creature that snores! Blakiston's Fish Owl *Bubo blakistoni* is especially revered as *Kotan-kor-kamuy*, the god of the village, no doubt because both owls and Ainu settled and occupied similar riverside locations and confluences of rivers.

For a people who historically lived very close to the land, the rivers and the sea, who were dependent on the bounty those habitats provided, and who revered their native land, it is not surprising that the Ainu language recognises the wildlife and edible plants that they encountered, and relied upon. Nor is it surprising that amongst such tribal people there were regionally different dialects and words for the same things. So for some Ainu, Steller's Eagle *Haliaeetus pelagicus* was the revered deity known as *Kapatcir-kamuy*, while others referred to it as *Ekay-cikap*.

It is clear though that even the Ainu were not the first to settle in Hokkaidō. Archaeological investigation of dwellings, shell middens, and pit graves, and findings of stone micro-

Ainu Elder Nishida Masao of Akan © Nick Szasz

16 As only one species of crane is resident in Hokkaidō, hereafter they are referred to simply as cranes.

blades provide evidence of palae-olithic presence in Hokkaidō from 30,000 years ago and, in the Shire-toko area, from more than 23,000 years ago, when nomadic peoples hunted megafauna there such as Naumann's Elephants *Palaeoloxodon naumanni* and Woolly Mammoths *Mammuthus primigenius*. Perhaps these were ancestral Jōmon people colonising from the south and even-tually reaching Hokkaidō.

Established settlement in Hok-kaidō may only have come once the

Carved Inau mark Ainu sacred sites Please respect them

Blakiston's Fish Owl, the World's larg-est owl, is an Ainu deity

overwhelming influence of the last major ice age receded, some 15,000 years ago (approximately 13,000 BCE) close to the beginning of what is known as the Jōmon period (approximately 16,000 to 2,900 years ago). Cultural continuity and their genetic lineage, which is basal to both ancient and present-day East Asians, indicates that the Jōmon people were direct descendants of Upper Palaeolithic people and ancestors of later Ainu. They were it seems early migrants who followed a coastal route from Southeast Asia to East Asia[17,18].

Humans were here in Hokkaidō even before the formation of modern Lake Akan, the Mashū caldera, and Kushiro wetland. Early Jōmon period sites have been found in Eastern Hokkaidō dating back more than 8,000 years, while an Epi-Jōmon or post-Jōmon culture lasted here from the first to the seventh century CE. This was followed by the Okhotsk culture from the sixth to the eleventh century, which was derived from northern Sakhalin, then the Ainu culture. The relationships between these Jōmon and Okhotsk peoples, their land and the sea, and the bounties derived from each, are believed to have influenced subsequent Ainu culture.

The name Kiritappu, for this cape in southeast Hokkaidō is, like so many others, derived from the Ainu language

Salmon, such as this Cherry Salmon, are revered as an import-ant seasonal food resource © Kamada Sachiko

17 Kanzawa-Kiriyama *et al.* (2019).   18 Gakuhari, Nakagome and Rasmussen *et al.* (2020).

parks protect approximately 15 percent[19] of the national territory including some of the country's most iconic natural landscapes and some of its rarest wildlife species. Together these natural parks welcome over 900 million visitors every year[20].

Japan's natural parks include, in addition to forest, riverine and wetland habitats, agricultural land, areas of forestry, communities and their surroundings, scenery with historical and cultural value, and coastal regions. The parks are intended for a combination of conservation, recreation, tourism and education, and as such an emphasis is placed on a symbiotic relationship between regional communities and the area to be preserved. The management goal of Japanese national parks is a balance between conservation and sustainable use of natural resources in a cooperative partnership between stakeholders.

Hokkaidō is richly provided with areas of great wildlife value. Included in this book are the three jewels of the east, the national parks of Kushiro Shitsugen, Akan–Mashū and Shiretoko, along with two quasi national parks one at Abashiri and one at Akkeshi. In addition, mention is made of two prefectural natural parks, Mount (Mt) Shari and Notsuke–Fūren, a designated wilderness area known as the Mt On-ne-betsu nature conservation area, and a number of national wildlife protection areas. Some of these are separate from and others included within previously mentioned natural parks: Lake Tōfutsu, Shiretoko, Notsuke Peninsula and Notsuke Bay, Lake Fūren, Yururi and Moyururi islands, Daikoku Island, and the Akkeshi–Bekambe-ushi, and Kiritappu wetlands. The landscape here lends itself to exploration and adventure travel.

Eastern Hokkaidō is also richly provided with ancient Jōmon sites and historical and current cultural sites of great significance to the Ainu, making it possible to combine wildlife, adventure and cultural tourism here.

Top Five Wildlife Watching Tips

Binoculars are the most helpful field equipment you can carry

1. Your best equipment is a pair of binoculars — 8x or 10x magnification is highly recommended.

2. Field guides to the birds and mammals of the region will enhance your experience, as will exploring with an experienced wildlife watching guide.

3. Early morning soon after dawn and late afternoon until dusk are the best times of day for watching birds and animals. Butterflies and dragonflies are best seen during the warmer parts of the day, from mid-morning to mid-afternoon.

4. Wear neutral colours and move slowly and quietly to avoid disturbing the wildlife you hope to watch.

5. Be patient, and listen carefully. Animals and birds may be shy or reluctant to show themselves; so learn about their behaviour, their sounds, their tracks, and their droppings to increase your likelihood of finding them.

---

19 Data received from the Ministry of the Environment 2020. 20 In 2018 (the most recent year for which numbers are available), there were 905,138,000 visitors to natural parks. This total includes 371,508,000 to National Parks, 288,108,000 to Quasi-National Parks, and 245,522,000 to Prefectural Natural Parks. Data received from the Ministry of the Environment 2020.

Top Five Precautions — Be Sensible

1. Protect the environment — stay on trails; take your trash (and also any that you might find along the way) away with you; refrain from picking plants.

2. Drive slowly — avoid collisions with Japanese Deer *Cervus nippon*[21] and Red Foxes *Vulpes vulpes*[22] and any other wildlife that may be attracted to the roadside. DO NOT feed wild animals at the roadside.

3. Respect private property — refrain from entering farmland; do not disturb farming or fishing activities or related equipment.

4. You are in bear country — be aware, be cautious, be respectful. Bears are mostly shy and will do their best to avoid you. If you encounter a bear, avoid startling it by running, making sudden moves, or sudden sounds. If the bear does not notice you, move slowly and carefully away. If the bear notices you talk calmly or sing softly so that the bear will

Take the signs seriously; deer are a driving hazard © The Hokkaido Shimbun Press

The Brown Bear is Japan's largest land mammal

Bear warning sign Akan–Mashū NP

recognise that you are there and that you are not a threat. When entering areas with dense undergrowth talk or sing to avoid encounters.

5. You are in Asian Giant Hornet *Vespa mandarina*[23] country — be aware, be cautious. These, and other species of hornets, are far more dangerous than bears (but *not* as dangerous as traffic accidents). Hornets can be aggressive and they may sting multiple times; their stings are immensely painful and potentially life-threatening. If you are approached by a hornet, stay very still until it leaves. Do not wave your hands or flap your arms in an attempt to deter it because you are more likely to excite it to become aggressive instead.

Asian Giant Hornet

21 As only one species of deer occurs in Japan, hereafter it is referred to only as deer.   22 Referred to as fox from now on.   23 This is the largest hornet species in the world, growing up to 4 cm in length.

1

Eastern Hokkaidō: An Overview

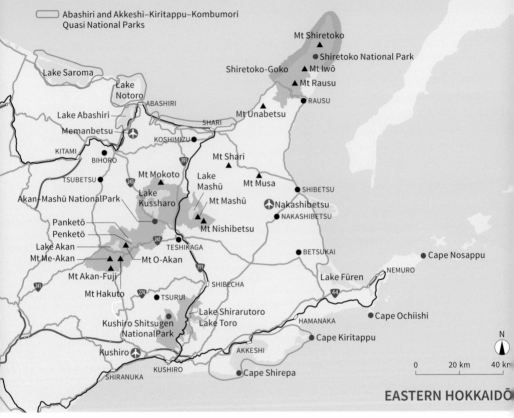

Ababashiri and Akkeshi–Kiritappu–Kombumori
Quasi National Parks

Mt Shiretoko
Shiretoko National Park
Shiretoko-Goko Mt Iwō
Mt Rausu
Lake Saroma
Lake Notoro
ABASHIRI
RAUSU
Lake Abashiri
SHARI Mt Unabetsu
Memanbetsu
KOSHIMIZU
KITAMI
BIHORO
Mt Shari
TSUBETSU Mt Mokoto Lake Mashū Mt Musa
Akan-Mashū National Park Lake Kussharo Mt Mashū SHIBETSU
Nakashibetsu
NAKASHIBETSU
Panketō
Penketō Mt Nishibetsu
Lake Akan TESHIKAGA
Mt Me-Akan Mt O-Akan BETSUKAI Cape Nosappu
Mt Akan-Fuji NEMURO
Lake Fūren
Mt Hakuto SHIBECHA
TSURUI Cape Ochiishi
Lake Shirarutoro
Kushiro Shitsugen National Park Lake Toro HAMANAKA
Cape Kiritappu
Kushiro AKKESHI
KUSHIRO Cape Shirepa
SHIRANUKA

N

0   20 km   40 km

EASTERN HOKKAIDŌ

Hokkaidō is Japan's wild island, blessed with great expanses of natural habitats and considerable areas of protected landscapes. This book, while mainly about the three great national parks of eastern Hokkaidō — the wildest parts of Japan's wildest island — also includes many other areas of natural and scenic beauty. All of them can be visited while travelling a circuit around the eastern quarter of the island, a region that repays spending at least a week or even ten days at any time of year.

In order to appreciate the natural history of this region it helps to have a little understanding of the land itself and the forces that have shaped it. Earth's rigid outermost crust and upper mantle are broken into tectonic plates. The motion of the plates relative to one another, and the boundaries and interactions between them, cause mountain-building, the formation of deep ocean trenches, earthquakes, and volcanic activity.

Japan is situated where several crustal plates converge. Japan's proximity to these plate boundaries makes it one of the most active tectonic zones on Earth. The Pacific Plate to the east and the Philippine Plate to the south are subducting beneath the continental plates on which most of Japan rests. Frequent volcanic activity, earthquakes and tsunami are all consequences of Japan's position, and seismic activity is a daily occurrence here.

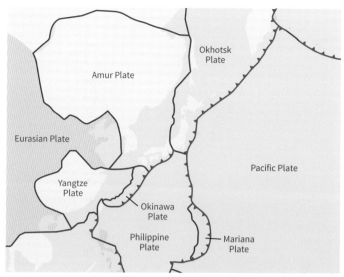

Japan is one of the most active tectonic zones on Earth

Hokkaidō, and Eastern Hokkaidō in particular, represents a microcosm of Japan. Beneath the landscape of Eastern Hokkaidō, ancient and modern tectonic forces are ongoing, shaping the land and providing various bounties. These include fertile volcanic soil, supporting the region's agriculture, the geothermal energy that provides the innumerable hot springs of the popular *onsen*[24] resorts, so beloved of residents and visitors alike, and the pleasing scenic landscape.

Here in Hokkaidō, the Pacific Plate to the east is sliding beneath the Amur Plate to the west and the Okhotsk Plate to the north, with most of Hokkaidō belonging to the Okhotsk Plate. Volcanoes form in relation to plate activity so they are not randomly distributed. They erupt along fronts known as volcanic belts or arcs, typically parallel to and 'inland' of plate boundaries. A unique characteristic of Hokkaidō is that whereas the western two-thirds of the island belongs to the Hokkaidō–Honshū Arc, the eastern third — the focus of this book — belongs to a separate domain, the Kuril and eastern Hokkaidō Arc. This latter volcanic arc stretches for more than 1,000 km between central Hokkaidō and

Volcanoes are prominent features of Eastern Hokkaidō: Mt Akan-Fuji from Me-Akan

the Kamchatka Peninsula.

Eastern Hokkaidō's delightful landscape is a result of volcanic forces. It is dotted with the evidence of geological forces including volcanoes, craters,

24 Hot springs specially used for bathing.

Hokkaidō's volcanic landscape is in constant turmoil: Mt Me-Akan from Akan-Fuji

calderas, hot springs and steam and sulphur vents — all features that tell the story of continual upheaval and eruption, constant turmoil — and it offers extensive plains, rivers, forests, and rugged coasts. The dominant features include enormous Lake Kussharo, and the extraordinarily beautiful Lake Mashū, both of which are key features of the Eastern Hokkaidō landscape. The Kussharo eruption, approximately 400,000 years ago[25], generated Japan's largest caldera, measuring 26 km by 20 km. It ejected an unimaginably large quantity of material. The single most voluminous pyroclastic flow is estimated to have had an astonishing volume of 175 km^3, which covered the whole of eastern Hokkaidō. The smaller Mashū Caldera only 7.5 by 5.5 km, formed on the eastern rim of the Kussharo Caldera about 7,500 years ago. It is estimated to have ejected approximately 18.6 km^3 of tephra[26]. Hokkaidō has the reputation of Japan's wild frontier, its natural biodiversity has been defined by the geological processes that have shaped the land along with its diverse seasonal climatic conditions.

Associated with volcanic activity are spectacular steam vents (as on Mt Me-Akan[27]), geysers (at Rausu in Shiretoko NP), brilliant sulphur-yellow fumaroles (at Iwō-zan[28] in Akan–Mashū NP), bubbling mud pools (at *bokke* beside Lake Akan in the same national park), and geothermally heated soil, beaches, and many warm springs at various locations around the region. Some of these springs

25 And every 20,000 to 40,000 years from 210–40,000 years ago: see Nakada et al. (2016). 26 See Nakada et al. (2016). Some volcanoes erupt lava, others gases, and some tephra. Tephra consists of dust and rock fragments that were ejected into the air. 27 As there is no standardisation of signage you may find this written as Mt MeAkan and Mt Meakan. For ease of pronunciation for non-Japanese speakers I have used Mt Me-Akan throughout. 28 Also written variously as Mt Iwo, Mt Io and Mt Iou. For ease of pronunciation for non-Japanese speakers I have used Mt Iwō throughout.

appear on land, forming hot pools and streams. Others arise underwater, keeping lakes ice-free in winter, still others beside the sea. Wherever they are, it is likely that human or animal life will be taking advantage of them.

Outdoor hot springs, known as *rotenburo*, are often set amidst trees, or in valleys in the mountains, so while you take an early morning dip, they make an ideal base from which to watch local wildlife. On the Shiretoko Peninsula at Rausu, it is possible to watch both wintering species of eagle while indulging in a hot spring bath. From the hot spring at the south end of Lake Kussharo, in the depths of winter it is possible to watch Whooper Swans *Cygnus cygnus* while listening for tiny[29] Band-legged Ground Crickets *Dianemobius nigrofasciatus* chirping[30]. The latter survive in the micro-climate at ground level where geothermal activity keeps the surface soil warm enough for them to survive year-round.

Beautiful Lake Mashū, with Mt Kamuinupuri to the right

Hokkaidō with its active volcanoes and winter sea ice is truly a land of fire and ice situated on the Pacific 'Ring of Fire'. Japan's northernmost island forms the southern border of the Sea of Okhotsk, and is Japan's sub-arctic zone. Until about 60,000 years ago Hokkaidō was connected to the Asian continent by way of a land bridge to the north and north-west across what is now the shallow La Pérouse Strait, Sakhalin Island, and the even shallower Strait of Tartary[31]. Subsequent warming led to sea levels rising and submerging the land bridge, but because of its past existence, Hokkaidō today shares many of its natural characteristics with the adjacent continental coastal region, making it very different from the rest of Japan from a natural history perspective.

Bubbling mud springs, called *bokke*, in Akan–Mashū NP

In contrast to the land bridge to the north, a barrier lay to the south. The relatively deep Tsugaru Strait[32] connects the Sea of Japan with the Pacific

Kotan *rotenburo* beside Lake Kussharo © Ministry of the Environment

---

29 Only 6–12 mm long.   30 The technical term is stridulating.   31 Ono (1990).   32 The Tsugaru Strait, or Tsugaru Kaikyō, is only 20 km across in places. It is 140 m deep in the east, and 200 m deep in the west, and at its deepest it reaches 449 m making it the most significant of the channels separating Hokkaidō from other land masses.

Silver-washed Fritillary is a common sight in Eastern Hokkaidō

Asian Skunk Cabbage flowers emerge soon after the snow melts and well before their leaves appear

Japanese Whitebark Magnolia bloom and leaf at the same time

Ocean, and separates Hokkaidō from Honshū, explaining why Hokkaidō's fauna shares more northern than southern affinities. Many northern species reach their southern limits today in Hokkaidō. Conversely, many species range north through Japan to the northern tip of Honshū but have been unable to cross to Hokkaidō. This line of biogeographical separation is known amongst biologists as Blakiston's Line[33]. From a natural history perspective, Hokkaidō is a unique place.

Though Hokkaidō represents just over 20 percent of Japan's total land area, it is home to less than five percent of Japan's total population. Today, Hokkaidō's main industries are fishing, farming, forestry, mining and tourism, and for many of these Hokkaidō's distinct seasonality is crucial. In particular, its cold boreal winters contrast with its warm, humid summers. Winter reigns for six months of the year in the mountains and for four in the lowlands. The brief summers are glorious and spring and autumn are both rich and colourful.

Spring comes to Hokkaidō during late April and May, when the snow melts in the mountains, and when the first perennial flowers of the year appear, such as the Asian Skunk Cabbage *Lysichiton camtschatcensis* and the yellow flowering evergreen shrub Kamchatka Daphne *Daphne kamtschatica* (a common species of the forest undergrowth). The forests of Eastern Hokkaidō are of two basic types: boreal evergreen coniferous and cool-temperate deciduous. Long before the latter break leaf in spring, Kobus Magnolia *Magnolia kobus* puts forth its delicate creamy flowers and Sargent's Cherry (or North Japanese Hill Cherry) *Prunus sargentii* provides splashes of pale pink on the mountainsides. In coastal meadows the golden-yellow candles of perennial Siberian Lupins *Thermopsis lupinoides* begin to appear.

Then, Japanese Whitebark Magnolias *Magnolia obovata* bloom and their enormous leaves become noticeable, while cascades of white-tipped leaves

33 Named (as is the fish owl) after the English explorer and naturalist Thomas Wright Blakiston (1832–1891).

Summer in Akan–Mashū NP

The wide open scenery of eastern Hokkaidō in early summer

draping forest trees are those of three species of vine: Hardy Kiwi Vine *Actinidia arguta*, Variegated Kiwi Vine *Actinidia kolomikta* and Silver Vine *Actinidia polygama*[34]. As soon as the early summer days turn hot and become humid during late May and June, Japanese Cicadas *Terpnosia nigricosta* first become noisy, producing an almost deafening high-pitched drilling sound.

As summer proceeds, from July onwards, the soft buzzing of the Small Hokkaidō Cicada *Lyristes bihamatus* becomes more noticeable and a wide range of butterfly and dragonfly species begin to emerge including species such as the spectacular Alpine Black Swallowtail *Papilio maackii*, Black-veined White *Aporia crataegi*, Boreal Dragonfly *Leucorrhinia intermedia*, Red-eyed Damselfly *Erythromma humerale* and the very large Subarctic Darner *Aeshna subarctica* dragonfly. The forest herb layer is now rich with flowers and coastal grasslands become delightful with the varied colours of their many wildflower species that include yellow Siberian Lupins, pink Wild Roses *Rosa rugosa* and beautiful purple irises (both Japanese Iris *Iris laevigata* and Japanese Water Iris *Iris kaempferi*). The fresh greens of spring turn deeper and darker during summer (June, July and August). Meanwhile in the mountains, in the alpine zone, the array of colourful wildflowers changes steadily

week by week.

Late summer can be unsettled with frequent rainy days and generally increasing heat and humidity, but by mid August mornings may turn cool and hints of autumn appear. One of those hints is the chirping sound of the Ussuri Bush Cricket *Gampsocleis ussuriensis*, as it gives brief bursts of stridulation from areas of dense grassland.

By mid September the colours of autumn begin a rapid descent from the higher mountains and steadily approach the lowlands. Erman's (or Stone) Birches *Betula ermanii* in yellow, or Japanese Rowan *Sorbus commixta* in red, contrast beautifully with Japanese Stone Pines *Pinus pumila* in dark

Wild Rose: the prefectural flower of Hokkaidō

34 Also called Silverleaf Vine.

Autumn colours of Japanese Stone Pine and Japanese Rowan in Akan–Mashū NP

The huge leaves of Asian Skunk Cabbage after flowering

green as the general appearance of the forest begins to turn tawny. Here and there the cascades of deep red draping down the trunks of various host trees are the large leaves of the delightful Crimson Glory Vine *Vitis coignetiae*. While salmon are running in the rivers, the roadsides and forest edges are rich with the final flowers of the year.

The first snows of the winter may dust the highest peaks during September and steadily the local world turns white. The dwarf bamboo, the common ground cover in East Hokkaidō forests, bows under the weight of accumulating snow and eventually disappears beneath it. The rigid stems of the Heartleaf Lily *Cardiocrinum cordatum*[35], which flowered in July and August, stand tall and dry now, ready to rattle and vibrate in the wind and scatter their wafer-like seeds across the frozen

35 This species, along with many other common plants of east Hokkaidō, serve as traditional elements of Ainu cuisine and medicine. The bark of some trees is even used to make cloth.

snow surface.

The approaching sea ice eventually arrives, damping the coastal waves and silencing them, as it stretches in such a broad white expanse that it is difficult to know where land ends and sea begins. The winter drift-ice on the Sea of Okhotsk is the southernmost in the northern hemisphere. It reaches the shore of the Shiretoko Peninsula and flows into the Nemuro Strait[36] between East Hokkaidō and Kunashiri Island. Drifting ice is a harbinger of deep winter; it contributes to the further chilling of Hokkaidō and brings with it a web of life ranging from macro-planktonic Sea Angels *Clione limacina* to marine mammals, including sea lions and seals. The sea beneath the drift-ice is rich and plentiful with plankton and associated fish, but it is in late winter and early spring when the ice begins to melt that the explosive increase in phytoplankton occurs followed by a proliferation of zooplankton and finally yet more fish and the species that prey upon them.

Much of Eastern Hokkaidō is mountainous with extensive boreal forests, but it also has coastal wetlands, craggy cliffs, and offshore islands. The forests are dominated by a mixture of northern species including subarctic conifers, such as the Ezo Spruce *Picea jezoensis* and Sakhalin Fir *Abies sachalinensis*, and hardy deciduous trees including Mizunara Oak *Quercus crispula*[37], Father David Elm *Ulmus davidiana*, Manchurian Ash *Fraxinus mandschurica*, Späth's Ash *Fraxinus spaethiana*, Katsura *Cercidiphyllum japonicum*, Japanese Wingnut *Pterocarya rhoifolia*, Japanese Walnut[38] *Juglans ailantifolia*, Erman's Birch and Siebold's Beech *Fagus sieboldii*[39]. The undergrowth is typically dominated by evergreen dwarf bamboo (otherwise known as bamboo grass), the species mix depending on the elevation. At lower elevations the forests support more cool-temperate hardwoods, such as oaks, maples, elms, limes and magnolias,

Stone Pine grows at low elevation near Kawayu Onsen

Autumn beside Lake Kussharo

along with Prickly Castor Oil Tree *Kalopanax pictus*[40], Koshiabura *Acanthopanax sciadophylloides*, and Amur Cork Tree *Phellodendron amurense* with a shrubby undergrowth of Forked Viburnum *Viburnum furcatum*, Oval-leaved Blueberry *Vaccinium ovalifolium* and Japanese Rhododendron *Rhododendron brachycarpum*. Colourful woody vines such as Climbing Hydrangea *Hydrangea petiolaris*, various kiwi vines, Oriental Bittersweet *Celastrus orbiculatus* and Climbing Lacquer or Climbing Sumac *Rhus ambigua*, and colourful shrubs such as Siebold's Spindle or Hamilton's Spindletree *Euonymus sieboldianus*, with its bright orange fruits,

---

36 Also called the Notsuke Strait or the Kunashirsky Strait.   37 Sometimes considered a subspecies of Mongolian Oak *Quercus mongolica*.   38 Also called Heartnut.   39 Also called *Fagus crenata*.   40 Also called Castor Aralia and *Kalopanax septemlobus*.

Drift ice on the Sea of Okhotsk

Boreal forest in Akan–Mashū NP

bring an added dash of vividness to the forests at various seasons.

Thanks to the extent of forest, lake and marsh-land habitats protected as nature parks, Eastern Hokkaidō supports populations of bears, deer, foxes, Tanuki and Sable, and is visited by wintering flocks of waterfowl such as Whooper Swans. It is also famous for its breeding population of graceful cranes[41].

Mixed deciduous forest near Kushiro Shitsugen NP

41 For further general background see Higashi, Osawa & Kanagawa (1993) and Brazil (2021).

Ten Additional Attractions in Eastern Hokkaidō

1. In Kushiro City, the Kushiro City Museum[42] is excellent with fascinating exhibits well displayed. It has a very fine natural history floor and an interesting collection of Ainu artefacts.
2. In the Akan–Mashū NP, the small Kussharo Kotan Ainu Museum[43], beside Lake Kussharo, is engaging. Open only in summer.
3. Nearby, at Marukibune in Kotan, you can enjoy a modern Ainu music and dance performance by *Ainu Moshiri*.
4. A little further north, in Kawayu Onsen, there is the engrossing Taihō Sumo Museum[44] dedicated to a famous grappler from the town — the great Taiho.
5. In Abashiri City, the Hokkaidō Museum of Northern Peoples[45] is well worth a visit. Its extensive scope helps put the presence of the Ainu in Hokkaidō in a broader context
6. The Drift Ice Museum[46], also in Abashiri City, is worth a brief stop and has a splendid view from the roof terrace.
7. In Shibetsu Town, the Shibetsu Salmon Science Museum and Salmon Park[47] offers an opportunity to learn much about this very special group of fish and, during summer and autumn, to watch them heading upstream.
8. In Shari Town, the rather old-fashioned Shiretoko Museum[48] has extensive exhibits on the history and natural environment of the town and the Shiretoko Peninsula, though there is little labelling in English.
9. In Utoro Town, the Shiretoko World Heritage Conservation Center[49] presents interesting background information on, and provides an excellent overview of, the Shiretoko Peninsula and the wildlife of the region.
10. In Rausu Town, the Rausu Visitor Center[50] has a small selection of exhibits and information on the local area. A very short walk behind the visitor centre reveals a geyser that erupts approximately once an hour.

Ainu ikupasuy (spatula), Kushiro City Museum

The great Taihō, outside the Taihō Sumo Museum, Kawayu Onsen   Ainu necklace, Kushiro City Museum

42 42.974562, 144.403345   43 43.5633354, 144.3422241   44 43.635321, 144.4376919   45 43.996801, 144.239537   46 44.000499, 144.238997   47 43.659719, 145.1158841   48 43.912766, 144.67275   49 44.0694826, 144.991301   50 44.0320183, 145.1613934

2

Chapter Two

Kushiro Shitsugen National Park

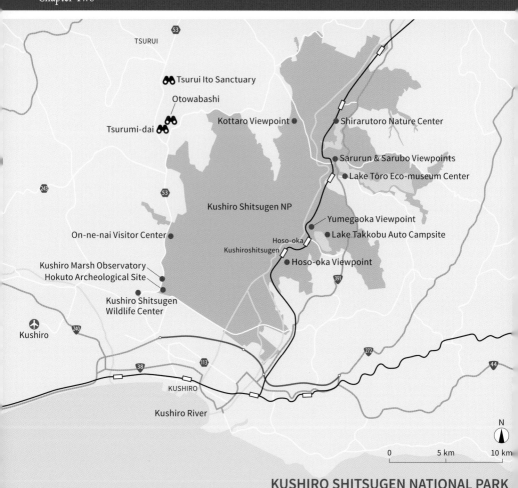

TSURUI

Tsurui Ito Sanctuary

Otowabashi

Tsurumi-dai

Kottaro Viewpoint ●

Shirarutoro Nature Center

● Sarurun & Sarubo Viewpoints

● Lake Tōro Eco-museum Center

Kushiro Shitsugen NP

Yumegaoka Viewpoint

On-ne-nai Visitor Center ●

● Lake Takkobu Auto Campsite

Hoso-oka

Kushiroshitsugen

Kushiro Marsh Observatory

● Hoso-oka Viewpoint

Hokuto Archeological Site

Kushiro Shitsugen
Wildlife Center

Kushiro

KUSHIRO

Kushiro River

N

0   5 km   10 km

KUSHIRO SHITSUGEN NATIONAL PARK

Hokkaidō's Wetland Heaven

Not all of Eastern Hokkaidō's landscapes are mountainous; in south-east Hokkaidō, north of the coastal city of Kushiro (population c 166,000[51]), lies Kushiro Shitsugen NP[52]. This is Japan's largest wetland of 22,070 ha, stretching 36 km from north to south and 25 km from east to west, and spanning parts of Kushiro City, Kushiro Town, Shibecha Town, and Tsurui Village.

Approximately 10,000 to 6,000 years ago, what is now an enormous peaty mire was merely an inlet of the sea. From 4,000 years or so ago, the sea retreated. Steady silting from the outpourings of volcanoes in eastern Hokkaidō, carried by the many streams and rivers that feed into Kushiro Marsh, created the swampy delta of the Kushiro River. It has subsequently become overgrown and morphed over the millennia into the freshwater wet-

51 September 2020 per Ministry of the Environment.   52 Designated as a national park on 31 July 1987 as Japan's 28th national park.

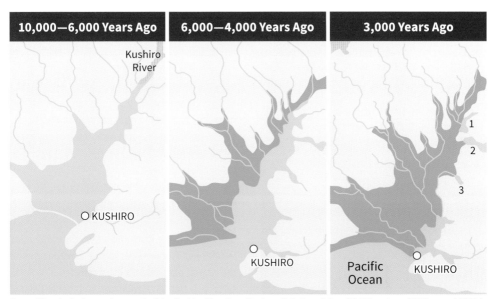

| 10,000—6,000 Years Ago | 6,000—4,000 Years Ago | 3,000 Years Ago |

Kushiro River

○ KUSHIRO

○ KUSHIRO

1
2
3

Pacific Ocean   ○ KUSHIRO

Over millennia the bay at the mouth of the Kushiro River has silted up. Only three lakes, (1) Shirarutoro, (2) Tōro, and (3) Takkobu, survive today

When summer comes at last to Kushiro Shitsugen NP it turns emerald green

land we see today, with three relict lakes (Takkobu, Tōro, and Shirarutoro) along the eastern side. The escarpments around today's wetlands were once coastal cliffs and slopes, and the whole area has a tendency to rise to the west and subside to the east, which is why water accumulates there in the Kushiro River and in the lakes.

Kushiro Shitsugen NP encompasses Japan's largest remaining natural lowland habitat, and the largest swamp forest and lowland marsh in Japan.

It includes the marshland itself, the three relict lakes and some of the surrounding woodland habitat. It also overlaps an internationally recognised wetland site. A total of 7,863 ha was listed under the Ramsar Convention in 1980, making it Japan's first wetland to be listed under the convention. It is a rarity amongst Japan's national parks, as most are in the mountains. The Kushiro wetlands are not only low-lying, they are also lower than much adjacent land, very close to human settlements, agriculture and industry, so that the impacts of human activities flow in from the surrounding areas. Fortunately, there is local awareness of the value of the wetland for water absorption, flood control, wildlife habitat and tourism.

Kushiro Wetland is dominated by reed marsh and swamp forest

Today, the area of Kushiro Shitsugen NP consists mostly of reed-sedge marshland, swamp forest mostly of alder, and peat swamp through which flows the Kushiro River and an intricate web of its tributaries. The pristine natural environment of the central portion is strictly protected as a Ramsar site, a Natural Monument, a National Wildlife Protection Area, and as a National Park Special Protection Zone. The surrounding areas have experienced differing extents of environmental deterioration resulting from land development and past river improvement projects that have led to changes in the wetland vegetation. To counter these issues, restoration projects including of the

Kushiro River meanders through Kushiro Wetland

surrounding woodlands and the meanders of the Kushiro River have been implemented.[53]

The wetlands filter and purify the water that falls here as rain, and more than 20,000 springs around Kushiro Shitsugen deliver an average of 5–10 tons per day per spring of never-freezing freshwater. Several of these springs and their streams can be seen if you walk the Yume-ga-oka trail along the interface of the hills and the wetlands from Takkobu Auto Campground. The winding streams and rivers follow mostly natural courses through the wetland and are flanked by riparian alder woodland as they meander through extensive reed marsh and peat swamp. The iconic species of the marshland here is the crane.

The Hokkaidō Brown Frog is a typical wetland inhabitant

Viewpoints to the west (at Hokuto[54]), east (at Hoso-oka[55]), and north (at Cape Kirakotan and Cape Miyajima[56]) provide opportunities to grasp the enormity of this beautiful landscape and to visualise the ongoing ecological processes here[57]. The entirety of central Tōkyō could be lost in this national park.

Canoeing is possible along Kushiro River from Lake Kussharo to Kushiro Wetland and beyond © Ministry of the Environment

Kushiro draws thousands of visitors each winter determined to watch and photograph the stately cranes at their regular feeding grounds in their cold season home. A railway line, between Kushiro and Abashiri cities, runs alongside the eastern flank of the marsh and is served for part of its length in winter by a steam locomotive and tourist train, which is attractive to riders on and photographers of such engines. But there is much more to Kushiro than cranes and steam locomotives.

The wetlands of the national park are easily understood as a natural sponge for flood control and as important wildlife habitat, but they are also Kushiro's main tourist attraction. The wetlands provide sought-after opportunities for relaxation and recreation, for experiencing the healing sounds of the wind, the rustling reeds, the summer

Swamp forest with sedge tussocks

53 Kushiro International Wetland Centre (2016) provides excellent information on Kushiro wetland. 54 43.074010, 144.320690 55 43.098130, 144.449234 56 See http://tsurui-kanko.com/pdf/pmf-eng-2016.pdf: 43.156690, 144.360759 57 Both Hokuto and Hoso-oka can be visited easily. However, Cape Kirakotan and Cape Miyajima require special permission from Tsurui Village because they are within special protected natural monument areas managed by the national government or involve private property.

Red-crowned Crane — Deity of the Marshes

The stately and elegant Red-crowned Crane is an ancient and potent symbol of long life and happiness. Known as *Sarurun Kamuy* to Ainu and *Tanchō* to Japanese, its stronghold today is in Eastern Hokkaidō.

It once occurred much more widely in Japan, but despite its cultural significance, this crane — the only one resident in Japan — which stands about 1.5 m tall and has a wingspan of 2.4 metres, was hunted and nearly exterminated before conservation measures were put in place a century ago. From a critical low of fewer than 30 birds that survived in the Kushiro wetland area in the early twentieth century, its numbers have recovered to almost 2,000 today and its range has spread both westwards and northwards from Kushiro thanks to a combination of legal protection, habitat protection, and winter feeding.

During summer, monogamous crane pairs disperse widely and occupy large territories in the wetlands of Eastern Hokkaidō, where they breed. They build an enormous nest on the ground in which the female lays two white eggs. There are many challenges to raising their chicks successfully and whereas some pairs may raise both, some may raise only one, and others may fail entirely.

In the lush green of the summer reed beds even these tall birds are well hidden. From midsummer onwards the surviving crane families wander away from their nesting areas and along streams and wetland edges in search of food. Eventually, as the waters of the marshes cool in autumn, they will forsake their breeding grounds entirely and move to agricultural land to glean food from the post-harvest waste. During autumn they gather into ever larger groups and ultimately move to their wintering grounds where flocks gather during the day and number 100 or more birds at a time. Each evening they fly off to roost at safe sites in nearby rivers. Three important viewing sites north of Kushiro, two in Tsurui village (the Tsurui Ito Tancho Sanctuary[58] and Tsurumi-dai[59]) and one in Akan town (Akan Tancho no Sato[60]), allow visitors to watch and

The supremely elegant Red-crowned Crane gathers in Tsurui Village in winter © Wada Masahiro

58 43.227973, 144.331720   59 43.178410, 144.319397   60 43.144065, 144.149529

photograph the cranes at very close range.

Images of this iconic crane can be found gracing a wide range of items from saké labels to gorgeous silk wedding kimonos. Shintō shrines are frequently draped with leis of thousands of colourful origami representations of cranes. Although other species of cranes do occur in Japan, the Red-crowned Crane has been the most popular subject in traditional Japanese art because of its beauty, and as a symbol of conjugal love. Not only is it an ancient symbol of happiness, but myth tells us that it lives for a thousand years.

As winter progresses adult crane pairs, the epitome of grace, duet and dance as they engage in their winter courtship displays to re-kindle and reinforce their pair bonds and prepare for the breeding season that lies ahead. By late winter they spend more and

An adult crane carefully guards its growing youngster

more of their time engaged in courtship. Few sights are more inspiring than the spectacle of graceful monochrome snow ballerinas leaping, dancing and pirouetting in gently falling snow, creating a wonderful winter spectacle on the fringe of Kushiro Marsh.

Bare red skin on the crown becomes more conspicuous when excited

Crane legs and feet are covered with scales

Black wing feathers hang over and hide the white tail

In flight, cranes reveal their black wing feathers and white tails

The graceful courtship dance of the Red-crowned Crane
The crane is the prefectural bird of Hokkaidō © John Williams

bird song, and for feeling the wellbeing derived from relaxing natural movement. Canoeing on the lakes and rivers has become popular, and hiking, cycling and horse trekking on the tracks and trails are increasingly attractive. All are low-impact non-polluting activities that offer 'slow time'.

A cold ocean current (the Oyashio) flows down from the Bering Sea passing offshore just south of Kushiro. Warm, humid winds from the south cool rapidly as they pass over this cold water current and, as a consequence, waves of fog are generated that roll inland on more than 100 days of the year, mostly in summer. These fog banks can reach the lakes of Kushiro Shitsugen, and even as far north as Lake Mashū, settling in over the water and sometimes lasting all day. Elsewhere inland, fog tends to be a morning phenomenon that burns off with the sun. Frigid winter temperatures and cooling fog in summer leave the Kushiro area with a rather cool climate and an annual mean temperature of only

Reeds are pioneers, occupying wet and poorly drained areas

$6°C$[61]. This greatly influences the flora and fauna of the Kushiro Plain.

The main sources of the water flowing through Kushiro Wetland are the numerous streams arising from the northwest, north and northeast and seasonal rainfall; however the main inflow is that of its largest river — the Kushiro River. This river arises fully formed, from the southeastern corner of Lake Kusshato in the Akan–Mashū NP (see Chapter Three), and draws to itself many smaller rivers and streams before eventually flowing out to the Pacific Ocean at Kushiro City.

Kushiro's wetland, once a large bay, then a delta, has been formed by the steady inflow of silt, carried by many streams from the surrounding uplands and volcanoes. Over a period of several thousand years the delta has silted up almost completely. Ecological succession, and the year-round cool conditions experienced here, have allowed the steadily shallowing wetland to develop initially as a peat swamp topped with reed marsh. Subsequently, as Common Reeds *Phragmites australis* have helped to dry out the swamp, it is now being colonised steadily by alder forest.

It is well worth following the course of the Kushiro River. As you leave behind the stunning scenery of Akan's volcanic peaks, you enter a slow, quiet world, the greatest expanse of wetland habitat that remains in Japan, where the enormous fish, the Japanese Huchen *Hucho perryi*[62], three cold-adapted native amphibians Hokkaidō Brown Frog *Rana pirica*, Japanese Tree Frog *Hyla japonica* and Siberian Salamander *Salamandrella keyserlingii*[63], and as many as 48 species of dragonfly live[64].

On cool summer nights, the calling of the frogs from below, the bizarre sounds of Latham's Snipe *Gallinago hardwickii* displaying above and, on misty summer mornings, the far-carrying calls of

---

61 An interesting read, if your interests include geography is: Ito et al. (2011).   62 Also called the Sakhalin Taimen *Parahucho perryi*, they grow to a metre in length and weigh up to 30 kg.   63 See Sato (1993) for more on salamanders in the Kushiro wetlands.   64 See Ubukata (1993) for more on dragonflies in the Kushiro wetlands.

Subnivean Life

If you notice a fox in winter leaping into the air and punching down through the frost-crusted snow layer covering a field, then it is almost certainly hunting voles. Voles, such as the Grey Red-backed Vole *Myodes rufocanus*, are small rodents that are active throughout the year, but in winter they take up a subnivean existence. Their burrows, runs and dens are at the surface of the ground, but beneath the snow — half ground burrow, half snow burrow.

In spring, after the snow has melted the movements of the voles can be traced in the strange grooved patterns they leave in the dried grasses at the surface. The long grooves are the bottom halves of their winter burrows used for travelling between feeding areas, their den and their latrine. A ball-like bundle of dried grasses will be the den, and the separate area with concentrated piles of droppings is clearly their latrine.

In woodland, voles also winter beneath the snow. There they take to chewing the bark of certain trees

Foxes patrol open fields in search of voles beneath the snow

and branches where they are buried beneath the protective niveous layer. Once their feeding sites are exposed in spring you will notice how neatly they have nibbled off the outer and inner bark leaving a clear border around the nibbled patch, which is typically low down on the trunk near the base, or along branches that have been lying beneath the snow.

the Common Cuckoo *Cuculus canorus* and Black-browed Reed Warbler *Acrocephalus bistrigiceps*, all serve to bring the marsh to life. In winter these sounds are replaced by brittle Common Reed stems rattling, frosted river ice cracking, and the soughing of the wind. In the brief interlude between winter and summer, impressive cries echo across the marshes — these are the powerful duetting calls of the graceful cranes.

The main gateway to Eastern Hokkaidō is through Kushiro — either at Kushiro Railway Station[65], the adjacent bus station, or at Tancho Kushiro Airport[66]. The airport, named after the crane, is situated on low hills to the northwest of Kushiro

City, where it avoids much of the summer fog. It makes an ideal starting point for exploring the region. Rental vehicles are readily available there.

Leaving the airport, a broad, cherry tree-lined road descends gently towards Kushiro Plain. A large statue of a pair of cranes stands in the central reservation of the road and mixed woodlands spread to either side. The large rhubarb-like leaves found beside this road from spring to early autumn, and beside roads and streams elsewhere, are those of the Japanese Butterbur *Petasites japonicus* (see page 76) and the forest floor is carpeted with more butterbur and dwarf bamboo. Dwarf bamboo is the dominant ground cover in Eastern

65 42.990695, 144.381791   66 43.045088, 144.196729

Oriental Crow (L) and Japanese Crow (R) are common throughout Eastern Hokkaidō

Hokkaidō. In May, the forest is dotted with the pink of mountain cherries and the white of flowering magnolias blooming here and there in the forest with some forest trees just beginning to open their first leaf buds.

Continuing from the airport on Route (Rt) 952 the way is signed to Tsurui 31 km and Central Kushiro 20 km. As you cross the low plain, the scenery is dominated by Japanese Alder *Alnus japonica* woodland and occasional pasture land. In summer Stejneger's Stonechats *Saxicola stejnegeri* can be seen beside the road and occasionally Common Cuckoos can be seen flying across. In winter, the whole area is white with snow and occasionally it is possible to see foxes patrolling open areas. Solar

farms dot the landscape and you may notice Eastern Hokkaidō's only Ferris wheel. To the north and ahead there are low hills, while to the south lies Kushiro City. Turn right onto Rt 666, cross the Akan River, then continue until meeting the junction with Rt 53.

Two common species of crows the Oriental *Corvus orientalis* and Japanese Crows *Corvus japonensis*[67] can frequently be seen at the roadside, in the fields, and in the woodland throughout Hokkaidō. Look out for occasional cranes, and, if you visit during migration season, look for flocks of Whooper Swans on the fields. In May, bright yellow Common Dandelions *Taraxacum officinale*[68] line the roadside. Notice the red and white arrows

Hokuto Archaelogical Site has a museum, woodland trails and a viewpoint overlooking Kushiro Wetland

67 Sometimes referred to as Carrion Crow *Corvus corone* and Large-billed Crow *Corvus macrorhynchos*.   68 A non-native species.

White-tailed Eagle

This enormous eagle is Japan's second largest bird of prey (after Steller's Eagle) with a wingspan of between 1.9 and 2.4 metres. It can be seen year-round in Eastern Hokkaidō where a number of pairs breed near rivers, lakes and coastal lagoons, placing their huge stick nests in tall trees commanding broad views. Numbers are supplemented in autumn when birds that have bred in eastern Russia migrate into Hokkaidō for the winter months from November to March before migrating back northwards. Eagles spend the winter along ice-free sections of coasts and rivers, hunting for fish, duck and gulls, and scouring shores and inland forests for carcasses (seal and deer) at which they scavenge.

Wherever one travels in Eastern Hokkaidō during winter, there is always the chance of seeing a magnificent eagle soaring overhead.

White-tailed Eagles spend considerable time soaring (centre © Fukuda Toshiji) while searching for prey. In winter, lake ice, and coastal drift ice provide convenient surfaces on which to dismember prey

pointing down towards the road edge and the barriers on the side of the road standing taller than a vehicle; these are snow fences to prevent blizzards from blocking the road and arrows to mark the road edge — they are invaluable during white-out conditions brought on by blizzards.

In winter the landscape appears bleak, snow-covered and windswept, but there are other exciting things to look for in addition to the cranes. Watch out for occasional eagles flying lazily across the landscape. Here and there, dairy farm land gives way to the natural swamp vegetation — Common Reeds that stand one to two metres tall and line the ditches and streams.

Take a turn to the left (northwards) onto Rt 53 which is signposted to Tsurui Village and Teshikaga. Along the way notice that the roadside embankments are covered with dwarf bamboo and that the native forests of this region consists of oaks, Japanese Limes or Japanese Lindens *Tilia japonica*, Father David Elms and a mixture of other summer green broadleaved species.

Approximately 1.5 km ahead, to the left of the road, you will find the Kushiro Shitsugen Wildlife Center[69], a public facility which provides treatment for injured raptors and other birds with an exhibition hall where visitors can learn about the natural history of the area. Just over a kilometre further on along Rt 53, those interested in the history of human presence in the area may wish to turn off to the right at the sign to the Hokuto Site[70]. A short drive takes you to the Hokuto Archaeological Museum[71], behind which a wooden walkway leads up steps to a low hill 700 m away. The trail continues through open woodland and eventually reaches a

The view to the east across Kushiro Shitsugen NP

low wooden tower from which there is a view to the east across the open floodplain and the alder woodland that now covers much of it. In the foreground there are reconstructions of ancient dwellings with thatched roofs indicative of where and how people used to live.

The forest here offers pleasant walks on clear, well-marked trails. In summer look for numerous butterfly species including the Old World or Yellow Swallowtail *Papilio machaon* and others. Birds include the Great Spotted Woodpecker *Dendrocopos major*, Eurasian Treecreeper *Certhia familiaris*, Eastern Crowned Warbler *Phylloscopus coronatus*, and Sakhalin Leaf Warbler *Phylloscopus borealoides*. In spring, low-lying wet areas are enlivened by the enormous blooms of the Asian Skunk Cabbage, a member of the Arum family. The same areas support tall tussocks of the grass-like perennial Tufted Sedge *Carex cespitosa*, these tussocks are known locally as *yachibōzu* meaning bald head of the marshes.

Back on the main road once more, continuing uphill northwards, a large sign on your right announces Kushiro Shitsugen NP. Just beyond the sign Kushiro Marsh Observatory[72] is clearly signposted on the right. The unmistakable observatory

building, situated on the top of the hill, is shaped like a cross between a silo and lighthouse, but with pillars and castle-like crenellations! To the left of the entrance, a boardwalk leads down into the forest and offers views of Kushiro wetland.

In the low-lying low moor, there is a mixture of reed marsh and alder woodland which is slowly colonising the wetland area. A pleasant stroll along the boardwalk takes you to 'Satellite Tenbō-dai' (Satellite Viewpoint) from which there is a wonderful panoramic view east across Kushiro Wetland. Far out in the middle of the marsh a small area of open water glints in the sunlight.

In spring the woods are open, airy and seem exposed, though a few months later they are lush with dense knee-high vegetation. Look on the forest floor in spring for the large, pleated leaves of the White Hellebore[73] *Veratrum album*, and the tiny blue bell flowers of Blue Corydalis *Corydalis fumariifolia*. Although the hellebore is poisonous, the tall whitish flower spikes provide nectar for numerous insect species. The forest route loops back eventually to the parking area and the base of the strange observatory from which the view south is to Kushiro City and beyond it the Pacific Ocean.

A further kilometre along Rt 53, north of the

72 43.073650, 144.320446   73 Also called False Helleborine.

Mt Akan-Fuji (L) and Mt Me-Akan (R) are prominent features on the skyline

marsh observatory, there is a parking area on the east side of the road with a sign for the Kushiro Shitsugen NP. There is a rather pleasant vista here eastwards across the wetlands, which can be admired without having to walk through the forest. As Rt 53 continues northwards towards Tsurui Village (the winter crane capital and home of a superb hot spring at the cosy and welcoming Hotel Taito), there are occasional glimpses of the marsh through the trees to the right before the summer leaves become so dense that they obscure the view.

Keep an eye also to the northwestern horizon for the first glimpses of the Akan volcanoes. Once you have located the dramatic volcanic complex, you will see that at the western end there is a conically shaped peak: this is Mt Akan-Fuji[74]. Immediately to its right is the compact massif of Mt Me-Akan. This volcano is constantly active, billowing varying amounts of steam from vents high on its flanks and from its caldera. Farther off to the right of Mt Me-Akan you may glimpse through the trees

another large volcano isolated on the horizon: this is Mt O-Akan[75].

Whereas Kushiro wetland is a low-lying peat swamp, almost at sea level, it is surrounded by low hills. The wetland itself is somewhat like a spread hand with the palm to the south reaching the sea and the fingers (swampy river and stream valleys) extending northwards.

Approximately four kilometres further north from the marsh observatory is the parking area for the On-ne-nai Visitor Center[76] on the right. From here there are boardwalks and trails[77] through woodland and down to the low-lying reed-sedge marsh and peat bog with its associated swamp forest of willows and Japanese Alder trees. Here it is possible to relax and savour the natural soundscape while learning about the three habitats that make up the wetlands.

Two kilometres further north the road passes a convenience store on the right and about one kilometre further a small hotel (Hotel Yume-kou-

74 Also sometimes written as Mt Akanfuji. 75 Also sometimes written as Mt Oakan. 76 43.110574, 144.327277 77 Nakashima (1993) provides excellent information on the area.

Ecological Succession — From a Delta to a Swamp Forest

Ecosystems undergo a continuous and gradual process of change, known as ecological succession, during which the species composition of their communities changes over time. That time frame may be of months, decades, millennia or millions of years. A few pioneering species begin the process in newly exposed habitats. Turnover of species within the ecological community continues, but eventually stabilises with a self-maintaining climax community. Each species that becomes established in the community has an impact on its own environment in ways that may make that environment more or less suitable for subsequent species.

Black-browed Reed Warbler favours wetlands and reed beds

Wet peat swamp © Ministry of the Environment

A rare fish, the Japanese Huchen, is at home in the rivers of Kushiro Wetland © Kamada Sachiko

Kushiro Shitsugen NP is a fine example of this process. It consists of a silted-up delta that has been colonised by a range of species including Common Reed. At first sight, the marsh appears as a simple uniform grassland surrounded by low, forested hills. Only on closer observation does it become clear that the marsh consists of three main vegetation types — peat bog, reed marsh and swamp forest — in an ecologically dynamic association of wetland habitats.

Common Reeds are particularly successful colonists of open shallow water areas and flooded swamp areas where the ground water level is high. The reed community very effectively filters and purifies the ground water and the high rate of evapotranspiration from the reeds leads to drying of the substrate. The considerable leaf litter layer that reeds deposit as they age eventually reaches above the water table providing dryer conditions that can then be colonised by other species.

As aquatic and marshland vegetation grows and decays each year, it steadily accumulates as layer upon layer of partially decomposed organic matter that we call peat. Peat develops in wetland areas with stagnant water or where flooding occurs and limits oxygen from the atmosphere accessing the organic material thus slowing its rate of decomposition. Common contributing components of peat are mosses — species in the genus *Sphagnum* — which are sponge-like holding considerable moisture, although other plant species are involved too. Peat layers accumulate over thousands of years and as they do so they preserve plant remains and pollen, making it possible to study aspects of the region's past and reconstruct past habitats.

Over time, sphagnum moss-filled peat swamps have developed in some areas. In the wet and acid conditions of the swamp, vegetable matter only partly decomposes and the remains form layer upon layer of peat. That process began about 3,000 years ago, and peat has accumulated now to between one and three metres in depth at a rate of about one millimetre a year.

Swamp forest is a key indicator revealing the ongoing ecological change in the area. In lowland areas, where rivers meander and where flooding occurs, silt is deposited and accumulates atop the river banks where stands of Japanese Alder trees then become established. These trees are clones that are tolerant of acidity and water around their roots,

Kottaro Wetland is a summer home for cranes and other wetland birds

but very sensitive to soil quality such that where floods and rivers deposit deeper, richer and more nutritious soils, the alders grow taller, with larger trunk diameters.

The accumulation of vegetation over time, the drying effects of reeds (through evapotranspiration), and the establishment of alder-based swamp forest can easily be imagined when viewing the patchwork of open water, swamp vegetation and woodland visible today from the various viewpoints around Kushiro Shitsugen NP.

Swamp Forest consists mostly of Japanese Alder

Cranes roost in the Setsuri River downstream from Otowabashi | Spring and cherry blossoms arrive late in Eastern Hokkadō

bou) on the left. A further four kilometres ahead turn right following the sign to Kottaro Viewpoint. After two kilometres you will reach a bridge (*Otowabashi*[78]) which spans the slow-flowing Setsuri River. The shallows downstream from the bridge are favoured by cranes for roosting in winter and the foot bridge parallel to the road bridge was built specially as the ideal point from which to photograph them. This site attracts wildlife photographers from around the world in the hope of clear weather, heavy frost and dancing cranes. Please note that approaching any closer along the river sides than the bridge is forbidden, as any disturbance will cause the cranes to desert the roost.

About one kilometre ahead a narrow road off to the right leads to some wonderful forest and two rather special capes[79] (Miyajima and Kirakotan) that overlook the northern part of Kushiro Marsh. Two kilometres from the turning, an opening in the landscape provides good views of the Akan volcanoes to the northwest while isolated in a lush green

meadow in the foreground a single, large cherry tree stands. It makes for a beautifully stunning scene in spring when the cherry tree is in blossom and the volcanoes are still capped with snow.

After seven kilometres the road ends at a small parking area with toilets. It is from here that the trail to beautiful Cape Miyajima begins — a walk well worth making, but only from spring to autumn. This is a strictly protected area requiring permission arranged in advance via Tsurui Village. One way to enjoy this remote forest and wetland landscape is by joining a horse trekking excursion for the day. A loop road carries on to the Kirakotan Misaki trailhead. The forest along the way has so many beautiful cherry trees that a spring visit is especially attractive. Where the natural mixed deciduous forest has been felled, it has been replaced with plantations of Japanese Larches *Larix kaempferi*.

As you continue towards Rt 243 watch for cranes in the fields and another fine view of Mt O-Akan to the northwest. A kilometre after crossing the Kuchoro River a turning to the right onto Rt

78 43.187833, 144.334480   79 The term 'cape' is used because long before the marshes developed here these two protruded into the sea.

1060 is signposted, and from this junction it is three kilometres to Kottaro Marsh. Rt 1060 leads towards Kottaro Marsh but first passes a small farm[80] where you may find heavy Hokkaidō *Banba* horses in the paddocks near the farm buildings. Further on there are open fields on the right hand side and low woodland on the left, then eventually you will see another sign marking Kushiro Shitsugen NP. Beyond this you will begin to see out to the left across a very broad, shallow valley with a low moor of reed and sedge. Cranes often breed in this area.

After a while the road descends gently and reaches the Kottaro viewpoint parking area[81]. Behind the small building situated here (the toilets are only open in summer) there is a steep track going first up steps then along an earthen trail towards the Kottaro Wetland viewpoint. Looking down from the viewpoint across the Kottaro River towards the north and the east, you see that the expanse of reed marsh seems vast. The reed beds are a pale tawny grey-brown for much of the year, only the new growing stems and leaves are green. In the distance, alder trees can be seen growing where they have colonised the swamp. This is a great spot from which to listen and watch for birds and other wildlife. In the foreground there is a small area of open water and here you may see cranes or Grey Herons *Ardea cinerea* foraging, and sometimes herds of deer are pushing their way through the marshland vegetation. Through the trees to the south in spring and winter you can just make out the buildings of Kushiro City.

Continuing along the road, you are likely to encounter more herds of deer browsing amongst the trees and reed beds near the river and in the wetlands. In summer the reed beds are noisy with chattering Black-browed Reed Warblers and the calls of Common Cuckoos, whereas in winter the brittle, brash sounds of ice flowing down the river

are the backdrop for the occasional barking call of a passing eagle. Eventually you will cross Kushiro River by the Nihon-matsu Bridge, then a railway track, before joining Rt 391, which is the main road from Kushiro to Shibecha and Teshikaga.

After exploring Kottaro wetland it is well worth visiting the lakes on the east side of the national park before ending up at the splendid viewpoint at Hoso-oka. To do so, join Rt 391 and head south in the direction of Kushiro.

Turn west, off Rt 391, towards the Hoso-oka viewpoint[82] and Takkobu-numa[83], the road is un-numbered but clearly signed. Both sites repay visits. From the eastern end of Takkobu-numa the view west is across reed beds and in the far distance over the lake the Akan volcanoes are prominent again in clear weather. Takkobu-numa, with an area of just 1.31 km², is the smallest of the three lakes found in Kushiro Shitsugen NP. Extensive reed meadows fringe the lake, while the road itself is lined with willows[84] and alder trees.

In winter, everything here is frozen, including the lake, but in summer the whole area is carpeted with lush and vibrant green vegetation. Black-eared Kites are typically soaring over the lake and as eagles breed nearby they also may be seen throughout the year. Look for cranes along the lake shore and in the marshes around the lake. On the wooded slopes beside the lake in spring look for the snowy blooms of White Trilliums *Trillium camschatcense*. Watch for Barn Swallows *Hirundo rustica* and Sand Martins (or Bank Swallows) *Riparia riparia* low over the water, as they hawk rapidly for flying insects, and for Pacific Swifts *Apus pacificus* as they swoop down at high speed to drink from the lake or splash-wash at the surface. In summer the peripheral marshland vegetation is noisy with singing Masked Buntings *Emberiza personata* and Black-browed Reed Warblers and around the

---

80 43.226044, 144.436503   81 Also known as the Kottaro Wetland Observatory: 43.191018, 144.466101   82 Also known as the Hosooka Observatory: 43.098151, 144.449241   83 Also known as Takkobuko, or Lake Takkobu: 43.1050286, 144.4803158   84 Several species in the genus *Salix* grow in the region. Their identification is difficult.

Japanese Deer

Japanese Deer stag in summer coat and antlers in velvet

Japanese Deer stag in winter coat

Japanese Deer female in summer coat

The commonest large mammal in Hokkaidō, and in fact throughout most of Japan, is the Japanese Deer (also called Sika Deer[85]). The local Hokkaidō subspecies is widespread and has become especially common since the 1990s in Eastern Hokkaidō, where it benefits from milder winters and reduced snow cover. This is the largest of the various subspecies in Japan with males weighing up to 130 kg; the females are smaller and weigh considerably less.

Males give a strange whistling call during their autumn rutting season making it the best season to listen for them and to watch their behaviour. Females give short sharp whistles in alarm when they are disturbed. During autumn, the stags shed the velvet from their antlers and compete by calling and jousting to gather and possess their harems for mating rights.

During winter the deer have pale grey-brown fur. They forage for dwarf bamboo leaves and other edible vegetation by pawing down through the snow, and may resort to nibbling and stripping the bark of various kinds of broadleaf trees. Their distinctive feeding method, chewing at the bark low down, then nibbling and pulling upwards, leaves a ragged fringe of torn bark at the higher end; such signs can often be seen even from the road. The most challenging time of year for the deer is during late winter (March and early April). By then their energy resources are mostly depleted after months spent eating poor quality food. Many die of starvation before spring's bounty becomes available for them.

Once the snow begins to melt in spring, herbaceous plants are increasingly abundant so the deer are able to begin to regain their strength after the long winter. They exchange their winter coat for richer, orange-brown fur adorned with rows of

85 This name uses the Japanese name for deer (*Shika* pronounced She-ka), so literally means Deer Deer!

white spots along their flanks. At this time of year, the stags drop their old racks of worn and even broken antlers[86] and their new velvet-covered antlers begin to show. During June, the females give birth to one or two fawns, which they hide at first amongst dense thickets to avoid disturbance and predation. During July, the fawns emerge to accompany their mothers as they wander and forage. Deer can be seen foraging along forest margins, in marshes, and in agricultural fields; they are regularly encountered as they cross roads and as a consequence are often involved in traffic accidents.

When snow is deep, deer may be reduced to feeding on tree bark

Deer have increased considerably in Japan and their negative impacts on vegetation are significant. In low-lying areas of Eastern Hokkaidō, such as at Hashirikotan and Shunkuni-tai, Lake Fūren (see Chapter Six), deer have grazed so extensively that they have almost completely eradicated Crowberry *Empetrum nigrum* and many other coastal plant species such as Wild Rose have suffered with knock-on effects including impacts on small bird populations. In adjacent dune forest dominated by Japanese White Birch *Betula platyphylla* and Siberian Crab Apple *Malus baccata* browsing and bark stripping by deer kills many

Winter herds are commonly segregated. Here a group of females is moving together

maturing trees and small saplings are eaten out. Such impacts are not confined to Eastern Hokkaidō, but are found now across wide areas of rural Japan wherever there are long-persistent deer populations and short snow periods[87]. Deer hunting takes place legally each winter in Hokkaidō from 1 October to 31 March[88]. This period was deliberately chosen to reduce shooting accidents as there are fewer leaves on the trees, allowing greater visibility, fewer workers in the mountain forests, and because it avoids the breeding and migration seasons of birds and other wildlife. If you enter the backcountry during the winter be cautious, wear bright colours, and keep a watch for deer and hunters.

Stags thrash at vegetation and anything on the ground, sometimes becoming entangled, though only rarely as badly as this male trapped in abandoned ropes

86 The shed antlers are an important source of minerals and are often nibbled by mice and squirrels.   87 For example, Misaki *et al* (2006) and Ohashi *et al* (2014).   88 The dates vary from region to region; these are the earliest and latest dates.

Black-eared Kite

Of Japan's many birds of prey, the Black-eared Kite *Milvus lineatus* is by far the most widespread and frequently seen in a wide range of habitats. The kite's wings and tail are long and broad with a large surface area for its low weight allowing it to soar rather effortlessly for long periods.

Frequently seen with a noisy mob of crows in pursuit, the kite's shape alone is sufficient to elicit a mobbing response from them. The unforgiving crows swoop and harry the kites in the air and even while they are perching.

Although classified as a bird of prey, this kite is in fact a scavenger. It has sharp eyesight, but weak feet and a relatively small bill. It can be found soaring over open areas of farmland, or drift-

Black-eared Kites scavenge for their food

ing along casually above any road, river, estuary, or stretch of shoreline in search of food. A spell of soaring may end in a sudden spiralling descent to the ground where it will scavenge a wide variety of food items including amphibians, reptiles, road-killed rodents, tide-washed fish, as well as bugs, beetles, and (especially after rain) earthworms. The kite will eat almost anything as long as it is dead.

Steam Locomotive C11 171

marsh edge there may be small herds of deer.

Four kilometres after leaving Rt 391, the road to Hoso-oka crosses the railway tracks and then runs for a while alongside the Kushiro River. This pretty area with native riparian woodland is popular with fly fisherman and canoeists. Introduced American Mink *Neovison vison* are sometimes seen in this area. They may appear on the riverbank or

they may be swimming in the water where they are sometimes mistaken for River Otters *Lutra lutra* — except there are none of the latter species in Hokkaidō.

A kilometre further on the road crosses the railway tracks again, then a short distance later there is a large car park (with toilets). Park here and continue southwards uphill on foot along the gently inclining narrow road for another 300 m, and then turn right (to the west) onto the well-marked trail out to the Hoso-oka viewpoint. In winter, a steam locomotive (C11 171, a 2-6-4T Adriatic built between 1932 and 1947) travels between Kushiro and Shibecha making a nostalgic sight as it puffs its way along the east side of Kushiro Marsh directly below the viewpoint. An excellent vantage point is the railway crossing near Rt 391 that you cross when entering or leaving the Kottaro Marsh road or the viewpoints beyond Lake Tōro.

Hoso-oka Viewpoint provides an excellent perspective with wonderful views of the expanse of the wetlands. The broad Kushiro River winds its way through the wetlands below the viewpoint. In

The Japanese Larch

The Japanese Larch is a native conifer tree of the main islands of Japan (Honshū, Shikoku, Kyūshū). It was introduced to Hokkaidō where it is widely grown in plantations and you will see many of them as you travel around Eastern Hokkaidō. A related species in North America has many names but is usually called Tamarack. The larches are unusual conifers in that they are deciduous. In autumn their needles turn a delightful golden yellowish-orange before being shed. In spring their young needle leaves emerge as a very vibrant pale green.

Rows of Japanese Larch trees serve as important shelter-belts (windbreaks) in snow country

Kushiro Shitsugen NP seen from the Hoso-oka viewpoint

the far distance to the north-west, there is a panoramic view of all of the Akan volcanoes: O-Akan to the north, with Me-Akan and Akan Fuji[89] further to the west. On the near side of the river, there is much Japanese Alder woodland; on the far side lies the specially protected area of the wetland that extends into the far distance. Scan across the reed marsh with your binoculars and you will find the occasional crane and small herds of deer. In win-

ter the cranes will be absent but instead there's a good chance that you might see either eagle species soaring over the wetlands. Looking due west, on the far hillside, you can see the strange tower of the Kushiro Marsh Observatory and down to the southwest you can see Kushiro City and the tall, steaming chimney stacks of its paper mill.

Turn back from the Hoso-oka viewpoint and retrace your steps. After three kilometres you will

89 Also known as Mt Akanfuji.

The distribution and nature of the lakes of Kushiro Wetland

Today, the enormous expanse of Kushiro Shitsugen NP consists almost entirely of reed swamp, swamp forest, and peat bog with only small areas of open water. However, for reasons of topography three large lakes survive along the eastern edge of the Kushiro wetlands, which decline gently from west to east. The largest of the three, Lake Tōro, is aligned roughly east-west and stretches just over 6 km from end to end. The second largest, Lake Shirarutoro, is aligned roughly north-south and measures approximately 2.5 km from end to end. The smallest of the three, Lake Takkobu, is more oval, but aligned northwest-southeast, and is about 2 km long. Four smaller ponds are associated with them — all just west of Lake Tōro. All of these lakes lie close to the largest river of the region — the Kushiro River, which flows down from Lake Kussharo south to Kushiro. Hokkaidō's giant salmonid, the Japanese Huchen, can be found both in the lake and the river.

Birds found here include large numbers of migratory waterfowl passing through on their way south in autumn before the lakes freeze and returning north in spring as the lakes thaw. During winter, once the lake ice is reliably thick, you may notice the tents of ice-fishers out on the lakes, and see eagles soaring overhead as they search for carrion.

View of Lake Shirarutoro © The Hokkaido Shimbun Press.

pass Lake Takkobu once again. Across the lake, near the north shore, you can see the Takkobu Auto Campground[90]. You can reach it by way of an-

other turning off Rt 391 a little to the north of the lake. From the campsite take the boardwalk and trail (a round trip of c 5 km) along the edge of the

90 43.109392, 144.488523

Ural Owl

Ural Owl pair at their day roost

The Ural Owl *Strix uralensis*, Japan's second largest breeding owl species, is reasonably common throughout Eastern Hokkaidō. This nocturnal species hunts in woodland and around farmland margins for voles and mice. During the daytime it typically roosts out of sight in a tree cavity, but on winter days it may spend long periods sitting at the cavity entrance warming itself in the sun. With its eyes partly open it appears half asleep and half awake; periodically it may rouse to look around, preen or, more rarely, cast a pellet. Owls typically swallow their prey whole; then occasionally they regurgitate the hard parts; in the case of the Ural Owl it is the bones and fur of their prey that are regurgitated as a dense, often shiny, dark grey or black pellet.

hills and through the forest to the Yume-ga-oka viewpoint[91] for another very fine view of the Takkobu and Kushiro wetlands.

After visiting Lake Takkobu, rejoin Rt 391 and drive northwards. The next point of interest is Lake Tōro[92] (6.27 km²). Along the way, note that the slopes of the roadside embankments are covered with dwarf bamboo, a very hardy plant that survives the winter beneath a thick blanket of snow.

In the small community of Tōro[93], Rt 221 turns east from Rt 391 and is signposted to Kami-oboro. This road takes you along the south side of Lake Tōro where you will pass a roadside Grey Heron colony up in the trees. White-tailed Eagles breed in a huge stick nest in this area too. At the western end of the lake there is an extensive reed meadow and in its shallow pools there are often flocks of duck. In summer the beautiful Falcated Duck *Mare-*

The view towards Lake Tōro (distant left) and the Sarurun-tō Marsh from the Sarurun Viewpoint

91 Also known as the Yumegaoka Observatory: 43.115924, 144.468009   92 43.153123, 144.521201   93 43.151626, 144.498451

Red Fox

The fox is nocturnal throughout most of its Japanese range, but the endemic subspecies in Hokkaidō is largely diurnal and in Eastern Hokkaidō in particular it is the most likely mammal to be seen after the deer.

Red Foxes in Hokkaidō are frequently diurnal

The fox is an opportunistic predator, willing to eat almost anything including small insects, beetles, grasshoppers, and earthworms, berries and fruits, rodents and occasionally birds and even Mountain Hares *Lepus timidus*. They are territorial, patrolling and marking their hunting domains.

During the short winter days they patrol the snowfields hunting for voles and other small mammals that might be active. On hearing one beneath the snow, the hunter becomes tense, then after a brief rush forwards it suddenly leaps high into the air, dropping down with all four paws focussed to punch through the snow crust and burst through the roof of a vole's winter quarters. It then digs and scrabbles downwards, its foreparts disappearing deep into the snow layer. It reappears with a vole in its mouth, or, having failed, sets off once more on patrol.

Red Fox in heavy winter coat

Foxes will also scavenge for almost anything edible, from dead fish on a beach, to a dropped glove beside a road. Their scavenging behaviour places them at risk as drivers are often tempted to feed them at the roadside. This practice leads to the foxes associating roadsides with food, spending more time there where they fall victim in subsequent traffic accidents. Watch them, but please do not feed them at the roadside. The fox experiences irregular population ups and downs, so whereas in some years it is difficult to travel far without seeing one, in other years it may take effort to search for them. Foxes may also carry *Echinococcus* tapeworms, which they pick up from their rodent prey and which can, in rare cases, be transferred to dogs and humans. It is best to avoid close contact.

In Japanese folklore foxes are deemed to be secretive, sly, and capable of shapeshifting. They exist on many planes, as godly messengers, as tricksters, deceivers, and as wild and wily animals.

Red Fox pair courting

Red Fox litters average 6–8, but range from 1–12

ca falcata, an east Asian speciality, can be seen here. Watch then for Black-eared Kites and White-tailed Eagles, and in winter, while noting the ice fishermen camped out on the lake ice, watch for both eagle species soaring overhead.

Lake Tōro has become a popular area for canoe tourism both on the lake and along the Kushiro River.

Head northwards along Rt 391. A kilometre from the western end of Lake Tōro, you will pass once more the turning across the railway tracks to Kottaro Marsh. Where Rt 391 curves around the west end of Lake Tōro, a small parking area[94] beside the road provides access to an easy trail that climbs up into the low forested hills to the Sarubo[95] and Sarurun[96] viewpoints.

Early in the summer, before the trees have put out their leaves, the view back from this trail takes in the length of Lake Tōro and overlooks the Sarurun-tō marsh near the foot of the hill at the entrance of the Kottaro Marsh road. This small wetland is excellent for dragonflies in summer and autumn, and is a breeding area for Red-necked Grebes *Podiceps grisegena* and other wetland birds in summer. In winter it freezes over completely. After a short walk (about 10 minutes) the trail reaches the ridge top where there is a sturdy concrete and wooden tower from which you will have excellent views of Lake Tōro. There are flowering Kobus Magnolia and Sargent's Cherry trees near the tower. These early spring flowers (May in Hokkaidō) are attractive to both insects and birds. From the tower it is a further 770 m to the Sarurun viewpoint[97] along a very easy woodland trail with wonderful views back to Lake Tōro and down to Kottaro with plenty of birds to watch for and listen to. This is a very pleasant mixed forest with an early ground cover of Japanese Butterbur, White Trillium and White Helle-

bore. Later in the year here and elsewhere you may find tall blue Japanese Gentians *Gentiana triflora var. japonica* and Hokkaidō Monkshoods *Aconitum yezoense*, tall yellow Alpine Ragworts *Senecio cannabifolius*, and the tall, nodding spires of Bugbane *Actaea simplex*[98].

Two kilometres further north Lake Shirarutoro[99] comes into view to the west of the road with the Akan volcanoes silhouetted in the far distance across the lake. In late winter and again in autumn, the lake is a very important resting site for geese and swans migrating between their wintering grounds in Honshū and their breeding grounds in northeast Russia. Eagles are usually in the area, as they nest nearby, and in winter the magnificent Steller's Eagle can also be seen. Towards the north end of the lake there is the Shirarutoro-numa parking area[100] on the west side of the road (just before the road crosses a bridge). On the way there you can enjoy a panoramic view across the lake to Kottaro Marsh and to the tall peak of Mt O-Akan peeping above the hills and treetops. To the east of the road there is a small settlement of summer houses and a little restaurant. Just after the north end of the lake there is a turn-off towards the west to Kayanuma and the Shirarutoro Nature Information Center[101]. The hot spring hotel near the end of the road has closed down, but the area is a good one for walking and birdwatching. Cranes also breed in the marsh below, at the north end of Lake Shirarutoro.

Rt 391 continues northwards to the towns of Shibecha and Teshikaga (population 6,976[102]) and the Akan–Mashū NP beyond it. Approaching Teshikaga from the south, you can see a distinctive high hill (Mt Birao 554 m) just beyond the town, with communication antennae on the top, while the peak of Mt O-Akan is now prominent to the west.

---

94 43.163320, 144.497470   95 43.164926, 144.497736   96 43.164660, 144.490430   97 Also known as the Sarurun Observatory.   98 Formerly *Cimicifuga simplex*.   99 43.1773017, 144.5008598   100 Also known as Shirarutoroko: 43.1809465, 144.5054732   101 Open from May to October: 43.191188, 144.498943   102 As of August 2020.

Akan–Mashū National Park

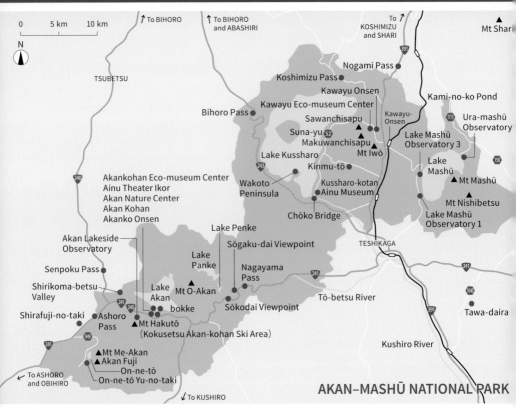

A tremendously explosive period in Hokkaidō's geological history occurred between 200,000 and 30,000 years ago, creating a series of volcanic cones that subsequently collapsed and formed the prodigious craters we now see in the region (and further west in Hokkaidō too). Subsequent volcanic activity has produced new volcanoes that now provide the antithesis to the deep craters and their lakes. These gigantic craters have since become carpeted with thick boreal forest that supports considerable plant and animal diversity. The scenery here is world-class and widely recognised as among the finest in Japan. The region is pocked with peaks, hot springs and even sulphur springs.[103]

Akan NP was one of the first to be designated in Japan, in 1934. This enormous protected area was extended (it is now 91,413 ha) and renamed the Akan–Mashū NP in 2017. Many consider this to be Japan's most attractive national park.

Three spectacular caldera lakes form the key features of this wonderful park — enormous Lake Kussharo, pretty Lake Akan, and clear Lake Mashū. Understanding the proximity and significance of the volcanic landscape and the geological activity here is crucial to understanding the significance of this park.

The western portion of the park is dominated by the paired peaks of Mt Me[104]-Akan (1,499 m; the

---

103 An excellent resource, for Japanese readers, is Satō et al. (2017). 104 Pronounced as in met, *not* as in meet.

The dramatic Kussharo Caldera from the Mt Mokoto viewpoint

female mountain), Mt O-Akan (1,370 m; the male mountain), and beautiful Lake Akan. The Me-Akan stratovolcano, the highest point of the Akan complex, consists of nine overlapping cones with two active summit craters — Ponmachineshiri and Naka-Machineshiri. It is highly active with the most recent major eruption in 2008[105]. Me-Akan erupts constantly and often dramatically spews steam and gas, in 2015 there were many local earthquakes and steam and gas were particularly noticeable.

Nearby, to the south, stands the satellite cinder cone of Akan-Fuji (1,476 m). Some 15 km to the northeast stands Mt O-Akan with Lake Akan on its western flank and lakes Panke-tō and Penke-tō on its northeastern flank. Because of its relative isolation and prominence from so many perspectives, Mt O-Akan appears the taller of the park's volcanoes.

Mt Me-Akan with Akan-Fuji reflecting in Lake On-ne-tō

The national park, thanks to its intensely active geological history, has such stunning volcanic scenery that it is surely worthy of being listed as a global geopark and as a World Heritage Site too.

Akan–Mashū NP is the next logical destination after exploring Kushiro Shitsugen NP. Continue your journey northwards on Rt 391 first to the town of Teshikaga. Wherever you see open fields look for

Mt O-Akan and Lake Akan from the approach to Mt Hakuto

105 Japan Meteorological Agency https://www.data.jma.go.jp/svd/vois/data/sapporo/105_Meakan/105_history.html

foxes hunting for voles in the grassland and watch too for cranes and deer. Very occasionally Mountain Hares (a mostly nocturnal creature in Hokkaidō) can be seen in late winter and early spring lying in the fields or running across them.

The landscape around Teshikaga combines flat areas of farmland, low hills with natural forest and forestry plantations. In between the fields, stand rows of Japanese Larches planted as wind shelter belts during the early years of Japanese settlement. Here and there in the tops of roadside deciduous trees you may notice balls of Japanese Mistletoe *Viscum album coloratum*

Before reaching Teshikaga, in the village of Isobunnai, turn off northeast onto Rt 1040 and follow the signs to the Tawa-daira viewpoint[106]. The approach to Tawa-daira is through rolling hills and dairy farmland — the region is home to thousands of Holstein cattle (see page 124). While the Shibecha region certainly is home to many cattle, their exact numbers are difficult to estimate as the animals are mostly kept indoors in barns year-round, except for the short summer period when some are turned out into lush grass pastures.

At Tawa-daira there is a spacious if simple campsite and in a paddock near the viewing tower a surprising flock of Suffolk sheep. Sheep are a rare sight in Japan and these black-faced, hornless sheep are raised mostly for their meat for the fa-

The Tawa-daira viewing tower overlooks extensive rolling countryside

mous Hokkaidō barbecue dish 'Jingisukan'.

Although the Tawa-daira viewing tower[107] is only at an elevation of 195 m it is set on the top of a prominent hill commanding a tremendous 360° panoramic view. The vista is across the hills and farmland of Shibecha to various mountain groups in each direction (see photos) including west to the volcanoes in the Akan–Mashū NP. On a clear night, a visit to the tower can be an excellent choice if you enjoy stargazing.

A large car park, toilets, a shop and the Green Hill Tawa café-restaurant all bear witness to the popularity of this destination on summer weekends. The shop also doubles as the reception area for the campsite, which opens in late April in time for the Golden Week holidays and remains open until late November (open 09:00–15:00). Access to the viewpoint is year-round.

Next, either retrace your steps to Rt 391, or continue seven kilometres on Rt 1040 to join Rt 243 and head to Teshikaga that way. Approximately one kilometre before reaching Rt 243, there is a soft sand cliff to the east situated opposite Kon Farm and behind the Watanabe Farm. The upper levels of the cliff are riddled with Sand Martin nest burrows with birds very active around the colony in spring and summer.

In Teshikaga, turn westwards onto Rt 241 towards Akanko Onsen. Leaving town, Rt 241 is at first lined with cherry trees, azalea bushes, and Japanese Stone Pines. Then it passes along the broad flat Tō-betsu River valley and through Okushun-betsu with dairy farmland on either side and low hills in the far distance ahead. The Tō-betsu River arises much higher in the park and joins the Kushiro River in Teshikaga. As you drive through the farmland you may see slender-billed Oriental Crows along the wires or foraging on the ground, or perhaps their larger and more aggressive cousins

106 43.437152, 144.588603   107 It is approximately 35 km between the Tawa-daira and Kaiyō-dai viewpoints making it possible to visit both easily in one day. The Ura-mashū viewpoint on the east side of Lake Mashū is also about 35 km away from Tawa-daira, an approximately 40 min drive.

Berries and Birds

If you have noticed the glob-ular green masses of short branches in many roadside trees in Eastern Hokkaidō, here are some great words for you. Those green masses are Japanese Mistletoes all of which are *obligate* stem *hemiparasitic* shrubs with *haustoria*! Put plainly, that

Japanese red-berried mistletoe

A roadside tree laden with mistletoe

means they always live on the branches of other tree species (typical-ly broadleaf deciduous trees), and although they tap into their host's branches for nutrients and water, by way of their own modified root system (or haustoria), they are also capable of photosynthesising and producing some of their own energy.

In Japan, mistletoes produce berries of two colours — greenish-yel-low or reddish-pink. Although the berries are toxic to humans, several species of birds are not only immune but also consume them in con-siderable quantities and become important dispersal agents for them.

Mistletoe berries are extremely sticky, but the berry pulp seems particularly attractive to birds. The most likely species to be seen feeding on them in East Hokkaidō are Dusky Thrush, Bohemian Waxwing *Bombycilla garrulus*, Japanese Waxwing *Bombycilla japon-ica* and Brown-eared Bulbul *Hypsipetes amaurotis*. The waxwings in particular feed on the berries and swallow them whole, excreting the sticky seeds that become glued to tree branches. The thrushes tend to separate the nutritious pulp from the sticky seeds, but the birds must

Brown-eared Bulbul feed heavily on berries

then wipe their beaks on branches to rid themselves of the seeds and in doing so effectively plant the next mistletoe generation. Trees, mistletoe and birds have become entangled in a three-way relationship.

Waxwings (L Japanese; R Bohemian both © Stuart Price) gorge on rosehips, and mistletoe and rowan berries, often stripping them completely before moving on

Summer Visitors — Winter Visitors

Hokkaidō has relatively few resident species of small birds. The region's cold winters are too severe for many species, which migrate south in autumn to spend the winter in milder regions of Japan, or elsewhere in Asia or Australasia. In spring they return, becoming our summer visitors.

Long-tailed Duck

After the prolonged winter silence, the forests of Eastern Hokkaidō begin to fill in spring with the songs of various thrushes, flycatchers, warblers and buntings. Grasslands become temporary homes for Stejneger's Stonechats and Common Cuckoos, mountains and seaside cliffs host Pacific Swifts and sandy banks are where Sand Martins excavate their tunnel nests. Latham's Snipe (see page 133) is a prominent summer visitor because of its visible and audible displays, but the most colourful summer birds are the snazzy Narcissus *Ficedula narcissina* and Blue-and-white Flycatchers *Cyanoptila cyanomelana*. The window of opportunity to watch for all of these birds lasts from May to August.

In contrast to those birds arriving for the short summer, other species migrate here for the long winter

Black Scoter © Stuart Price

having bred in northeast Russia, a region that experiences even harsher winters. These winter visitors include the enormous and magnificent Steller's Eagle (see page 116), the dramatic White-tailed Eagle, and the angelic Whooper Swan. Around the coasts many different species of sea ducks, such as Long-tailed Duck *Clangula hyemalis*, Harlequin Duck *Histrionicus histrionicus*, Siberian Scoter *Melanitta stejnegeri* and Black Scoter *Melanitta americana* gather for the winter and during spring and autumn they are joined by a wide range of other waterfowl visiting temporarily on migration.

Blue & White Flycatcher

Narcissus Flycatcher

Latham's Snipe

the hatchet-billed Japanese Crow.

As the valley narrows and the hills become closer, you may also notice snow gates, snow fences and snow poles at the roadside, snow arrows pointing downwards towards the road edge, and other forms of roadside 'furniture'. They are extremely helpful when driving in winter.

After 10 km or so the road (known locally as the

Snow Country 'Furniture'

The roadside 'furniture' of Eastern Hokkaidō exists entirely because of the winter climate. As you journey around the region, you cannot help but notice the red and white snow poles beside the road. These are invaluable during winter white-out conditions as they mark the road edge and are close enough together to make it possible to drive from one to the next at a walking pace and remain on the road. Taller poles arch over the side of the road and have red and white snow arrows near their tips. These arrows also indicate the road edge and are often fitted with solar panels powering flashing lights that are immensely helpful during night-time winter driving in blizzard conditions.

Here and there you may notice large heavy metal gates. Mostly these are kept in the open position, parallel to the road, but if snow falls too heavily or too frequently for municipalities to keep the roads ploughed clear then they may shut these gates temporarily, thereby closing off a section of the road.

Because of the local topography and wind conditions, some sections of certain roads were notoriously prone to being blocked by snowdrifts after winter storms in the past. This explains why in summer you might suddenly find yourself driving through a strange tunnel that doesn't pass under anything. Such snow tunnels are vital in winter when they may be buried under snowdrifts, but they do not pass underground.

Snow Pole

Snow Fence

Snow Tunnel

Snow Arrows

Akan Ōdan Dōro) begins to climb steadily, winding its way higher with mixed forest on either side containing many coniferous trees. The steep slopes support forest with many stone birch and spruce making an attractive colour contrast at any time of year. As in other parts of Hokkaidō, the commonest forest ground cover is dwarf bamboo.

A further 5 km on, the winding mountain road

passes through snow tunnels. This area experiences heavy snow in winter, and even in May snow remains in shady stream gullies. The views ahead are of forested hillsides; the view back is down the Tō-betsu Valley towards Teshikaga. Soon you will cross the Nagayama Pass (750 m) then reach two viewpoints.

From a small parking area on the north side of the road, the Sōgaku-dai viewpoint[108], there are views of the forested mountains ahead including Mt O-Akan and Mt Me-Akan. A further 3 km on, there is a parking area on the south side of the road for the Sōkodai viewpoint[109], situated upslope from

Mt O-Akan from the Sōgaku-dai Viewpoint © Ministry of the Environment

the parking area, with views over lakes Penke and Panke. After the Sōkodai viewpoint, the road begins to descend quite steadily towards Lake Akan; then in 9 km it reaches a junction with traffic lights where you will join Rt 240 turning right towards Akan.

The road passes just south of Mt O-Akan. One kilometre from the Rt 241 / Rt 240 junction is the turning for the base of the mountain. Turn in here and proceed about 100 m to where the broader track ends. Here, where a rushing stream emerges from the lake, you will find the entrance to the mountain hiking trail (see page 163). This hike will take approximately six hours round trip — depending of course on your level of fitness.

Three kilometres on you will reach the little town of Akanko Onsen[110]. There is a parking area (fee required) on the right from where you can walk to the museum and the Lake Akan mud springs (known locally as *bokke*[111]). If you turn right here, just before the convenience store, you can follow the road into central Akan-kohan. There you will find the hotels and shops of this hot spring resort town and views of the lake.

Akan-kohan, on the shore of Lake Akan is an important hub being famed for its scenic views,

Lake Akan with Mt Me-Akan beyond, seen from Mt O-Akan

The shore of Lake Akan near Akan-kohan

108 43.448738, 144.203730   109 43.448738, 144.203730   110 The cluster of hotels and other buildings beside the lake itself is known as Akan-kohan, literally Akan lakeshore. 43.433349, 144.097772   111 43.438417, 144.102638

Marimo

Lake Akan is said to have been home to Setona, an Ainu maiden who, when bereaved, wept tears which became the mysterious Marimo. In reality these are globes of a fine, fila- mentous green alga, formed by an interplay of water currents and physical rolling of the algal threads into spherical velvety green balls that grow slowly year by year as an aggregation until they reach diameters of up to 34 cm[112].

Marimo © Wakana Isamu

The origins, mythology and history of Marimo are myste- rious and confusing. It was only officially discovered in 1897, and has been said to have had no Ainu name (because it was not edible), though today Ainu dispute this and call it *Torasampe*. The alga is the subject of an annual festival held on 10 October.

Though Akan is generally considered a freshwater lake, it is surrounded by active volcanoes and has several partly saline springs with minerals derived from magma. Marimo is dependent on these springs and several other coincident factors. Chief amongst these are the wave-forming winds that blow across the lake. The dominant wind from the south, from the Pacific Ocean, is channeled between the Me-Akan and O-Akan volcanoes across the lake forming waves beneath which micro-currents occur. Those micro-currents, the clean water, and the sandy lake bottom substrate are three essential factors causing and allowing the slow rolling formation of Marimo. The lake averages a depth of 17 metres and is 45 m at its deepest point. In shal- lower water Marimo are small while in deeper water they are larger. The larger lake balls are hollow with the photosynthesising algal threads forming an approximately 5 cm thick outer layer.

Marimo also grows in other lakes in Eastern Hokkaidō, such as Lake Kussharo and the three lakes of Kushiro Shitsugen NP. It is also found elsewhere in Japan, such as in the Fuji Five Lakes and Lake Biwa, but rarely forms balls. It is even found elsewhere in the world in places such as at Lake Myvatn in Iceland, where spherical Marimo grew to 10 cm in diameter. Unfortunately they were declared extinct there in 2014. How- ever, in Lake Akan, where it has been designated a Special Natural Monument, unique conditions allow it to grow into the largest algal spheres in the world. Though protected, Marimo declined during the twentieth century. One of the problems was the impact of grey water contamination from the lakeshore settlement (a problem now solved). Another problem was the spread of organic silt on the lakebed leading to aquatic plants encroaching and reducing the area suitable for Marimo to form and grow. Today the Marimo popula- tion seems stable, though not yet increasing.[113]

the locus of the local Ainu community, a centre for multi-focussed tourism with a complex of modern hotels, a geological site with several small bubbling mud springs, and the lake itself which supports an extraordinary spherical algal aggregation known locally as Marimo *Aegagropila linnaei*[114].

A boat excursion to admire the magnificent scenery of Lake Akan takes in the southeast cor- ner of the lake and provides opportunities to see Daurian Azaleas *Rhododendron dauricum* and var- iegated kiwi vines in summer and resplendent red maple trees in autumn. The boat calls in briefly at

112 Some literature even claims diameters of 40 cm. 113 To learn more about ball formation by Marimo read Togashi et al. (2014). 114 Named as such in 1897 by researcher Kawakami Takiya. It is also called Lake Ball and was previously given the scientific name of *Cladophora sauteri*.

Chūrui Island in the northern part of the lake allowing time to visit a small museum dedicated to Marimo.

A walkway along the shore of the lake from the boat dock, or from the Akankohan Eco-museum Center, passes another geological feature, though this one is on a small scale. The *bokke* trail passes naturally bubbling mud pots. Pools of sloppy ash-grey mud heave and spit as steam and gas rise sluggishly from the depths, creating glutinous bubbles of mud that form, rise and burst at the surface. It is an oddly mesmerising slow-motion effervescence

Lake Akan *bokke*

Hiking the route from Akan-kohan to Mt Me-Akan

and the local name, *bokke*, is in imitation of the sloppy popping sound of bursting mud bubbles.

Current Lake Akan is merely a small remnant of a once vast lake that filled much of the Akan Caldera[115] about 150,000 years ago[116]. Later eruptions, about 20,000 years ago, began the formation of Mt O-Akan with the mountain developing its strato-volcano shape from about 13,000 years ago when it intruded into and re-shaped the southern part of Lake Akan. After an 8,000-year-period of inactivity, subsequent activity and lava flows from about 5,000 to 2,500 years ago uniquely re-shaped the once great lake, dividing it into western and eastern portions and confining the western portion into the present shape of Lake Akan. Continuing activity of Mt O-Akan separated the lake's eastern portion into two and formed the current much smaller lakes — Panke and Penke — north and east of Mt O-Akan[117]. Travel away from Akanko Onsen, beside Lake Akan, bound for Teshikaga and you will glimpse these lakes down to the north as you head up to the Nagayama Pass.

Lake Akan is a crater lake[118] located between two active volcanoes. The lake[119] was listed as a Ramsar site in 2005 because it is home to various rare aquatic species including Marimo and Japanese Huchen. The lake's surrounding dense boreal forest is home to two more Natural Monuments — Blakiston's Fish Owl and Black Woodpecker *Dryocopus martius* — and it provides habitat for bears. The streams, rivers and ponds in the area are attractive not only to bears, but also to catch-and-release fly-fishers who come for the golden-coloured White-spotted Char *Salvelinus leucomaenis*. The lake freezes over in winter. Then it is possible to hike on the ice to admire the astonishing frost flowers that form overnight, or to fish through the ice. Much of the Lake Akan area was subjected to considerable logging in the early twentieth century,

---

115 The explosive activity that formed the Akan Caldera lasted more than one million years from approximately 1.5 million years ago to approximately 150,000 years ago (see Nakada et al. 2016). 116 Sato et al. (2017). 117 Wada (2017) in Sato et al. (2017). 118 With a surface area of 13 km^2 a perimeter of 25.9 km, and a depth of 44.8 m. 119 1,318 ha.

Woodpeckers

Hokkaidō's woodpeckers range in size from Japan's smallest — the Japanese Pygmy Woodpecker *Yungipicus kizuki* — to Japan's largest — the Black Woodpecker. The former can be found in forests of all types, in gardens, parks and roadside trees. The latter is far more exclusively associated with shadier old growth forests. In between these two in size are Grey-headed Woodpecker *Picus canus*, an olive and grey rather vocal species with a ringing whistled call, and three pied species in declining order of size: White-backed Woodpecker *Dendrocopos leucotos*, Great Spotted Woodpecker and Lesser Spotted Woodpecker *Dryobates minor*. The first three are reasonably common and quite likely to be encountered on woodland walks in the region, but the Lesser Spotted Woodpecker is scarce, secretive and seemingly associated with deciduous woodland close to rivers and lakes.

All six species feed on insect larvae excavated from rotting wood and they all excavate their own nesting cavities with their chisel-like bills, leaving behind cavities that are frequently used by 'secondary cavity nesters' that include many species of small bird, and also the Siberian Flying Squirrel *Pteromys volans*, while old Black Woodpecker nest holes may provide small owl species with suitable nesting sites.

Japanese Pygmy Woodpecker   Black Woodpecker   Grey-headed Woodpecker   Great Spotted Woodpecker

but 3,593 ha around the lake are now owned and protected by the Maeda Ippo-en Foundation. Access to the area is restricted to those with a guide accredited by the Maeda Ippoen Foundation such as those from the Akan Nature Center[120].

Akan-kohan is home to an indigenous Ainu community and the town showcases Ainu culture through its museum and *Ikor* theatre[121]. At Lake Akan's Akanko Ainu Kotan, Ainu-guided tours that focus on the cultural wisdom of the people that lived in the natural environment of this boreal region are also available. Daily theatre performanc-

Ikor Theatre performance © Akan Ainu Craft Union

120 43.434591, 144.089725   121 43.434037, 144.088787

Spruce Forest in the Akan–Mashū NP

Looking from Lake On-ne-tō to Mt Me-Akan (L) and Akan-Fuji (R)

On-ne-tō Hot Falls rich in moss and manganese oxide

es include traditional dances designated as an Important Intangible Folk Cultural Property. The town is a focal point for a range of outdoor activities from forest walks and mountain hikes to cross-country skiing, snowshoe trekking and, once the lake has frozen sufficiently in winter, to pond smelt fishing through the ice.

Two kilometres further along Rt 240 a left turn takes you up to the Kokusetsu Akan-kohan Ski Area[122], and beyond that a trail to Mt Hakutō.

A kilometre beyond the turning for the ski area is a turning up another track that continues for about 4 km to the parking area[123] for one of the hiking trails to Mt Me-Akan (see page 162). The track itself makes for a very pleasant walk through mature mixed forest; here and there you may notice some ancient Katsura trees, and in the wet, swampy areas of the forest there are also giant Asian Skunk Cabbages.

The hike up from Lake Akan over the Me-Akan and Akan Fuji peaks and down the other side to Lake On-ne-tō affords spectacular views at any season, especially in autumn when paintbox colours add to the scenery. O-Akan is a more serious hike, but also manageable in a day.

Route 240 leads you westwards away from Akanko Onsen and 5 km after the turn for the Mt Me-Akan hike rejoin Rt 241 turning southwest over the Ashoro Pass (645 m) towards Ashoro and Obihiro. After 5 km take the turning to the south (left) towards Lake On-ne-tō on Rt 949. After 3 km, and just before the hot spring hotel buildings, another trail for Mt Me-Akan turns off to the left uphill through Sakhalin Spruce *Picea glehnii* forest. Two kilometres ahead Lake On-ne-tō[124] will come into view. The strikingly clear waters of this volcanic lake reflect Mt Me-Akan on a clear day and seem to fluctuate in colour[125] though they are mostly a delightful blue. Light and shadow play across the water surface making this one of the most beautiful scenes

122 Also known as the Akankohan National Ski Area: 43.424743, 144.085043   123 43.409521, 144.061932   124 43.384707, 143.968645
125 Locally the lake has the nickname *Goshikinuma* meaning five-coloured pond.

Eurasian Red Squirrel

In Japan, the wide-ranging Eurasian Red Squirrel occurs only in Hokkaidō. This typically solitary creature is found in mixed deciduous broadleaved and coniferous evergreen forests where it forages in the trees for buds, flowers, fruits, nuts, and even large insects such as beetles or cicadas. It descends to the ground to gather from the abundant autumn harvest that includes fungi, fallen acorns and walnuts. Weighing 300–410 g, it measures 38–47 cm long including its long tail, which it often holds in an elegant S-shaped curve over its back.

In summer its short coat is a rather dark, and red-tinged, chocolate-brown, whereas its denser, longer winter fur is greyish-brown. In winter it also grows long, prominent ear tufts, giving it an impish look. These tufts are lost in summer, revealing that its ears are actually short and rounded.

The period from late winter into early spring is their mating season and soon after successful courtship they den, gathering a large ball of twigs, leaves, and bark high in the fork of a tree, or in a tree hole to serve as a nest in which to raise their litter of up to half a dozen young.

Eurasian Red Squirrel

Entrance to the Mt Me–Akan trail from Lake On-ne-tō campsite

in the Akan–Mashū NP. A walk along the path and road beside the lake is pleasant at any time but in early summer, it is especially delightful with rhododendrons and other wildflowers in bloom.

The narrow road continues for another kilometre around the lake with occasional places to stop and admire the view before eventually reaching the camping area. Just before the campsite building there is a hiking trail that turns off to the right uphill through mixed forest with a sign board at the entrance with a map of the trail, the lake and the volcanoes. This trail offers a particularly pleasant route up Mt Me-Akan.

A little further along Rt 949, beyond the campsite, there is another trailhead parking area (with toilets) this time to a rather special location known as On-ne-tō Yu-no-taki[126] (On-ne-tō Hot Falls). It takes just 20 minutes from the car park along an easy, broad trail to reach this unusual Natural Monument. It was designated as such in 2000 because here natural manganese oxide (normally found on the ocean floor) is found at the surface over a large area (approximately 150 m x 70 m) and as much

as two metres thick[127]. The mineral is precipitated out from hot spring water at about 40°C that arises about 30 m upslope and forms two waterfalls, through the action of special bacteria and algae in a process known as biomineralization[128]. This is the largest recent manganese deposit in the world, and the only place on Earth where you can see the

126 43.3674262, 143.9727004   127 Miura *et al.* (2004).   128 Miura *et al.* (2004).

Siberian Chipmunk

The Siberian Chipmunk is a small, mostly terrestrial squirrel, with a long, straight, furry tail. This active little creature reveals its presence as it scampers across the forest floor with its tail erect like a flagpole. Erratic dashes are interspersed with sudden hesitant, watchful pauses when it stands upright with its small fore-paws tucked up on its white chest, bracing itself on the tripod of its tail and hind legs as it scans its territory. It produces a high-pitched squeak, so attenuated as to be almost impossible to locate and easily dismissed as the squeaking of a hidden vole or shrew.

This endearing little creature weighs just 71–116 g and is a mere 12–17 cm in length, with an additional 8–15 cm of tail. It occurs widely throughout Hokkaidō in a wide range of habitats from lowland parks with woodland and bushy understory, through various forest types up to the sub-alpine zone, and even among stabilised coastal dunes. Its diet includes nuts, seeds, berries, buds, fungi and grains, which it transports in its cheek pouches.

Siberian Chipmunk

Diurnal Siberian Chipmunks are most active on warm summer days. Their seemingly constant active behaviour changes abruptly during October. From late October onwards, until the following April, they hibernate in an underground burrow. They emerge in spring, build up their body reserves once more, mate and nest. After 35–40 days the females give birth to a single litter of 3–7 young that will remain with her until it is time to hibernate once again. For chipmunks the summer is a rush — to breed, to rear young, and then to store food.

According to Ainu legend, Hokkaidō's chipmunks sprang from the slippers of the gods, which were accidentally left behind when the Earth was made.

blackish-brown manganese oxide deposits above ground. Manganese precipitation began at Yu-no-taki more than 4,500 years ago and for a while in the early 1950s approximately 3,500 tons of manganese ore was mined in the area.

The forest in the Akan–Mashū NP rings to the calls of six species of woodpeckers, including the huge Black Woodpecker and the diminutive Japanese Pygmy Woodpecker. Many other forest birds occur here too, along with foxes, Eurasian Red Squirrels *Sciurus vulgaris*, Siberian Flying Squirrels and Siberian Chipmunks

Steam and moss are an unusual combination on Mt Hakutō

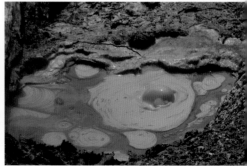

Mt Hakutō *bokke*

Sable — Hokkaidō's most voracious predator

The Sable is a member of the family Mustelidae, related to the Japanese Marten *Martes melampus*, the Stoat *Mustela erminea*, the Least Weasel *Mustela nivalis* (the smallest member of the genus), and the introduced American Mink. Despite its apparently gentle face it is a formidable predator capable of chasing down animals larger than itself, such as the Mountain Hare. More typically though, especially in winter, it hunts rodents living beneath the snow. Strong, fast, agile and as nimble as a squirrel, the Sable is an excellent climber allowing it to hunt in the trees and on the ground.

Males are slightly larger than females, which appear slighter and gentler. They measure 67 cm long and weigh up to 1.5 kg. They live solitarily or semi-socially in extended families in mixed deciduous and coniferous forests from the lowlands to the tree line. Although the Sable is an aggressive and rapid pursuit hunter, it is not entirely carnivorous. It also eats invertebrates during summer, fruits and nuts in autumn, and seeds in winter, making it an opportunistic forager.

The seemingly gentle Sable

Eutamias sibiricus. Haunting night-time wavering whistles here are the loud penetrating calls of rutting male deer that roam the forests in search of females.

Retracing your way along Rt 949 to Rt 241, 2 km after the junction, on the way back towards Akanko Onsen, a sign indicates a broad track off to the left to Shirafuji-no-taki (Shirafuji Waterfall)[129]. The track passes through pleasant mature forest with lots of feeding signs of Black Woodpeckers in the trees. It is also a good area in which to look for Hazel Grouse *Tetrastes bonasia*, which can be found here and elsewhere in the Akan–Mashū NP. The waterfall is clearly audible from the end of the track from where it is a short walk (about 5 mins) down a narrow trail to view the cascade.

Five kilometres further north you will reach Rt 240. To the left the road climbs up to Senpoku Pass and then descends along the Abashiri River Valley towards Tsubetsu and Bihoro. To the right the road returns to Akanko Onsen. Straight ahead is a minor dirt road that takes you on a pleasant 5-km loop through forest, along the Shirikoma-betsu Valley[130],

Shirafuji Waterfall

towards Lake Akan and then back to Akan-kohan. The road around the far side of the lake, although shown on many maps, is private and closed to the general public.

129 43.425071, 143.980639   130 43.453754, 144.032897

Lake Kussharo in the enormous Kussharo Caldera seen from Bihoro Pass

The geological features of the surrounding area, the natural ecosystem, and Marimo, all make Lake Akan especially interesting. However, to grasp the grand scope and scale of the volcanoes, the caldera, the lake, and the astonishing diversity of its environs, it is best experienced by hiking up to the

The visitor site at Mt Iwō

Mt Hakutō (Hakutō-zan) viewpoint[131]. Here, amidst the volcanic landscape, geothermal activity is so great that the high ground surface temperature allows subtropical mosses to grow. In contrast, just a few kilometres away near the start of the hiking trail for Mt O-Akan and no higher than 400 m there are alpine flowers, while higher on the flanks of the same mountain there are permanent snow fields on the surface and here and there natural wind holes amongst the rocks chilling the permafrost below. So, within just 2 km of the lake there are huge temperature differences and a tremendous range of vegetation types.

East of Akan, over the pass towards Teshikaga, an attractive drive in itself, there are splendid views back to the volcanoes. Another 25 km northeast of Akanko Onsen, as the crow

Approaching the Mt Iwō visitor site during a special guided walk

131 43.411553, 144.078611

flies, lies enormous Lake Kussharo, which is several times larger than either Lake Akan or Lake Mashū.

The Kussharo Caldera features not only the lake of the same name but also panoramic viewpoints at Bihoro Pass[132] on the western rim and Koshimizu Pass[133] on the northern rim. The eastern rim is much degraded and poorly defined, but to the east of the current lakeshore are several low, round-topped 'mountains' including the somewhat more rugged Mt Iwō (or sulphur mountain, 508 m)[134]. The latter, a fascinating geological spot with dramatic sulphur springs bubbling boiling water, spouting steam and condensing heaps of pure sulphur, is easily reached by car, or on foot along the Tsutsuji-ga-hara Nature Trail, from Kawayu Onsen. From May to July the frothy white flowers of Milky Way Rhododendrons *Rhododendron diversipilosum*[135] carpet the area and contrast beautifully with the dark green of the Japanese Stone Pines here.

From Teshikaga Town, Rt 243 passes the southern shore of Lake Kussharo on its way to the Bihoro Pass. Near the southeast corner of the lake, Rt 52 turns off to the north and follows the eastern shore of the lake. Just less than 1 km from the junction the road crosses the Chōko Bridge[136] over the Kushiro River which arises here from Lake Kussharo. The river is a popular attraction for canoeists and fly fishers. Continuing northwards the road passes Kotan with its little Kussharo-kotan Ainu Museum[137] and hot spring. Six kilometres from the start of Rt 52, a gated forest trail known as Ikeno-yu Rindō[138] turns off to the right. This dirt road winds its way eastwards and eventually emerges on Rt 391 (the road between Teshikaga and Kawayu Onsen). In a straight line this is about 5 km,

Milky Way Rhododendrons and Japanese Stone Pines with Mongolian Oak

though the track is rather longer because it winds considerably. Approximately halfway along it there is a short walking trail to the south to secluded Kinmu-tō[139], an attractive small lagoon surrounded by beautiful forest.

Jutting from the southern shore of Lake Kussharo is the Wakoto Peninsula[140] around which there is a pleasant woodland trail providing a 'forest-bathing' experience that includes the strange repetitive buzzing sounds of Min-min Cicadas *Hyalessa maculaticollis* on warm summer days. Nearby, at the narrow base of the peninsula, hot spring bathing is possible at a pleasant outdoor pool. If you take a guided canoe trip onto the lake, you will see the steaming vent at the waterline at the tip of the peninsula and perhaps even cook your lunch there in a natural geothermal steam oven!

Halfway up the eastern shore of the lake following Rt 52 there is another area of geothermal activity known as Suna-yu[141]. During summer the campsite is very popular with visitors, but in winter Suna-yu draws a different kind of visitor — swan

132 43.648374, 144.248862   133 43.702795, 144.358860   134 43.616390, 144.441258   135 Previously considered to be Labrador Tea *Ledum palustre var. diversipilosum*, but that genus is now incorporated within the rhododendrons and the uniqueness of this species is recognised.   136 43.558954, 144.339494   137 43.563300, 144.342154 Open in summer only.   138 43.605724, 144.356196 Open in summer only. Rindo means a forestry road.   139 Also known locally as Kimuntō: 43.597151, 144.405258   140 43.5857133, 144.3146139   141 43.624290, 144.359766

Lake Kussharo

Lake Kussharo, a year-round beauty spot, is situated at an altitude of 121 m above sea level in the municipality of Teshikaga. It is not merely the largest caldera lake in the Akan–Mashū NP, but also the largest caldera lake in Japan, and Japan's sixth largest lake of any type. The lake has a surface area of just over

79 km^2 and a shore length of 57 km. Although reaching a depth of 118 m, much of the lake is shallow so the average depth is only 28.4 m. A single island, Nakajima, is very prominent, as is the single river that flows out of the lake from its southeast corner — the Kushiro River.

This enormous lake may freeze over almost entirely in winter[142]. Then, the weird singing sounds of the ice and the snaking cracks and pressure ridges of ice across the lake are special features. Thermal vents keep portions of the lake ice-free, enticing flocks of Whooper Swans to remain during the cold winter months. The swans are very vocal, giving soft contact calls by day and at night, and much louder clamouring or bugling calls whenever excited. They look ethereal in the early morning mist rising off the tiny strips of open water, and their beauty has earned them the sobriquet *Angels of Winter*.

A pressure ridge of ice snakes across Lake Kussharo in mid-winter

Whooper Swans gather during winter at Sunayu

142 Once an annual guarantee, as winters have become milder the period during which the lake is frozen is shortening and is becoming less predictable.

photographers. Heat rising through the sand at the lake's edge keeps the shore ice-free all winter making it attractive to a highly photogenic flock of Whooper Swans that spend the season here.

Rt 52 not only follows the eastern shore of Lake Kussharo, but also loops up and along the western rim of the Mashū Caldera. From Teshikaga Rt 52 climbs uphill through farmland then forest to the first Lake Mashū viewpoint[143]. It then continues northwards beside the rim to reach the third viewpoint[144] (strangely there is no second viewpoint). From there Rt 52 descends in a series of hairpin bends eventually to cross the railway tracks and rejoin Rt 391 just south of Kawayu Onsen. Approximately 1 km north of this junction and opposite Hotel Parkway you will pass the turning to Kawayu Onsen Station. A little further on you will find the left turn for Mt Iwō and the small town of Kawayu Onsen. The road tunnels through woodland then curves and breaks out into the open so that you can now see steam billowing from Mt Iwō (Ato-sa-nupuri — the naked mountain), and the neighbouring rounded, and forested mountains of Maku-wanchisapu (Kabuto-yama 574 m), Sawanchisapu (Bōshi-yama 520 m) and just to the west the adjacent Ponpon-yama (256 m).

The eastern portion of the national park includes attractive Lake Mashū, which I consider to be the most beautiful of all Japan's lakes. The Ainu called this *kim-ta-an-kamuy-tō* meaning the lake of the gods in the mountains. Mashū is a crater lake within a caldera whose walls rise 300–400 m above lake level. The views from the caldera rim take in much of Eastern Hokkaidō and make this one of the greatest scenic spots on the island — it is a very special place indeed. When the weather is kind, it is truly spectacular. The lake itself is a closed basin fed by precipitation falling within the caldera, but with no surface outflow. Rainwater accumulates within the caldera and feeds directly into the lake,

and is lost mostly by seepage through the volcano itself down to the water table (feeding many freshwater springs in the region) and by evaporation.

The Mashū crater's steep internal cliffs encircle and rise 200 m above the lake, while the pumice covered floor of the crater lies 212 m below. The water is an astonishingly clear blue[145], and this is one of only two lakes registered as a United Nations Global Environment Monitoring System (GEMS) Water Baseline Monitoring Station in Japan. The panoramic view from the Mashū crater rim takes in Mt Shari to the north, the Shiretoko Peninsula to the north-east, and Lake Kussharo and beyond to the Akan volcanoes to the west.

The deep, clear waters of Lake Mashū and its surrounding forests beautifully frame *Kamui-nu-puri* (Mt Mashū; 857 m)[146] which stands on the southeastern rim. The mountain rises steeply and jaggedly from the shore of the lake and makes a fine destination for a day hike along the rim from the Mashū crater rim viewpoint, perhaps taking in also the wildflower haven of Mt Nishibetsu (799 m)[147]. The tiny island (Naka-jima) in the centre of the lake is also called *Kamuishu* in Ainu, while the name of the mountain beyond means mountain of the gods.

Lake Mashū is one of the essential elements of a visit to Eastern Hokkaidō. Although many visitors are thwarted by the fog that sometimes blankets the crater in summer, in winter, with mostly sun-

Whooper Swans on Lake Kussharo

143 Also known as Lake Mashū Observation Deck No. 1: 43.556564, 144.507197 144 Also known as Lake Mashū Observation Deck No. 3: 43.583243, 144.503796 145 Known locally as Mashū Blue. 146 43.572351, 144.561197 147 43.553451, 144.581969

The Mashū Caldera with Lake Mashū and Kamui-nupuri is one of the most beautiful scenes in Japan

ny weather and clear blue skies, there is much to watch for in addition to the spectacular scenery. The caldera rim provides the perfect viewpoint from which to search for migratory birds of prey moving between the Sea of Okhotsk coast and the lowlands, capes and lakes of south-east Hokkaidō. The lake is picture perfect and completely remote in the sense that there are no trails down to the shore from the crater rim and hence no boats on the lake. Mere mortals may not disturb the home

Lake Mashū sometimes freezes over completely in winter

of the gods.

The seasonal variation in climate in the park is so extreme that in summer the temperature may rise above 30°C whereas in winter it may drop below -30°C. In summer, Lake Mashū, and even Lake KusshARO, may be filled with a sea of cloud, while in winter each of the lakes may freeze over, presenting an entirely different aspect.

The cold and dry atmosphere here in winter lends itself to the production of beautiful hoar frost, which coats the trees around the springs, diamond dust (fine, barely visible crystals of ice drifting on the breeze), and also causes the extraordinary explosive sound of tree trunks freezing and cracking!

The western side of Lake Mashū is the most frequently visited as it is easily accessible from Teshikaga or Kawayu Onsen by way of Rt 52 and is on the popular tourist circuit. In summer the road is open all the way, but in winter the northern part, beyond the No. 1 observatory viewpoint, is closed, leaving access only from Teshikaga. The less frequently visited eastern side of the lake, known as Ura-mashū, also has its attractions. After visiting Tawa-daira, turn right onto Rt 243 then left onto Rt 885 before turning again onto Rt 150, which will take you to Ura-mashū.

The Mashū-ko–Shari Line (Rt 150 then Rt 1115),

passes to the east of dramatic Lake Mashū, passing through forestry plantations and boreal forest. A sign on Rt 150 indicates 3 km to Ura-mashū Observatory[148]. The turn is just north of the end of a long snow tunnel. At the end of the road is a small car park with toilets, a visitor centre, and a wooden platform giving views westwards across Lake Mashū past the flank of *Kamui-nupuri*. The view of the lake is sometimes brilliant and blue, but drifting fog occasionally shrouds a mysterious scene or may hide the view completely. During summer the birch, oak, Japanese Rowan, and spruce forest here is noisy with the loud songs of Japanese Bush Warblers *Horornis diphone* while there are sometimes Pacific Swifts overhead. Once winter arrives it is a quiet spot and eventually only accessible to those with snowshoes or cross-country skis when snow closes the road.

Looking west across Lake Mashū from the Ura-mashū viewpoint

Having come as far as Ura-mashū don't miss Kami-no-ko Pond (Kami-no-ko-ike)[149]. Approximately 6 km further north of the turn to Ura-mashū, a track turns off to the southwest to Kami-no-ko (Child of the Gods) Pond, which is signposted as 2 km away. The gently inclining track through Ezo Spruce forest and beside a stream makes for a pleasant drive or a walk to the pond. The small pond at the end of the track is circumnavigated by a wooden boardwalk. The pond is spring-fed and the upwelling water causes the fine sand at the bottom to billow up forming patterns in the deeper blue depths. You may find Brown Dippers *Cinclus pallasi* along the valley, or even at the pond, and in summer the forest is loud with Eurasian Wren *Troglodytes troglodytes* and Japanese Robin *Larvivora akahige* song.

Kami-no-ko Pond

Rejoining Rt 1115 the road continues northwards towards Midori and then Sattsuru. About 7 km south-southeast of Sattsuru Station in Kiyosato, along the Shari River, there is a three-metre-high waterfall called Sakura-no-taki[150]. It can be a little tricky to find as none of the signs to it along Rt 1115 are in English, but tall blue signs at first

Cherry Salmon ascending Sakura-no-taki

148 43.600566, 144.570818   149 43.645085, 144.549964   150 43.731847, 144.523198

The Whooper Swan

Whooper Swan

The migratory Whooper Swan is a common winter visitor to Japan. These birds breed at boreal nesting grounds in Russia. Many pass through Eastern Hokkaidō during the spring and autumn migration seasons, with some lingering to winter at lakes and bays where they can find ice-free areas at which to feed. In autumn they arrive in family groups and small flocks that have been driven south by the arrival of freezing weather further north.

Migrant swans may be found at many wetland sites throughout Eastern Hokkaidō including Lake Tōfutsu[151] on the Sea of Okhotsk coast and in Akkeshi Bay on the Pacific coast. They even forage on farmland on post-harvest waste. However, they are most famously seen and photographed during winter along the eastern shore of Lake Kussharo, especially at Suna-yu, where geothermal activity warms the beach and keeps a strip of water ice free, or at sites elsewhere along the lakeshore where hot springs keep the water tepid and even raise mist on cold mornings.

Whooper Swans at hot springs beside Lake Kussharo

Winter Whooper Swan gatherings can be noisy, even aggressive, affairs. Clamouring swans stretch out their necks and make jousting thrusts at each other with their long necks and bills. They may grasp their opponent's feathers with their beaks, thrash with their wings and kick with their feet, sending water spraying and, eventually, their opponents fleeing. Pairs then turn towards each other to perform an emotional display strengthening their own bond while celebrating successfully having defended their family against intruders. Yet where food is plentiful, they put aggression aside and gather closely packed together with their creamy-white wings and backs appearing like densely arranged pillows of snow.

Whooper Swans tolerate the presence of people in winter

Families of two adults with 2–3 cygnets are very common and the cygnets will stay with their parents throughout the winter and during the first part of the northbound spring migration. They leave Japan as ice and snow here begin to thaw, to be ready on their northern breeding grounds when the thaw arrives there.

The very best way to watch these graceful and ethereal snow angels is from a piping hot *onsen* bath, as they swim through the morning mist rising from the edge of a sparkling, snow-covered frozen lake in Eastern Hokkaidō.

A Whooper Swan family arriving at Lake Kussharo

151 43.938375, 144.396057

Tanuki

The rather stocky, short-legged, short-bodied, and bushy-tailed Tanuki is an atypical member of the dog family, or Canidae, that lacks a bark, has a distinctive facial mask, and partly hibernates. This creature is also known by the less than satisfactory English name of Raccoon Dog — it is neither a raccoon nor a dog used for hunting them; it is more closely related to the fox. Tanuki occurs in heavily wooded habitat from the lowlands to low mountains, often close to water, and although closely associated with forest and forest edge, it also occurs in agricultural areas and even suburban gardens.

Tanuki

Superficially fox-like, Tanuki has a long muzzle and erect ears, but its face is rounder, its legs and tail much shorter and its coat is rather variably pale and dark brown, grey, tan and black. Those in Hokkaidō weigh 5–9 kg and measure 54–68 cm long plus a tail of 15–19 cm.

Tanuki is entirely terrestrial, foraging only on the ground, consuming plenty of plant food including fallen fruits and berries. It also catches small mammals, such as mice and voles and occasionally eats birds, but a high proportion of its diet consists of earthworms and insects, especially beetles.

Tanuki gains weight considerably in autumn, then retreats to a burrow, from November until about April, where it becomes torpid much like a bear. Mating takes place in the spring with young born two months later. Tanuki families remain together until the following winter.

They are most active throughout the evening and again early in the morning, and may wander many kilometres in search of food.

Whereas foxes leave their droppings randomly, Tanuki regularly use fixed latrine sites at which to defecate. Their latrines often glitter with the wing cases of the beetles they have consumed; the latrines also attract butterflies that gather for the minerals.

then square white signs for the final section do help along the way. Finally there is a gravel car park with toilets and a short narrow trail to the little waterfall viewing area that is big enough for about a dozen people. This is a renowned fish-watching and photographic spot.

Thousands of Cherry Salmon *Oncorhynchus masou* ascend this river to spawn from June to September and are faced with the three-metre cataract. While all leap, few succeed in the ascent of the falls. Watching them is mesmerising. Some leap and fall short, others reach halfway up the falls but are battered back down, others simply disappear into the spray. On some days there may

be hundreds of salmon leaping every hour. This is a lovely shady woodland spot at which to wait and watch for the action while listening to the constant refreshing background noise of the rushing river and the falls.

Drawn by instinct, Cherry Salmon ascend the river of their birth © Kamada Sachiko

Hokkaidō's Megaherbs

While exploring Eastern Hokkaidō in summer it is difficult not to notice, or be impressed by, several enormous plants that grow quite commonly beside the road and in the forests. The term megaherb is used most commonly for a group of herbaceous perennial plants growing on New Zealand's subantarctic islands. They share large size, huge leaves and often very large flowers, with adaptations to the local harsh conditions. Hokkaidō also has its own large, striking herbaceous perennials that are adapted to its harsh climate and equally deserving of the term megaherb.

The most conspicuous of these Hokkaidō megaherbs are the giant Asian Skunk Cabbage, the gigantic

Japanese Butterbur, Giant Knotweed, Branched Indian Plantain and Heartleaf Lily. Because of its thick stem and large, almost umbrella-like leaves, the Japanese Butterbur is frequently mistaken for rhubarb. This giant butterbur grows in damp or poorly drained soils beside streams, ponds, in damp areas in woodlands and at forest margins. It grows steadily from spring into summer becoming chest high and so densely packed as to be the dominant ground cover beside the road or in woodland by late July. The stems are much favoured as food both by bears and by people in the spring.

Japanese Butterbur sprouts appear soon after the snow melts

Japanese Butterbur flowers are among the first to appear, pushing up from chilly soils in early spring in concert with the

Butterbur leaves are as big as umbrellas
© Ministry of the Environment

The Hellebore is another of Hokkaidō's conspicuous megaherbs

Along with Japanese Butterbur, Heartleaf Lily (L), Giant Knotweed (Centre) and Branched Indian Plantain (R) are frequently encountered roadside megaherbs

large creamy white flutes of the Asian Skunk Cabbage that appear alongside streams and in swampy areas soon after the snow melts. The elongate, sky-pointing leaves of the skunk cabbage continue to grow and enlarge until they are enormous, like the butterbur, long after flowering has finished — making the giant skunk cabbage yet another northern megaherb.

In the slightly drier margins of the forest stand White Hellebore. At first, these tall plants show only their strangely pleated leaves; later they develop their tall spires of surprisingly delicate pale-green flowers.

In more brightly lit areas, often beside trails and roads, the Heartleaf Lily is quite common. It produces a rosette of broad, dark green leaves around the base of its tall stem and eventually, after several growing seasons, raises a tall two- to three-metre-tall spire of large creamy flowers. After fertilisation the flowers drop and finger-sized pods develop. These fill with densely packed winged seeds that will be scattered by the wind during the late autumn and winter.

Along riversides and at roadsides you don't need to look for the clumps of Giant Knotweed *Fallopia sachalinense*[152] as they are so common and obvious. Now infamous around the world, wherever it was introduced as an exotic garden plant, it has become an invasive alien species, but here it is at home in its natural environment. The tall stems extending two to three metres may clatter in any breeze. Their leaves are large and elongated and eventually at the nodding tips of their stems they produce inflorescences of fine off-white flowers.

Another tall plant of forest margins and roadside verges is the Branched Indian Plantain *Parasenecio robustus*[153]. This deciduous perennial grows up to three metres in height and produces enormous triangular leaves that may be as much as 35 cm across from tip to tip.

---

152 Also called *Polygonum sachalinense* and *Reynoutria sachalinense*.   153 Also called *Parasenecio hastatus* and *Cacalia hastata*.

4

Chapter Four

Abashiri Quasi National Park and the Sea of Okhotsk Coast

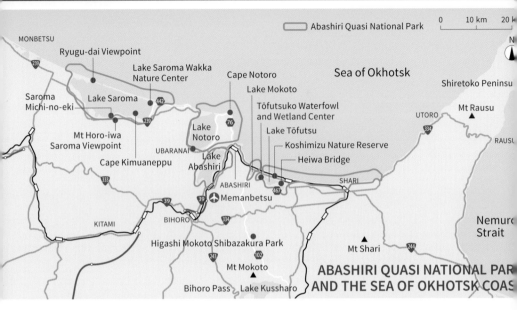

ABASHIRI QUASI NATIONAL PARK
AND THE SEA OF OKHOTSK COAST

From Monbetsu[154] to Shari, the coastline faces mainly northeast or north across the largely enclosed Sea of Okhotsk which is bounded by Russia on three sides and Hokkaidō in the south. In winter, this sea is renowned for generating the southernmost drift-ice in the northern hemisphere. The enormous volume of outpouring freshwater from the Amur River lowers the salinity of the northwestern part of the sea and hence raises the freezing point of the sea's surface water. Currents and wind carry the ice floes south down past Sakhalin until they eventually cover the southern part of the Sea of Okhotsk and reach the Hokkaidō coast. Ice breaks up and flows around the Shiretoko Peninsula (see Chapter 5) and into the Nemuro Strait. The ice brings a bounty of plankton and ice-related organisms, both directly and indirectly. The salt expelled during ice formation sinks and the heavier, more saline water carries nutrients and oxygen that support life as it flows south. Unfortunately,

ocean warming is particularly rapid in the Sea of Okhotsk shortening the sea ice period and driving certain fish populations northwards into cooler waters and away from the Japanese shore.

Hokkaidō's Sea of Okhotsk coastline varies between gently shelving dark sand beaches and moderately raised cliffs. There are areas of stabilised dunes and a number of large brackish lagoons each of which has associated salt marsh plant communities and adjacent wildflower meadows. It can be bleak, but dramatic, in winter, and from spring to autumn it is enriched by birdsong and colourful seasonal wildflowers. The cool summers and cold winters, along with the cool but rich volcanic soils here, make the area inland from the coast ideal for growing root crops and help to make the area a major producer of potatoes, beets and onions.

Seven lakes (Saroma, Notoro, Riyaushi, Abashiri, Mokoto, Tōfutsu, and Tōtsuru-tō), all of which used to be connected to the sea, now lie within the

154 Often also written as Mombetsu.

80

Abashiri Quasi NP. They share much in common, but they differ in size and each has unique features including special plants and insects. Some are more attractive to waterbirds, others to shorebirds, but all offer highlights, and each presents a different face during the passing different seasons.

From the Akan–Mashū NP there are multiple options for exploration. You could head directly to the Shiretoko Peninsula or straight to the Sea of Okhotsk coast at Abashiri via Koshimizu Pass[155] on the flank of Mt Mokoto (Mokoto-yama). However, if you have sufficient time then do explore the Abashiri Quasi NP beginning in the west with Lake Saroma.

Leave the Akan–Mashū NP northwards from Teshikaga on Rt 243 and you will pass first through farmland and forest, then along the south side of Lake Kussharo before the road winds its way up to the 493 m high Bihoro Pass and viewpoint. The broad view from here eastwards across the lake and volcanic scenery is spectacular on a fine day and strongly recommended as a special afternoon trip for photography at any time of the year.

Having crossed the pass, the road descends towards Bihoro Town running through arable farmland with crops of winter wheat, onions and potatoes and, in the lowlands beyond Bihoro, even some rice fields. From Bihoro follow Rt 39, then Rt 333 and short cut across country to join Rt 239 on the south side of Lake Saroma, where you will find Saroma Michi-no-eki (Saroma Road Station)[156].

Lake Saroma (Saroma-ko) is situated north of Kitami City in the Abashiri Quasi NP. With its 150 km² surface, it is the third largest lake in Japan (after lakes Biwa and Kasumigaura in Honshū), and the largest lake in Hokkaidō. It is also the largest brackish lagoon in Japan. Famous for scallops and, in the past, oysters, this vast lagoon is best seen and understood from Mt Horo-iwa[157] to the south of the lake. This vantage point also provides a superb spot from which to enjoy sunrise.

The Sea of Okhotsk from Cape Notoro

From the air the tapering shape of the coastal spit separating Lake Saroma from the Sea of Okhotsk is clear © The Hokkaido Shimbun Press

The shallow 25-km-long brackish lagoon is separated from the sea by two long spits to the northwest and northeast and, between them, a long barrier dune, well-stabilised and forested almost blocking off the lagoon entirely from the sea. The western entrance, once erratic and temporary, was made permanent by dredging, while the eastern entrance remains narrow and unpredictable. The whole lagoon is shallow, only 19.5 m deep at its deepest point.

155 43.697697, 144.371022   156 44.131342, 143.718875   157 44.097365, 143.836255

Lake Saroma seen from Mt Horo-iwa

It is 20 km from Saroma Michi-no-eki around the western end of the lake to the end of the north-western spit where you will find the Ryugu-dai viewpoint[158]. There are views from here over the Sea of Okhotsk to the north and south across Lake Saroma. A simple campsite (the Sanrihama Camping Ground), and a huge car park, make this an attractive stop.

Returning around the western end of the lake and along its south side to pass the Saroma Michi-no-eki again, you can next visit the Saroma viewpoint[159] which lies 20 km east of the road station. Turn inland and uphill from Toppushi, then take the turn just east of the village centre (one turn beyond the traffic lights) and follow the signs to the viewpoint.

This approach is 5 km up a mostly gravel, easily drivable, track or via hiking trails through mature mixed forest to Mt Horo-iwa. At the end of the track a viewing tower provides a wonderful panoramic

Lake Saroma seen from Cape Kimuaneppu

158 "Ryugu-dai Observatory Deck" 44.186528, 143.763531   159 44.097365, 143.836255

view of the whole of Saroma-ko from an elevation of 376 m. In fact, this is the only spot from which the entire lagoon and dune complex can be viewed. Even on a cloudy or hazy day the viewpoint allows a tremendous outlook on this enormous body of water, the spits and the long sandbar between them. The view also takes in the pretty patchwork pattern of low hills with hay fields, arable crop lands, forestry plantations and native woodland that spread inland from the southern margin of the lake. The long-range view to the east is to Cape Notoro and, rising beyond that cliffy cape, to the Shiretoko Peninsula.

The forest track and forested hills around the viewpoint offer pleasant birdwatching with chances of sighting various species such as Black Woodpecker, Oriental Cuckoo *Cuculus optatus*, Narcissus Flycatcher, Asian Stubtail *Urosphena squameiceps*, Goldcrest *Regulus regulus*, Hawfinch *Coccothraustes coccothraustes* and Japanese Grosbeak *Eophona personata*. As with most wild regions of Eastern Hokkaidō, there are indications that bears occur in the area, so do stay alert and take sensible precautions, especially if walking alone.

After descending from Mt Horo-iwa continue eastwards and make your next stop for a walk at Cape Kimuaneppu[160]. It is possible to camp at the Kimuaneppu Misaki Campsite, which makes a pleasant spot from which to explore the area. Kimuaneppu Misaki is the only cape jutting into

Lake Saroma from its southern shore. A short pathway leads around the cape. The proximity to the water, the carpets of wildflowers in season and the plentiful summer birds, combine to make this a peaceful place to stay or visit. Siberian Lilies, Siberian Lupins, Wild Roses and various irises present a delightful palette of colours while the birds here include eagles, Middendorff's Grasshopper Warblers *Locustella ochotensis*, Siberian Rubythroats, Stejneger's Stonechats, Black-browed Reed Warblers, Eurasian Skylarks *Alauda arvensis*, Long-tailed Rosefinches *Carpodacus sibiricus*, and Oriental Greenfinches *Chloris sinica*. Ponds at the base of the peninsula attract various duck including the delightful Asian speciality — the Falcated Duck.

Abashiri Quasi NP is specially protected because of its rich flora and there is no better place to enjoy this than at the Lake Saroma Wakka Nature Center and Wakka Primeval Flower Garden[161] situated near the northeast corner of the lake off Rt 442. It is open from April to mid-October and various trails allow summer walks or cycle rides[162] of different lengths over flat or gently undulating trails through wildflower meadows best viewed during peak flowering in June, July and August, though they can be pleasant also earlier and later. Siberian Lily *Lilium dauricum* or *pensylvanicum*, Wild Rose, orange-yellow Dumortier's Daylily *Hemerocallis dumortieri* and Siberian Lupin are all common here along with dozens of other species

Wakka Primeval Flower Garden

Wild lilies

Siberian Rubythroat

160 44.108278, 143.911806   161 44.135426, 143.960503   162 The centre had rental bicycles for ¥650/day in 2020.

Agriculture in Hokkaidō

Hokkaidō's agriculture, forestry, and fisheries are vitally important, contributing to a stable food supply and providing approximately 20 percent of the nation's domestically produced calories. The island's location, soil conditions and climate, its cold winters and cool summers, its long days and long hours of sunlight, and its considerable difference between daytime and night-time temperatures, make it naturally suitable for large-scale lowland farming, upland farming and dairy farming. Hokkaidō is, in fact, Japan's premier food production region with a total cultivated land area of 1,147,000 hectares.

Hokkaidō accounts for 25.5 percent of Japan's total cultivated land, and the prefecture is so productive that whereas the entire country's calorie-based food self-sufficiency ratio was as low as 38 percent (in fiscal year 2017), Hokkaidō's ratio was 206 percent! Only five other prefectures (mainly in northern Honshū), have ever reached self-sufficiency of more than 100 percent.

Hokkaidō has been developed predominantly for field crops and dairy farming, which is evident while travelling around Eastern Hokkaidō. The prefecture ranks number one annually for production of sweet corn, potatoes, Japanese yams, wheat and barley, long white radishes, known as daikon, carrots, asparagus, broccoli, pumpkins and onions, and ranks number two for rice, tomatoes, soybeans, and garlic, while coming in third or fourth for a range of other crops.

Early spring crops with Mt Shari beyond

Looked at in another way, the agricultural output of Hokkaidō has been valued at over ¥1 trillion annually since 1984, with Hokkaidō producing crucial percentages of the nation's agricultural output by volume (sugar beet 100 percent, kidney beans 94.6 percent, adzuki beans 93.1 percent, potatoes 78.6 percent, onions 62.1 percent, wheat 61.6 percent, milk 54.4 percent, dairy cattle 53.8 percent, beef cattle 13.7 percent, horses 97.5 percent, and rice 6.6 percent)[163].

of wildflowers. The birds include Japanese Bush Warbler, Black-browed Reed Warbler, Lanceolated Warbler *Locustella lanceolata*, Sakhalin Grasshopper Warbler *Locustella amnicola*, Siberian Rubythroat, Chestnut-eared Bunting *Emberiza fucata*, and many Eurasian Skylark. The eastern shore in spring and autumn offers superb sunset views across the lake.

From the Wakka Nature Centre it is just 18 km east along Rt 442 and Rt 239 to the Notoro Gensei-kaen (Notoro Wildflower Meadows)[164] and

the spit that almost closes off the mouth of Lake Notoro. This is a pleasant drive through coastal meadows and past shallow wetlands on both sides of the road, then through farmland with potatoes and winter wheat crops.

Notoro Koguchi, at the narrow entrance to Lake Notoro, is a sleepy-feeling headland with a breakwater where cormorants fish just offshore. There is also a view eastwards to the cliffs and headland of Notoro with its prominent black-and-white lighthouse. The whole area around this lake and Lake

163 Agricultural data from Department of Agriculture Hokkaidō Government (2020), Japan Crops (2020) and National Agriculture and Food Research Organization (2020).   164   44.1030444, 144.1841539

Lake Notoro is renowned for its extensive areas of colourful glasswort and wild irises

Saroma offers a lovely landscape for cycling. Driving back to Rt 239 you find wide views of the low coastal landscape around Lake Notoro and the rural farmland of this region.

Lake Notoro, at 58.4 km^2 is the 13th largest lake in Japan and the fifth largest in Hokkaidō. Along with Lake Tōfutsu, it is an important shorebird migration site in spring and autumn. At Ubaranai[165], at the southwest extremity of the brackish lake, there is a site just west of the Koshitoshi River that is renowned for Common Glasswort *Salicornia europaea* (aka Marsh Samphire or Coral Grass), a salt-tolerant plant. From mid September to early October this strange fleshy plant turns deep red

adding a touch of beauty and drama to what might otherwise be bleak wetland scenery.

Having looped around Lake Notoro, continue up the east side by turning onto Rt 76 in Futami-ga-oka and continue straight on for 24 km (approximately 30 mins) to reach Cape Notoro[166].

If, instead of visiting lakes Saroma and Notoro, you aim to travel northwards from the Akan–Mashū NP directly to the coast, then leave Teshika-ga towards Kawayu Onsen on Rt 391. The road here parallels the railway tracks although the railway is hidden in the forest off to the right. The forest consists mainly of birch trees with occasional Sakhalin Spruces and Kobus Magnolias.

The Kussharo Caldera seen from the Mt Mokoto viewpoint

165 44.0137237, 144.1167509   166 44.113051, 144.243422

Narcissus-flowered Anemone

From the traffic lights signalling the north end of Kawayu Onsen, continue approximately 4.5 km then turn left onto Rt 102 towards Mt Mokoto and the pass that leads north towards the coast. The low hills ahead are actually the crater rim of the Kussharo Caldera. There are a number of small farms in this area, but it is mostly forested with the usual mixture of birch, willow, oak, lime and spruce. As Rt 102 winds its way up towards the caldera rim, look out to your left to catch glimpses of steam rising from Mt Iwō, then of Lake Kussharo

Creeping Phlox or Moss Phlox at Shibazakura Park

and in the distance the peak of Mt O-Akan showing over the crater rim. Eventually the forest gives way to open areas of dwarf bamboo and scattered Japanese Stone Pine trees.

After about 8.5 km there is a parking area and viewpoint[167] to the left of the road providing a panoramic view of Lake Kussharo to the south and southwest. This view takes in Mt Shari to the northeast, the crater rim of Lake Mashū to the southeast, and the crater rim of the Kussharo Caldera. Rising to the northwest you can see the slopes of Mt Mokoto covered with Japanese Stone Pines and Erman's Birches. After another 1 km the view to the north is down to the shore of the Sea of Okhotsk. Rt 102 continues to climb through a series of switchbacks and a snow tunnel towards the pass. Another 1 km further on, a left turn will take you up to Highland Koshimizu. About 1 km from the turn you will reach a parking area, an observatory building, a separate toilet building, and the trailhead for Mt Mokoto. This is a rewarding short hike of just over an hour (one way). The top of the mountain offers fantastic views across the lake. In the Japanese Stone Pine and Erman's Birch forest along the way there are often interesting summer birds such as Spotted Nutcrackers *Nucifraga caryocatactes* and Japanese Accentors *Prunella rubida* as well as Siberian Rubythroats.

It is difficult to decide during which season the views are best — they are spectacular throughout the year. While driving back down towards Rt 102, you will find a lovely view of the various mountains of east Hokkaidō.

After re-joining Rt 102 and continuing north to Abashiri City (population c35,000) the road descends through Sakhalin Spruce forest with birch and dwarf bamboo. About 11 km further north, after rejoining Rt 102, you may notice an open hillside adorned with a strangely pink Shintō Shrine gate. You have reached the entrance to the small Higashi Mokoto Shibazakura Park[168]. If you visit

167   Oddly signed as the Mokotoyama Observatory Parking Park at 43.687690, 144.379829   168   43.782739, 144.310524

The Siberian Flying Squirrel

As twilight spreads in the forest, the day shift of insects, birds and mammals falls silent and gives way to the emerging night shift. Perhaps a Ural Owl will give its gruff hoots, or a dog fox may bark sending alarm and fear through the minds of voles and mice.

A hard to discern distortion of a tree trunk's silhouette and an almost subliminal flicker of movement may be the first sign that a nocturnal Siberian Flying Squirrel has just emerged from its day rest in a natural tree cavity or old woodpecker nest hole. Just 15–16 cm long, with a 10–12 cm tail, this flying squirrel weighs only 81–120 g.

The dark line along the flanks is the squirrels flying membrane

Its enormous limpid eyes reflect the whole forest; a wrinkled two-tone fold of fur along each flank is in fact a fold of skin known as the patagium, which can be extended tautly between the sides of the body and the outstretched limbs, making a kind of wing membrane. After leaving its roosting cavity, it will invariably scurry upwards to the treetops from where it will launch itself out. It stretches its arms and legs wide using its patagial membrane to sky-sail like a miniature base jumper wearing its very own squirrel suit that will carry it several trees further into the forest.

Siberian Flying Squirrels occasionally emerge during daylight

It will spend the night foraging in its territory for edible leaves, buds, flowers, seeds and nuts of deciduous broadleaved trees.

In Japan, this widespread Old World boreal species lives only in Hokkaidō, where it breeds twice a year. Males have large home ranges (up to 2 ha), and females have small ones (of about 1 ha). Females give birth to litters of 2–6 young in spring and summer. Their lives are short; they may only survive for three years in the wild.

during May you cannot miss the vibrantly pink hillside covered with Creeping Phlox or Moss Phlox *Phlox subulata*, a species introduced from North America, but very popular with Japanese tourists. For a brief period the entire hillside is covered with their small pink flowers and near the top of the hill is the small shrine gate (also pink!).

After the Shibazakura Park, you will descend through a broad fertile valley with numerous crop fields all the way towards the coast. Four kilome-

tres beyond the village of Higashi Mokoto another surprise is in store in the form of an Emu farm situated prominently beside the road.

Rt 102 continues straight on to join the coast at Mokoto, just beyond Lake Mokoto. During May many early plants are in flower, not only those pink Moss Phlox. Dandelions, considered a weed in many countries, are a golden delight beside country roads in spring, while in gardens and in the forests there are cherry trees and magnolia trees in

Shintō

Japan has an indigenous polytheistic and animistic religion known as Shintō or way of the gods. Supernatural deities (kami) are believed to inhabit all things, including creatures, rocks, trees and so on. These deities are worshiped privately by practitioners at home, at a household shrine, or publicly at more prominent public shrines. You may notice shrines atop mountains, on offshore rocks, or situated amongst trees on the edge of communities.

Shintō shrines are marked by distinctive entrance gates, known as *torii*, with two vertical posts and two horizontal top bars. The shrine sanctuary is where a particular deity has been enshrined and where sacred objects are stored. Worshipers approach only the outside; they do not step inside. They purify themselves with water and approach the shrine to make an offering (often in the form of money, as coins or notes) and to say a prayer. Some shrines are enormous and impressive for their scale, but among the most memorable are the miniature shrines to be found atop mountains where the whole peak is considered sacred.

The distinctive vermilion entrance gate of a Shintō Shrine in Abashiri

The Shintō shrine gate at Cape Shirepa

Cape Notoro with its lighthouse

flower too.

When you reach the coast, turn left to the city of Abashiri and there cross the Abashiri River and head out of town on Rt 76 following signs towards Cape Notoro. From the town it is approximately 11 km to the cape. As you leave town the road slowly climbs and, when not passing through mature, mixed deciduous forest, you will have views out to the Sea of Okhotsk on your right. Ten kilometres after crossing the Abashiri River you will find the final turning to the cape. From here it is a 1 km drive to the parking area. On the way you will notice the main feature of Cape Notoro — the black-and-white Notoro Lighthouse[169].

A post-and-rail fence marks the edge of the

169 44.112129, 144.243139

Dwarf Bamboo — a local indicator of Global Warming

The forest floor and roadside ground cover of Eastern Hokkaidō are dominated by dwarf bamboo. Three species are involved forming typical and essential components of the forest ecosystem, driving, to an extent, the composition of the forest herb flora. The dwarf bamboos of Hokkaidō in the genus *Sasa* (taken directly from the Japanese name) produce such dense leaves that they shade the forest floor making it quite dark and thereby suppressing the growth and regeneration of other low-growing species.

Dwarf bamboos regenerate more rapidly than most species after disturbance, such as fire, giving them a competitive edge. These species grow up to three metres in height and flower synchronously every 60–100 years, after which large quantities of seeds are produced before the plants die.

Eastern Hokkaidō's three widespread species are *Sasa senanensis*, *Sasa nipponica* and *Sasa kurilensis*. The first two are at home at low elevations and the third at higher elevations. *Sasa senanensis* produces simple branching stems and large leaves. It grows up to 2.5 m in height; it is highly flexible and adapts to different nutrient and environmental conditions. Thus, not surprisingly, it has the greatest distribution in Eastern Hokkaidō. *Sasa nipponica* is also widespread at low elevations in Eastern Hokkaidō, but has simple unbranched stems with large leaves and grows only to 1–2 m tall. It requires the fertile conditions of soils with a deep humus layer, but like *Sasa senanensis* can cope with those soils freezing. The third species, *Sasa kurilensis* is the hardiest of the three. It produces multi-branching stems, with small leaves and grows up to 3 m in height in shallow infertile soils corresponding to areas with deep snow and harsh conditions.

Warming conditions favour *Sasa kurilensis*. As snow melts more quickly each spring (research in the Daisetsu Mountains of central Hokkaidō has shown that this is now up to four days earlier per decade), the soils at higher elevations dry more quickly allowing dwarf bamboo to spread and out-compete perennial alpine plants in Hokkaidō's mountains. The dwarf bamboos themselves absorb large amounts of water further drying the soil and excluding alpine plants that require damper, more humid conditions.

Dwarf bamboo emerging after a winter beneath the snow

cliff and indicates a very easy, almost flat, loop walk around the cape. This takes in the lighthouse and a monument to the fishermen of the Sea of Okhotsk before returning to the car park in about 30–40 minutes. The views are delightful, in winter spectacular, and the almost constant breeze here makes it an excellent spot to fly a kite.

There are eagles around the cape throughout the year and in winter there are sometimes Steller's Eagles here too. If you look down into the surf just off shore you may see various sea ducks (including Harlequin Duck, Black Scoter, Red-breasted Merganser *Mergus serrator*) and perhaps even a Spotted Seal[170] *Phoca largha*. The natural sounds here are marvellous. They are dominated by the wind, the waves, and the rustling of the wind-blown

170 Also called the Largha Seal, and in Japanese it is the *Gomafu-azarashi*, named for its sesame-like spots.

Harbours and Birds

The many harbours of Eastern Hokkaidō attract a wide range of avian species at different times of the year. Some come to scavenge from the fishing fleets, some to shelter from storm winds and high seas, others to feed in their sheltered waters, and many to roost in safety along the harbour walls and ledges and on the roofs of harbourside warehouses.

Watch for both Temminck's *Phalacrocorax capillatus* and Pelagic *Phalacrocorax pelagicus* Cormorants roosting on the outer walls and fishing in the harbours; note the throngs of Black-tailed *Larus crassirostris* and Slaty-backed *Larus schistisagus* Gulls roosting with them, or the larger Slaty-backed Gulls raising their chicks in summer in messy nests atop the buildings and harbour walls. The two common species of gulls are occasionally joined by other, scarcer species — making harbours an excellent place to watch for unusual species.

Sea ducks take shelter in the harbours during rough weather, so that in winter it is often possible to find Harlequin Ducks, Long-tailed Ducks, Red-breasted Mergansers, Greater Scaups *Aythya marila* and Black Scoters close enough to photograph. Sometimes grebes and divers, auks and auklets, even swans, may be found sheltering with them.

Temminck's Cormorant © Kurita Masateru

Slaty-backed Gull

Harlequin Duck male

The Red-breasted Merganser is piscivorous — it eats fish — and has serrated edges to its bill © Peter Porazzo

dwarf bamboo, until the arrival of the drift-ice, which comes with its own indescribable sound — then there is silence. In summer you may hear Eurasian Skylarks singing here, while in winter there will be the crooning sounds of sea duck offshore or the brittle crashing sound of sea ice being washed against the rocks. Once the sea ice locks in against the shore the sound of the sea changes dramatically, as the ice first dampens, then completely masks, the waves so that the sea becomes silent.

Spotted or Largha Seal © Kamada Sachiko

Abashiri offers a number of enticing options ranging from the excellent Hokkaidō Museum of Northern Peoples, to the small but fascinating Moyoro Shell Mound Historic Site and Museum[171] dedicated to an ancient Okhotsk village where, amazingly, many Short-tailed Albatross *Phoebastria albatrus* bones have been found. In summer and autumn one may take a whale watching excursion to look for Northern Minke Whales, when there may also be thousands of Short-tailed Shearwaters *Ardenna tenuirostris*. In winter a sightseeing trip out to the sea ice may be taken by boat. Return to the city from walking at Cape Notoro and continue 12 km eastwards now on Rt 244 to Tōfutsu-ko. Rt 244 parallels the coast, so for much of the drive you can observe the Sea of Okhotsk to your left and the Shiretoko Peninsula ahead. The mountains there are white with snow from late October well into June. You will pass Lake Mokoto on your right before reaching the shallow brackish lagoon of Tōfutsu-ko, just east of Kitahama. Wakasagi or Japanese Lake Smelt *Hypomesus nipponensis* and Lake Shrimp *Palaemon paucidens* are important catches here, and Pacific Oysters *Crassostrea gigas* are cultivated too. This 900 ha brackish lagoon was formed some 1,200–3,000 years ago when a sandbar cut off a bay from the sea. Today, Tōfutsu-ko is a vitally important migratory stopover site for many species of waterfowl in spring and autumn and a good area to look for eagles in winter. Its 27.3 km shoreline is surrounded by coastal grasslands

An excavated dwelling at Moyoro Shell Mound

Large flocks of Short-tailed Shearwater gather offshore from Abashiri

and marshes. There are sometimes shorebirds here on migration and often one or more pairs of cranes.

Near the west end of the lagoon, signed as the Swan Park[172], there is the Tōfutsu-ko Waterfowl and Wetland Center and viewing area, and an observation tower on the escarpment above.

171 44.0247512, 144.269264   172 43.952438, 144.359049

Kamchatka Fritillary

Once renowned for the large number of Whooper Swans gathering here, feeding is no longer allowed and swans are only occasionally present, but it is still worth visiting as it is now a spot from which to watch various duck, gull, and shorebird species depending on the season.

At the western end of the lagoon Rt 244 crosses the bridge over the lagoon's only outlet channel, the Maruman River, with the JR Senmō railway line just beyond and the sea just beyond that. On the seaward side of the road there are stabilised sand dunes overgrown with coarse grasses, Wild Roses, and a host of other plant species. In summer, this is a wonderful area for wildflower watching and from late June to late July it hosts a profuse flowering of perennial Lemon Daylilies *Hemerocallis lilioasphodelus*. The small trees growing amongst the dunes are completely wind sculpted, leaning landwards from being continuously shaped by wind and the salt-laden air.

Eagles frequent the environs of the lagoon throughout the year, and watch for Eastern Marsh Harriers *Circus spilonotus* and other birds of prey over the extensive reed marshes with occasional low bushes on the landward side of the road. In winter there may be Short-eared Owls *Asio flammeus* too. Looking southwards across the lagoon you can see Mt Mokoto in the distance. Five kilometres to the east of the west end of the lagoon you will reach the Koshimizu Gensei-kaen (wildflower area)[173] and Koshimizu Nature Reserve. There is a parking area here (along with souvenir shops and

Looking across Tōfutsu-ko to Mt Shari

173   43.941007, 144.413737

Furetoi Observatory (© Koshimizu Tourist Association) in summer and the view of the Sea of Okhotsk from the observatory in February

toilets), from which a track leads across the railway lines up to a viewing area. From the viewpoint there is a short circular walk through the wildflower meadows and Wild Roses to the beach. In June, July, and August, the wide variety of wildflowers is spectacular with bright yellow Siberian Lupins, pink Wild Roses, purple wild irises, orange lilies, deep maroon Kamchatka Fritillaries *Fritillaria camschatcensis*, and many more species. From mid-July until the end of August this is one of the few places in Japan where you can listen to the brittle rattling sounds of the amazingly named Wart-biter Bush Cricket[174] *Decticus verrucivorus* (it occurs only along the Okhotsk coast). While admiring flowers and listening to the sounds of nature, also do note the hollows in the earth here too, as they are the remains of ancient pit dwellings.

At the east end of the lagoon a turning south onto Rt 467 leads to the Heiwa Bridge[175] (3 km from Rt 244), which gives fine views across the lagoon and is an excellent spot for birdwatching. The broad flow beneath the bridge is the Urashibetsu River which connects Lake Tōfutsu to Uratōfutsu, the extension of the wetland to the east. Both the main shallow lagoon and Uratōfutsu are reed-fringed and important resting grounds for migratory waterfowl and a breeding ground for one

or two pairs of cranes. The area supports a small population of Gadwall *Mareca strepera*, a species of duck that breeds here and in few other areas in Hokkaidō. In autumn, the sound from here of Bean Geese leaving their roost before dawn is one of the great natural events of Eastern Hokkaidō. Other special sounds here in late autumn and early winter are those of large flocks of Common Mergansers[176] *Mergus merganser* many hundreds strong, and dense packs of Black-necked Grebes *Podiceps nigricollis* group fishing, splashing and diving simultaneously. The view southeast to Mt Shari covered with the first snow of winter is also delightful.

Back on Rt 244 continue a little further east and, just before Hama-Koshimizu Station, the road station and Mont-Bell outdoor store, you will find a track that turns left across the railway lines to a parking area, picnic area and campsite. From there a short trail climbs steeply up the hillside to a white pyramidal building on top. This is the Furetoi Observatory which provides a panoramic view of the Sea of Okhotsk and the beaches east and west, and a long-range view back to the lagoon. In spring and autumn it can be interesting to watch for seabirds from here, and in winter it is an excellent place from which to view the sea ice.

174 So named because in eighteenth century Sweden, near the western end of their range, they were used to nibble off warts! 175 43.923353, 144.429251 176 Also called Goosander.

93

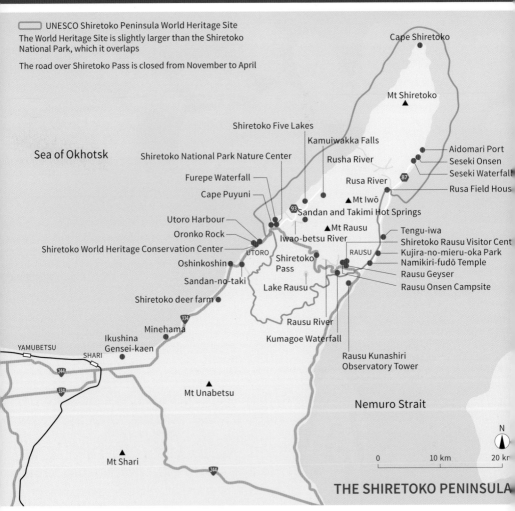

UNESCO Shiretoko Peninsula World Heritage Site
The World Heritage Site is slightly larger than the Shiretoko National Park, which it overlaps

The road over Shiretoko Pass is closed from November to April

Cape Shiretoko

Mt Shiretoko

Shiretoko Five Lakes

Kamuiwakka Falls

Sea of Okhotsk

Shiretoko National Park Nature Center

Rusha River

Aidomari Port
Seseki Onsen
Seseki Waterfall

Furepe Waterfall

Rusa River

Rusa Field House

Cape Puyuni

Mt Iwō

Sandan and Takimi Hot Springs

Utoro Harbour

Mt Rausu

Tengu-iwa

Oronko Rock

Iwao-betsu River

Shiretoko Rausu Visitor Center

Shiretoko World Heritage Conservation Center

UTORO

RAUSU

Kujira-no-mieru-oka Park

Oshinkoshin

Shiretoko Pass

Namikiri-fudō Temple

Rausu Geyser

Sandan-no-taki

Lake Rausu

Rausu Onsen Campsite

Shiretoko deer farm

Minehama

Rausu River

Ikushina Gensei-kaen

Kumagoe Waterfall

YAMUBETSU

SHARI

Mt Unabetsu

Rausu Kunashiri Observatory Tower

Nemuro Strait

N

Mt Shari

0   10 km   20 km

THE SHIRETOKO PENINSULA

The Shiretoko Peninsula and Shiretoko NP lie east of Abashiri Quasi NP, and north-east of Akan–Mashū NP. This remote finger of land, approximately 70 km long by 25 km wide, extends like a drawn broad-bladed sword and separates the Sea of Okhotsk from the Nemuro Strait. Named *Sir-etok* by the Ainu, the name means a promontory or, more romantically, the 'End of the Earth'[177]. The strictly repetitive consonant–vowel syllabic pronunciation of Japanese led *sir-etok* to become *Shirietoku* and now Shiretoko.

The peninsula's rugged spine consists of a well-forested mountainous ridge of volcanic peaks with three particularly prominent volcanoes — Mt

---

177 Perhaps this is a more modern interpretation, given that Ainu also lived in Sakhalin and the southern Kuril Islands (Kunashiri Island is easily visible from Hokkaidō), travelled between them, and so surely knew that this was *not* the end of the Earth.

Shiretoko (1,254 m), Mt Iwō[178] (1,562 m) and Mt Rausu (1,661 m). Mt Rausu, overlooking the town of the same name, dominates the steep volcanic Shiretoko Range, much of which rises above 1,000 m. The range extends almost to the tip of the peninsula at Cape Shiretoko. Mt Iwō is unusual in that it erupts molten sulphur. It last erupted from December 1935 to October 1936, during which time the mountain ejected approximately 200,000 tons of pure sulphur. It once was mined for this valued material. Traces of this bounty can be seen on the yellow seabed near the Kamuiwakka Waterfall on the Kamuiwakka River. The name of the river and falls are taken from the Ainu language meaning 'Water of the Gods'.

Snow lingers well into summer on the Shiretoko Peninsula

Shiretoko NP (61,307 ha[179]), perhaps the wildest national park in all of Japan, protects a complex and integrated ecosystem of interconnected mountains, forests, rivers and seas. It was designated as a national park in June 1964, and became a UNESCO World Natural Heritage Site in July 2005. Here the mountains and the sea are in very close proximity. In this landscape are diverse environments from the rocky shore to the alpine zone with mixed forest of needle leaved trees and deciduous trees in between. Local guides here urge us to take time, to walk, watch and experience the richness of nature on the peninsula, while maintaining a respectful stance towards the iconic bears living there. They also recommend walking in a different way (in a dry suit) amongst the drift-ice in winter when the colours and texture change daily.

The Shiretoko Peninsula is vibrant in summer, seen here from beyond Utoro

During summer the Shiretoko Peninsula is lush and immensely productive both below and above water. In winter it is icebound by the southernmost sea ice in the northern hemisphere. Maritime conditions strongly influence the local climate here. In summer, as humid southerly winds blow inland from the sea, considerable precipitation falls along the mountain flanks of the eastern shore, the Rausu side, which faces the Nemuro Strait separating Hokkaidō from the neighbouring island of Kunashiri just 20 km across the water to the east. The same winds blow across the mountain range towards the western shore of the peninsula, the Utoro side, facing the Sea of Okhotsk, which lies in the rain shadow and is drier with higher temperatures.

During winter, the ice that forms in the northwestern part of the Sea of Okhotsk, drifts southwards until it surrounds the peninsula for several weeks. The drifting sea ice reaches the Utoro coast first in January, thus the Utoro side experiences its most extreme impact with scouring and eroding of the rocky shoreline. Then the previously stormy

178 Also sometimes spelled Mt Iō or Mt Io.   179 Shiretoko NP was extended in 2019 and now includes 38,954 ha on land and 22,353 ha of the surrounding sea.

The Shiretoko Peninsula is spectacular in winter from the Nemuro Strait

Eagles, drift ice and Mt Rausu from the Nemuro Strait

grey sea is quietened and becomes a vast white field of ice and snow damping the waves completely and creating a magnificent scene all the way to the horizon. Currents then help the ice drift around the peninsula and into the Nemuro Strait on the

Rausu side; eventually it continues beyond Shiretoko reaching even as far as Nemuro, the city in Hokkaidō's southeast corner.

The year-round generally cool climate here exerts a strong influence on the vegetation. Natural grasslands on the coastal slopes with Painted Maples *Acer mono* along the cliffs give way to mixed montane forest on the lower flanks of the mountains. The primary mixed forests at lower elevations support a range of broadleaf and needle leaved species consisting largely of Ezo Spruce, Sakhalin Fir, and Mizunara Oak, Japanese Yew *Taxus cuspidata*, Prickly Castor Oil Tree, various maples and Japanese Rowan. At higher elevations the hardy Erman's Birch dominates and then at the tree line Japanese Stone Pines and Montane Alders *Alnus maximowiczii* take over.

Above the tree line, among the rocks and in the alpine meadows alpine flowers such as Wedge-leaf Primroses (or Pixie Eyes) *Primula cuneifolia*, Aleutian Avens *Geum pentapetalum*, Komakusa *Dicentra peregrina*, Meakan Cinquefoils *Potentilla miyabei* and the endemic Shiretoko Violet *Viola kitamiana* can all be found. The cool climate here

Lord of the Owls — Protector of the Village

Blakiston's Fish Owl is the size of a White-tailed Eagle © Fukuda Toshiji

The Ainu share their homeland with multiple deities including the magnificent Blakiston's Fish Owl, a secretive and enigmatic resident of mature riverside forest in Eastern Hokkaidō. They revere it as the deity, *Kotan Kor Kamuy* the defender or protector of the village. Like the similarly deified crane, this giant owl can still be found in Hokkaidō, but unlike the crane its numbers remain perilously low.

Arguably the world's largest owl, and one of the rarest species on Earth, it dwells in riverside forest where fish abound. There it nests in huge tree cavities in enormous trees (or today often in giant nest boxes set up specially for them by conservationists). Its traditional habitat coincided with Ainu settlements, close to freshwater with plentiful fish so that the deep sonorous calls of this nocturnal deity would have been a familiar sound for Ainu villagers.

As its name indicates, for much of the year it eats fish, but these long-lived birds live in Japan's harshest northern environment, so when ice covers the streams and rivers in winter it broadens its diet to include small birds, mice, voles and even flying squirrels. Pairs occupy year-round territories marking their presence with a far-carrying duet. They begin nesting during winter, raising at best only one or two young, and not every year.

means that many alpine plant species occur at lower elevations here than elsewhere in Hokkaidō, with some found as low as 400 m.

Thanks to the survival of its interconnected ecosystem from sea to peak, the Shiretoko Peninsula supports a small population of Blakiston's Fish Owls and one of the healthiest populations of bears remaining in Hokkaidō. Bears frequently forage along the coastal strip during spring, summer and autumn so they are most readily seen by taking a boat towards Cape Shiretoko from either Utoro or Rausu.

The wild forests of the peninsula, combined with its beautiful volcanoes, contribute greatly to the untamed, bountiful appearance of its scenery.

Winter brings drifting ice, and with it comes the phytoplankton that forms the base of the food web at the top of which are fish, seals and eagles. One creature of the macro-plankton, the Clione — the sea ice angel — has become a popular mascot for these waters, which can sometimes be seen during a drift-ice walk near Utoro. Eastern Hokkaidō's coastal waters are richly productive, but none more so than those around the Shiretoko Peninsula which provide some of the greatest catches of marine life in Hokkaidō. These are seasonally dependent, but include Pink

Seals and Sea Lions of Eastern Hokkaidō

Northern Fur Seal

Though ungainly on land Northern Fur Seals are graceful underwater © Kamada Sachiko

Steller's Sea Lion © Kamada Sachiko

The cold Oyashio current flows south from the Bering Sea and past northern Japan bringing with it many cold-associated species, especially during winter and spring (December to May). Various species of Pinnipeds (seals and sea lions) visit Japan in winter and these include especially Northern Fur Seals *Callorhinus ursinus*, Steller's Sea Lions, Spotted Seals, and Harbour Seals. The first two show extreme sexual dimorphism — males are enormous and dwarf their more slightly built females.

The Northern Fur Seal has a broad head with a sharply pointed snout; it is very much at home in cold water, and adopts an odd, but highly distinctive, jug-handle posture as it rests at the sea surface and thermoregulates, gripping a hind foot with a forefoot creating an arc. This sexually dimorphic seal has a silvery-grey to dark, blackish-brown coat. Adult males may weigh up to 210 kg and grow to 2.0 m in length, whereas females weigh only up to 44 kg and grow to merely 1.3 m in length. The Northern Fur Seal's fur is especially fine and dense which led to its being commercially harvested during the 18th and 19th centuries and thus populations became dramatically depleted.

The Northern Fur Seal is dwarfed by the impressive Steller's Sea Lion, which also reaches Hokkaidō in winter. This tawny brown animal is the largest eared seal in the world. Steller's Sea Lion has a broad flat-crowned head with a wide, blunt snout. The largest males can grow to nearly three metres in length, and weigh up to 1,000 kg, whereas adult females can grow to reach just over two metres in length and weight 300 kg. In Hokkaidō these sea lions are most frequently seen off the Shiretoko Peninsula in winter.

The common earless seal of Eastern Hokkaidō is the Spotted Seal. This is a fairly common winter visitor to coastal waters, most of them arriving with the sea ice drifting down from the Sea of Okhotsk. The head is broad across the crown and tapers to a rounded muzzle. The eyes are large and dark brown; the muzzle is furred, has extensive long stiff whiskers, and the nostrils can be completely closed. There are no external ears. This blunt-nosed creature — a medium-sized pale grey-brown seal with an irregular scattering of many small dark, oval spots — may float upright in the water, its bobbing head pointing upwards like a broad-based floating bottle. In water, it appears dark grey, and after hauling out for some time it becomes a lighter, sandy-grey colour as its fur dries. It feeds on a wide range of fish, and octopus. Males may reach 168 cm long and weigh 90 kg, whereas females weigh up to 75 kg and measure up to 162 cm.

True seals differ from the eared seals (fur seals and sea lions) in that they have short, broad, forelimbs modified as paddles and heavily modified hind limbs largely hidden within the body. They cannot be drawn forward beneath the body. This means that on land they can barely move beyond an ungainly wriggling motion. They are agile in water, moving by flexing the spine for propulsion, and using the forelimbs for directional control. In contrast, the eared seals have exposed outer ears, long forelimbs and hind limbs that can be drawn beneath the body making them supremely aqua-dynamic and also fast and agile on land over short distances.

Spotted Seals are sometimes joined by their larger and endangered local relative the Harbour Seal. Their range is much more restricted and in Eastern Hokkaidō they are most likely to be seen around the Nemuro Peninsula and at Daikoku Island near Akkeshi. Males of this species reach 190 cm in length and can weigh up to 170 kg.

Scarcer, even rare, seals are occasionally encountered along Eastern Hokkaidō shores in winter. These include Ringed, Ribbon and Bearded Seals, and even the accidental Walrus *Odobenus rosmarus*.

Spotted Seal © Kurita Masateru

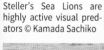

Steller's Sea Lions are highly active visual predators © Kamada Sachiko

Spotted Seals frequently float at the surface showing only their heads © Kamada Sachiko

Steller's Sea Lions are extremely sociable © Kamada Sachiko

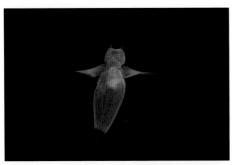

Clione © Kamada Sachiko

Orca in the Nemuro Strait off Rausu

Sperm Whale is the largest of the toothed whales

Salmon[180], Chum Salmon[181], Walleye Pollock[182] *Gadus chalcogrammus*, sea urchins and kelp. The kelp beds are important spawning grounds for numerous fish species thus contributing greatly to the bounty of the offshore ocean. These waters also support the largest population of marine mammals in Japan.

Northern Minke Whales are common in the southern Sea of Okhotsk between Abashiri and the peninsula, Killer Whale, or Orca, gather during winter in the Nemuro Strait, Sperm Whales *Physeter macrocephalus* migrate past the Kuril Islands and enter the northern part of the Nemuro Strait while various dolphins, porpoises and seals may also be encountered. Steller's Sea Lions and up to five species of seal visit the Shiretoko Peninsula. The commonest species here is the Spotted Seal, while Harbour Seals[183] *Phoca vitulina stejnegeri*, Ribbon Seals *Histriophoca fasciata*, Ringed Seals *Pusa hispida* and even Bearded Seals *Erignathus barbatus* have all been recorded too. As the sea ice nears, the seals travel with it and are increasingly seen from boats approaching the ice for eagle watching. Further out amongst the heavier ice the seals give birth and raise their pups far from land. In summer, currents and upwellings encourage a sumptuous bounty and it is then that Dall's Porpoises *Phocoenoides dalli* and Pacific White-sided Dolphins *Lagenorhynchus obliquidens* are most likely to be encountered.

Given the intensity of the human exploitation of the marine resources of these coastal waters, it is astonishing that there is still such wildlife profusion here. There is a wide range of climatic conditions on the steep-sided narrow Shiretoko peninsula. The terrestrial flora is diverse. The ocean is rich because of the currents and the winter drift-ice. The continuous natural environment extends from the ocean to the alpine zone with little or no human disturbance (which is rare in Japan). These are the underlying factors that make the Shiretoko

---

180 Also called Humpback Salmon.   181 Also called Dog Salmon.   182 Also called Alaska Pollock.   183 Also called the Kuril Seal *Phoca kurilensis*.

Peninsula so special. Spectacular scenery, deep snow, sea ice and magnificent wildlife combine to make Shiretoko NP one of the most exciting areas of Japan. Its very remoteness helps to retain its role as a haven for wildlife.

The Shiretoko Peninsula can be approached from several different directions, but in each case the saw-backed skyline is distinctive and clearly volcanic. Whether you approach from Teshikaga on Rt 391, or travel along the Sea of Okhotsk coast on Rt 244 and Rt 334 from the west, from the Abashiri Quasi NP, or enter via the east coast along Rt 335, you will see the wilder landscape ahead of you for much of your journey.

Travelling north from Teshikaga towards the district of Koshimizu and the coast will take you over the Nogami Pass (320 m)[184] and through boreal forest. Many of the roads in east Hokkaidō are only a few metres above sea level. So even when you cross inland passes, such as this one, they are only measured in hundreds, not thousands, of metres above sea level. As you descend to the coast, forest gives way to broad fields of sugar beet, potatoes, winter wheat, barley, daikon, peas and onions. The view eastwards takes in the sharp peak of Mt Shari.

As you reach the coast you will join Rt 244, the main road east between Lake Tōfutsu in the Abashiri Quasi NP and the town of Shari (population about 12,000). If you follow backroads closer to the coastline paralleling the shore wherever you can, you will see many fields that are important in spring and autumn for migrating families and flocks of geese and swans and perhaps find cranes foraging there too.

Just west of Yamubetsu Station, a track towards the coast leads to a forestry plantation (Yamubetsu Kaigan Chisan no Mori)[185] lying between the railway line (connecting the towns of Abashiri and Shari) and the coast. This forest was planted on the coastal sand dunes to help protect the area against

Looking southwest down the Shiretoko Peninsula © The Hokkaido Shimbun Press

storm surges. It consists mostly of Sakhalin Spruce and Japanese Emperor Oak *Quercus dentata* because they are hardy and tolerant of dry soils. The first plantings were made in 1937 with subsequent plantings over many decades. There is a 1.7-km trail around the plantation with open access; the trail is clearly marked on a map at the forest entrance.

As you continue eastwards from Yamubetsu Station, you begin to see the mountains again. The isolated peak, inland from the town of the same name, is Mt Shari, with its prominent sharp tipped peak rising to 1,547 m. Further east is another isolated mountain — Mt Unabetsu (1,419 m). Beyond the isolated peaks of Shari and Unabetsu are the mountains belonging to the Shiretoko mountain range, which continues almost to the tip of the peninsula.

Thirteen kilometres east of Yamubetsu Station you will cross Shari Bridge. Birdwatchers should explore left from here to the mouth of the Shari Riv-

184 43.688372, 144.466605   185 43.923021, 144.518071

Forest-covered stabilised dunes and flower meadows at Ikushina Genseikaen

Fringed Pink *Dianthus superbus* at Ikushina Genseikaen

Oshinkoshin Waterfall

er[186], often a good place to watch gulls, cormorants and sea ducks. It has the distinction of having had more records of the very rare winter visitor Ross's Gull *Rhodostethia rosea* than any other location in Japan. Two kilometres further east you will pass the Okhotsk cemetery and a further 2 km on, you will reach Ikushina Gensei-kaen[187]. You can access the beach here or take the trail that parallels the beach and loops through the stabilised dune forest for just over 1 km. The low swale just inland, between banks of dune forest, is a delightful wildflower meadow famous for its perennial Siberian Lilies and Wild Roses from mid-June to mid-July. Week by week the various flowers of the area continue to bloom in sequence until late August. There is pleasant walking here and birdwatchers should look out especially for Chestnut-eared Buntings in summer.

Continuing your journey, eventually join Rt 334 to the east of Shari and head towards Utoro. Twelve kilometres east of Shari the road rejoins the coast and passes through a small settlement called Mine-hama. A few kilometres further on the road rises and there is a view out to the Sea of Okhotsk from Hinode. From here the coast is increasingly rocky and there are usually Temminck's Cormorants along the shore and often eagles along the coastal escarpment.

Just over 25 km east of Shari you will pass the Shiretoko deer farm[188] and 1 km further on the On-ne-betsu River[189]. Here you can watch salmon running up the river in late summer and autumn and, if lucky, you might see bears hunting for them. The scenery now becomes ever more rewarding. Two kilometres beyond the On-ne-betsu River you will see an example of columnar basalt beside the road by the sea. Look out here for cormorants fishing offshore or resting on the rocks. Then, 1 km further on, to the right of the road, you will find the parking area for Oshinkoshin[190], one of Japan's 100

186 43.916426, 144.659184   187 43.917388, 144.700346   188 44.003389, 144.911366   189 44.012750, 144.918410   190 Public toilets and a souvenir shop are also located here 44.037279, 144.933838.

best-known waterfalls. A short flight of steps leads up beside the stream to a viewing platform from where you can see the falls at very close range. Three kilometres further on you will pass a smaller, but also attractive, waterfall known as San-dan-no-taki[191] with three small cascades.

Soon (after 4 km) you will reach Utoro. The Shiretoko World Heritage Conservation Center is on the seaward side of the road alongside the Utoro Road Station. Excellent displays here introduce the Shiretoko Peninsula. The scenic beauty of the Shiretoko Peninsula is perhaps best witnessed from the sea, so at the traffic lights in the centre of town, turn left towards the harbour and you will soon find the offices for the various companies that offer boat trips. Various boat excursions along the peninsula are possible from Utoro (in summer and autumn), some to the very tip, some as far as the Rusha River, which is a trip that can be good for bear watching, and others to see the Kamuiwakka Hot Spring Falls. They each provide excellent opportunities to see the dramatic cliff scenery that buttresses the peninsula's northwestern shore, the wild, forested montane landscape, and some of the local wildlife. Boat trips from Rausu on the eastern coast of the peninsula run for most of the year with good whale and dolphin watching opportunities.

Just opposite the port of Utoro is prominent Oronko-iwa (Oronko Rock)[192]. This huge rock rises about 60 m and can be climbed easily by means of a stairway. The view out over the rocky reef and towards the Shiretoko mountain range is well worth it. Birdwatchers will find this an excellent spot from which to search in summer for Spectacled Guillemots *Cepphus carbo*.

Leaving Utoro Harbour onboard your chosen boat excursion, you may notice two large boats moored nearby: these are the Aurora I and Aurora II, the icebreakers that are used for sea ice cruising from Abashiri in winter and for larger groups taking the long course to Cape Shiretoko in summer. The

The view from Oronko-iwa

The wine glass falls, Shiretoko Peninsula

Columnar basalt on the shore of the Shiretoko Peninsula

191 44.045329, 144.953619   192 44.073480, 144.990404

Brown Bear — Deity of the Mountain

Brown Bear on the Shiretoko Peninsula © Itō Akihiro

Brown Bears frequently patrol the shores of the Shiretoko Peninsula © Itō Akihiro

Beach-washed fish, seals and even cetaceans are readily consumed © Itō Akihiro

The Brown Bear is Japan's largest land mammal weighing from 150 kg to 250 kg with the very largest males exceeding 300 kg and measuring 200–230 cm in length. Its range is restricted to Hokkaidō where it is mostly shy and secretive. Its colour varies from pale tawny brown to dark blackish-brown; most have a paler neck and upper parts with darker legs.

Bears live all across Eastern Hokkaidō, but the intact environment of the Shiretoko Peninsula stretching from the shore to the alpine zone, the extensive shoreline, rivers and forest there provide particularly good habitat and a diverse food supply for them. They are mostly herbivorous, eating great quantities of a wide variety of plants, favouring fresh grasses and megaherbs in spring, and berries, fruits and nuts in summer and autumn. They are not entirely vegetarian as their diet also includes invertebrates, such as earthworms, ants, bees and sandhoppers[193]. They will scavenge for meat at deer, seal and cetacean carcasses, and especially like to eat spawning salmon in autumn.

During summer and autumn Hokkaidō's bears roam widely, foraging on a robust and varied diet, gorging when they can on the seasonal plenty, and converting excess food into an insulating and energy-storing layer of body fat. The autumn harvest, of Mizunara Oak acorns in the forest and Pink *Oncorhynchus gorbuscha* and Chum Salmon *Oncorhynchus keta* returning to spawn in the rivers of the peninsula, is an important and rich food resource for bears readying for hibernation. The arrival of winter weather, especially snow, and the declining seasonal bounty, leads the bears to seek out an underground den for hibernation, typically on a hillside or slope. They may choose a natural cavity beneath a fallen tree, a cave, or dig their own hibernaculum, in which they will remain torpid for several months, relying on their accumulated store of body fat as their energy supply

193 Any of a number of species of amphipods in the family Talitridae.

throughout their long, winter sleep.

Bears emerge in spring, usually in early April or, if they gave birth to cubs in late January or early February, during May. During spring they favour sunny coastal slopes from which the snow has melted and where there is an ample supply of fresh green vegetation, shoots and buds. During early summer male bears roam widely in search of females as June is their mating season.

The sounds of rushing mountain streams and the dense chest-high megaherb vegetation can easily mask the presence of bears, so be cautious when walking in such areas. Look for bear signs — tell-tale footprints on the trail, scratch marks on tree trunks, overturned logs, and prominent droppings. Watch especially for deer carcasses as bears may defend these as a food source and remain nearby, and look also for any disturbed ant nests as they too are an important food for hungry bears.

Muddy tracks where a bear has crossed a road

Among Japanese people bears are great fear-inducers[194], yet according to the Japan Bear and Forest Society, in a recent year (2017) only two people were killed by bears in the whole of Japan. In contrast, more than 20 people are estimated to die in Japan each year from hornet stings, and traffic accidents claim several thousand lives annually. Bears are definitely to be respected, but do keep a sense of perspective. To the indigenous Ainu the bear is revered as their deity of the mountains — *Kimun Kamuy*.

Autumn salmon runs are a major attraction for local bears
© Itō Akihiro

Brown Bear mothers frequently have twin cubs

194 News media sensationalised an incident in 1915 that occurred at Sanke-betsu during which a single bear killed seven settlers in the worst bear attack in Japanese history. It transpires that the bear had previously been shot and injured before it made the fatal attacks while searching for food.

Spectacular Seabirds

Tufted Puffin © Wakasa Masanobu

Spectacled Guillemot

Spectacled Guillemot © Terasawa Takaki

Two of East Hokkaidō's seabird species, Tufted Puffin *Fratercula cirrhata* or *Etopirika* and Spectacled Guillemot or *Keimafuri*, take their Japanese names from the Ainu language. The former is at the very southwestern limit of its North Pacific and Bering Sea distribution and considered critically endangered in Japan, whereas the latter is endemic to the Sea of Okhotsk and northern Japan where it is considered vulnerable[195].

Once numbered in their 100s in southeast Hokkaidō, the puffins have declined steadily from the 1970s to the 2000s. They suffer from predation by gulls on their nesting islands and are at considerable risk from entanglement in set nets at sea when they are diving for their main prey of small fish and squid. Now just one or two pairs may nest on offshore islands near the Nemuro Peninsula, so they are best looked for by taking a boat ride out from Habomai or Ochi-ishi. Spectacled Guillemots may also be seen there, but are best found in good numbers off the Shiretoko Peninsula in summer, either from land, such as from Oronko-iwa, or by taking a boat from Utoro towards the Rusha River. Shiretoko Peninsula remains something of a stronghold for them. Elsewhere they are in decline. They forage by diving for fish and molluscs close to shore, making them particularly vulnerable to accidental entanglement in set nets.

The puffin has the most colourful bill and face of any bird in Japan, but the guillemot has brilliant red feet, and a bright red lining to its mouth, contrasting with its black plumage and white 'spectacles'.

line of the Shiretoko Peninsula mountains is soon in view and just after passing a high spanning bridge to the right the rugged cliffs begin. Attendant black and sickle-winged Pacific Swifts swirl and scream around the cliffs in their hundreds. Within 15 minutes of leaving the harbour you will reach Iwao-betsu[196] and, weather permitting, you will have a view up to Mt Rausu. Close inshore, near the shading cliffs, where it is cool and damp from the streams and their fine spray, look for small groups of Spectacled Guillemots; your boat's route winds sometimes close to the cliffs sometimes out beyond the ends of the long

lines of nets set to catch Pink Salmon.

Beyond Utoro the steeper northwestern flank of the peninsula is so precipitous in parts that several of the numerous streams and rivers draining out of the mountain forests inland, though completely normal in their upstream sections, lack downstream sections. Their mid-stream flows cascade in waterfalls 80–200 m down the cliffs directly onto the rocks below or into the sea, with no river mouth. On a clear day, waterfalls, sea caves and curious rock formations in the cliffs, including Elephant Rock and Lion Rock, make for a pleasant

195 Also sometimes spelled Iwaubetsu.   196 Japan Wildlife Research Centre (2002).

scenic boat journey with the mountain range of the peninsula as the splendid backdrop.

After about an hour you will reach the Rusha River[197] with its *banya* or fishing huts. This river is a favourite site for foraging bears so if you haven't already spotted one before now watch especially carefully in this area.

Northeast of Utoro Town, Rt 334 crosses the Horo-betsu River, then loops and climbs uphill. Pause at Cape Puyuni viewpoint[198] because there is a lovely panoramic view here at any time of day, though it is particularly spectacular at sunset when the sun sinks across the Sea of Okhotsk. A kilometre further on you will reach the Shiretoko National Park Nature Center[199] from which a hiking trail starts to the coastal viewpoint overlooking Furepe Waterfall[200]. This is a pleasant short walk with great rewards on a clear day, with superb views of the peninsula and of the ocean. Spectacled Guillemots and Pacific Swifts can often be seen here in summer, and bears are frequently sighted (so do take precautions).

Just beyond the nature centre the road forks. Rt 334 continues up and over the peninsula via the Shiretoko Pass viewpoint[201] to the port town of Rausu on the Pacific coast of Hokkaidō, whereas Rt 93 branches left towards the Shiretoko Five Lakes[202]. Soon after the junction on Rt 93 the view opens up and there is a splendid panorama of the mountains of the peninsula and a particularly fine view of the first peak in the range — Mt Rausu. The road then winds down towards the bridge over the Iwao-betsu River (4 km beyond the nature centre) from which there are fantastic views upriver towards Mt Rausu and along the Shiretoko mountain chain.

Soon after the bridge you can turn right up a narrow winding road along the Iwao-betsu River Valley to the Sandan and Takimi Hot Springs[203]

(3.8 km from Rt 93). This route runs alongside the Iwao-betsu River and through lovely mixed forest and eventually reaches Chi-no-hate Hotel and hot spring at which there is a car park with a toilet. This is a pleasant walk with Brown Dippers and wagtails along the river and both Narcissus and Blue-and-white Flycatchers singing in the forest in summer. To the right of the hotel, when facing the entrance, is the trailhead for one of the routes to the top of Mt Rausu. This is a great hike, but only for experienced mountain hikers who have a healthy respect for bears.

A raised plateau, the Iwao-betsu Tableland, between the peninsula's mountainous spine and the coastal cliffs, is where one finds both lakes and swamps. From the Iwao-betsu Bridge continue 5 km on Rt 93 and you will reach a fork in the road. A sign indicates Kamuiwakka Falls[204] to the right.

Kamuiwakka scenery

197 44.197909, 145.195872   198 44.088779, 145.009834   199 44.091349, 145.023199   200 Also known as Furepe-no-Taki Falls: 44.095950, 145.012746   201 Shiretoko Pass Observatory 44.053986, 145.104750   202 Also strangely known as the 'Shiretoko Goko Lakes (Five Lakes)' even though Goko means five lakes!   203 44.110357, 145.089281   204 44.153936, 145.129136

Iwao-betsu Tableland and Shiretoko Goko © The Hokkaido Shimbun Press

Mt Rausu dominates the scenery at Shiretoko Pass

Numerous fast-flowing rivers drain from the mountains of the Shiretoko Peninsula

This hot waterfall is not to be missed by *onsen* lovers and it makes a great destination for a cycle ride[205]. The left fork leads to Shiretoko Five Lakes[206]. Very soon afterwards, to the left, you reach a parking area from which it is possible to walk through mature fir and oak forest to the five pretty lakes that are accessible via a raised boardwalk and an easy trail. There is also a guided tour available (reservation required) during May, June and July. The ponds which reflect the mountains of Shiretoko on clear days, are dotted with Small Yellow Pond Lilies *Nuphar pumila*. The surrounding marshes support plentiful wild flowers, including the delicate insectivorous Round-leaved Sundew *Drosera rotundifolia*.

After visiting the Shiretoko Five Lakes, Kamui-wakka, and perhaps hiking for an hour or so part way up Mt Iwō for a dramatic view of the old eruption crater on its flank, continue for 10 km up Rt 334 from the nature centre to the Shiretoko Pass (738 m)[207]. The road[208] across the peninsula connects Utoro on the Okhotsk coast to Rausu on the Pacific coast in less than an hour in summer. When the weather is clear the views are spectacular. Because of the depth of snow that falls here in the mountains and the icy conditions that persist even on

205 The road is closed to private vehicles for a short period each August. 206 44.121904, 145.079972 207 Viewpoint at Shiretoko Pass 44.053986, 145.104750 208 It was opened in 1980.

Lobelia (L) and Sundew (R) prefer damp habitats near water

Mt Rausu reflected in one of the ponds along the trail to Lake Rausu

spring mornings, it has one of the shortest seasons of any road in Japan, with the snow gates on each side opening sometime in late April and closing again by early November. During the closed season travelling between Utoro and Rausu requires a lengthy detour (112 km) across the base of the peninsula using Rt 244 and that takes two hours or more.

The road winds steadily up through mixed forest with spruce, oak, white birch, stone birch and finally, from just below the pass, stone pine. The almost conical peak of the Mt Rausu stratovolcano stands northeast of the road. It is a relatively modern volcano dating back to within the most recent geological epoch, the Holocene, that began some 12,000 years ago. This attractive peak, which last erupted between about 1750 and 1850[209], is the highest point on the peninsula and is listed among the 100 most famous mountains of Japan.

The weather may change dramatically on crossing the peninsula, from clear and sunny on one side, to dense cloud on the other when east coast fogs are forced through the mountain gap. More than likely there will be wind and fog at Shiretoko Pass. Calm days at the pass are rare and to be cherished. There are interesting birds to find amongst

the Japanese Stone Pines here if the weather permits looking for them! The most unusual is a large finch, the Pine Grosbeak *Pinicola enucleator*, the males of which are deep red. As you begin to descend towards the town of Rausu you may be able to enjoy the dramatic view across the Nemuro Strait to the island of Kunashiri, which is just 33 km away.

A few kilometres below the pass a hiking trail strikes off southwards for Lake Rausu[210]. Just above the town of Rausu another trail begins heading north for Mt Rausu, Mt Iwō, Mt Shiretoko and the cape beyond[211]. Whereas Mt Rausu is a manageable, though strenuous day-hike, the journey to the cape requires several days and very careful planning. The long cold winters and short summers make hiking possible only from June to September[212].

Thirteen kilometres down from the pass there is a sign posted 0.4 km to Kumagoe Waterfall[213]; this detour to the Shōun River[214] is well-worth taking. The hiking trail descends into the woods first via rickety stairs and then along a rocky trail that continues down through forest for about 400 m to an area with picnic tables. The trail continues a little further to where you can see the falls cascading

209 According to the Smithsonian Institution National Museum of Natural History Global Volcanism Program https://volcano.si.edu/volcano.cfm?vn=285082   210 44.031029, 145.080007   211 The trail to Mt Shiretoko and Cape Shiretoko is not maintained. Hikers should visit the Rusa Field House to obtain the latest information and local conditions before starting.   212 Once the winter snow has compacted, it is possible to hike in snow shoes in late winter and early spring.   213 Kumagoe-no-taki: 44.031150, 145.145107   214 Appearing as the Shokumo River on some maps.

Kumagoe Waterfall

down a cliff of basalt. Brown Dippers inhabit the river here. Several trees in this area are marked as being more than 200 years old, and one oak tree is said to be at least 250 years old.

A kilometre further on you will notice a small parking area beside the road and a footbridge leading across the river to your right, a narrow road up to the left leads to the Rausu Onsen campsite[215]. The small buildings across the river are changing rooms for the famous *Kuma-no-yu Onsen*[216] (hot spring) — a

particularly pleasant spot to warm up on a cold winter's day!

Continue downhill for 1 km and you will soon see the Shiretoko Rausu Visitor Center[217] building on your left. It is worth a stop here to learn more about the peninsula and to take the trail behind the centre. Another trail to Mt Rausu begins here. A short distance along it, cross the bridge over the first stream, then to your left you will find the Rausu Geyser.

It is 3 km down to town from the visitor centre along the Rausu River. In Rausu (population about 5,000) you will find a huge harbour and the offices of the companies that offer excellent boat trips along the peninsula for sightseeing, whale watching or, in winter, sea ice and eagle spotting.

As you leave the town of Rausu heading up the coast to the northeast, now on Rt 87, look out for the first tunnel. Just to the right of the entrance you can park near the Namikiri-fudō Temple[218] and walk a short distance to look into the Makkausu Cave in the cliff where extraordinary sculpted ice creates stalactites and stalagmites in winter. Wind blasted and sculpted

Ice Moomins and Ice Blades in Makkausu Cave

The pollock fleet in Rausu Harbour during the heyday of fishing

215 Like many other places it goes by several names including the Shiretoko National Park Rausu Onsen Campsite and the National Rausu Onsen Camping Site.   216 44.031864, 145.155508   217 44.031863, 145.161275   218 44.029914, 145.206004

Geyser — Ancient Plumbing with Modern Steam

The English word 'geyser' is derived from the Icelandic verb '*geysa*' to gush and the place called Geysir (in Iceland), where the first geyser to be known in Europe was described.

Geysers are rather rare natural phenomena as they are springs that spout boiling water and steam intermittently into the air reaching heights of several tens of metres. They occur in very few areas on Earth as they are found only near active volcanoes. Four factors combine to make them possible. First, magma must occur close to the surface (typically within about 2,000 m). Second there must be cracks and fissures in the rock forming the plumbing system for the geyser. Third, a cavity or reservoir space that holds the water under pressure during the heating process is a necessity. Fourth, geyserite or siliceous sinter must be deposited in the water-carrying plumbing system keeping the system pressure-tight and preventing the pressurised water and steam from being dissipated through the rock before it rises to and erupts beyond the surface. Although some areas of the world are volcanic and many of those have hot springs, fumaroles and mud pots, very few of those areas have erupting geysers. These exceptions can be found at such places as El Tatio in Chile, the Valley of the Geysers in Kamchatka, Russia, Rotorua in New Zealand, and Yellowstone National Park in the USA.

Rainwater percolates downwards until it eventually reaches hot rock which boils the water that is now under pressure. The superheated and pressurised water is forced back to the surface through the geyser's plumbing pipe where a hydrothermal explosion occurs through a narrow vent at the surface.

Earthquakes and the deposition of minerals in the natural plumbing of the geyser can affect the volume and frequency of a geyser's activity. Some are fairly frequent and even regular; others may be inactive for months or years and then spring to life once more.

The only geyser in Eastern Hokkaidō is located near the trail behind the Shiretoko Rausu Visitor Center. Although it is not on the scale of geysers in Iceland, or Kamchatka, nevertheless this fairly regular 8 m high plume is well worth the wait. It erupts predictably every 50–70 minutes and the expected eruption times are posted inside the visitor centre, so it's worth checking there first.

The geyser at Rausu

Kujira-no-mieru-oka Park

ice hangs like giant blades from the cave roof, or stands in Moomin-like shapes rising from the cave floor.

Four kilometres out of Rausu there is a sharp turn back and uphill on to a very narrow road that leads towards the lighthouse and Kujira-no-mie-ru-oka Park (Whale Viewing Park)[219]. This is a good viewpoint from which to watch for the whales that move through the Nemuro Strait. Less than 1 km up the hill, you will find a viewing platform looking out over the channel. Sign boards here show images of various possible species of whales, the most likely being Orca. To have a chance of seeing them, you need to be armed with patience and a good pair of binoculars or a telescope. Looking back along the peninsula to the south you can see the surprisingly large fishing harbour at Rausu and looking out across the channel you can see Kunashiri Island on the horizon, now just 26 km away.

Returning to Rt 87, the road continues 20 km further along the peninsula to Aidomari Port[220] (the end of the road). But first, after 5 km, you will find a strange-shaped rock on the seaward side of the road called tengu-iwa or goblin rock. Several species of gulls often gather at the river mouth below the rock to bathe, and it is quite common to see foxes foraging along the beach. Carry on another 15 km to the road's end at Aidomari. From the small harbour there, it is possible to take a boat ride along the final third of the peninsula to the

very tip for bear watching during the summer and early autumn months. Along the narrow strip of level land just back from the shore, there are huts used in summer by 'fishermen' from Rausu who take harvests from the sea such as giant kelp. An important ingredient in broth-making, giant Japanese Kelp *Saccharina japonica* from Shiretoko is a popular souvenir, so it makes a summer cash crop here and elsewhere around the coast of Hokkaidō.

Following the road from Rausu onwards towards Aidomari the coast has a rather forlorn appearance that is very different from the Utoro side. Most of the shoreline along the Pacific coast of the Shiretoko Peninsula is 'protected' and here that means reinforced with long and unsightly ranks of concrete tetrapods to resist wave and storm surges. Most of the uphill slopes are protected with snow and avalanche fences and where there are fairly tall rocky cliffs you will find them shrouded in protective metal mesh. There are almost continuous settlements of fisherman's houses or seasonal fishing huts, known locally as *banya*, on the seaward side of the road and, in some areas, on the landward side of the road also. This creates an atmosphere of urban sprawl even here in one of the more remote parts of Japan. Many of the finest views of the peninsula from land have been lost as sections of the coastal road have been abandoned in favour of tunnels; thus the best way of enjoying the scenery of the peninsula (if you are not a mountain hiker) is by boat out to the Nemuro Strait. From the sea the view to the peninsula is inspiring and a wide variety of wildlife can be found offshore throughout the year.

Three kilometres before Aidomari, the Seseki Waterfall cascades down beside the road. One kilometre further on is Seseki Onsen[221], which emerges between the rocks at the beach. At low tide there may be sufficient warm water to enjoy bathing here.

As you explore the Rausu side of the peninsula, you may notice fish hung up to dry beneath the eaves of houses. If you are lucky you may see small,

The Seseki Hotspring

Taking a winter boat trip from Rausu is highly recommended

narrow boats with a single outboard engine and long poles onboard, either pulled up on the shore or out in shallow water. These special boats are used by fishermen when they go out to collect sea urchins and the poles are thrust down into the water to harvest them. Keep your eyes sharp for wildlife too as foxes can appear at any time as can deer. Occasionally it is even possible to see bears on the slopes above the road. These slopes are covered with dwarf bamboo and mixed forest. Japan's cherry blossom wave begins in the far south in February with Okinawa the first place to enjoy the blooms. That same wave ends here in East Hokkaidō three months later, and Rausu is often the final area to see these iconic flowers — in late May.

In autumn, when the full palette of brilliant paintbox autumn colours dominates the scenery, Pink and Dog Salmon return from the sea, first thronging the brackish river mouths, then fighting their way up the sweet water rivers to spawn. As autumn's rush fades and winter's bleakness returns, the eagles arrive once more. Several pairs of eagle nest along the peninsula and, in winter, their numbers are swollen by hundreds more arriving from Russia. But even these large birds are dwarfed by the world's largest and most magnificent eagle — Steller's Eagle — which is best seen north of Rausu in winter.

Wild and tempestuous weather may obliterate the landscape with storm-blown snow in winter, but it is well worth driving the peninsula road as far as it is open (it blocks eventually with snow). Look for eagles perching in the trees on the coastal escarpment above the road and always also look offshore for seals and Steller's Sea Lions. When a high pressure system dominates, however, and frost crisps the snow, it becomes a magical, exciting winter land.

Despite the town of Utoro having an over-developed tourist feel, that side of the peninsula has a much more natural atmosphere. In contrast, long after leaving town and heading along the shore by boat, the Rausu side gives the feeling of being confined in a ribbon development of fishermen's houses, sheds and storage facilities. The main fishery in Rausu has until recently been the Walleye Pollock, but catches have declined; however, Rausu is also famous for its kelp and very tasty sea urchin.

Sixteen kilometres beyond Rausu, on the landward side of the road just before a bridge, you will find the Shiretoko World Heritage Rusa Field House[222] a small visitor centre related to the site. This is named after the Rusa River that reaches the sea here and it is where you will likely find a Brown Dipper upstream and pretty Harlequin Ducks near the river mouth. It is worth looking offshore here for other sea duck, seals and even sea lions in winter.

As you drive along the coast beyond Rausu

222 44.138745, 145.263849

Steller's Eagle

Steller's Eagle is the most dramatic of all raptors

Hokkaidō's most spectacular winter visitor

Steller's Eagle has a particularly massive bill and powerful talons

The magnificent Steller's Eagle breeds around the northern parts of the Sea of Okhotsk and on the Kamchatka Peninsula; however, because much of that region is inhospitable in winter, the eagles are forced south in search of food. As many as 2,000 of them migrate to spend the winter from November to March in Japan, and most of them are found in Eastern Hokkaidō.

This huge fish-hunting raptor, named in honour of Georg Wilhelm Steller, an 18th century German zoologist and explorer, can be found most easily along Hokkaidō's east coast from the Shiretoko Peninsula to the Nemuro Peninsula. They are especially numerous around Rausu and further south, at Lake Fūren. Along the Shiretoko Peninsula, a traditional wintering area for them, they spend winter days fishing the Nemuro Strait and perch on the drifting sea ice when it is available. Sea ice floating down from the Sea of Okhotsk makes a suitable feeding platform on which to dismember prey. Their stiletto-like talons are ideal for grasping slippery fish and their massive hatchet bill rips easily into their prey.

They forage for fish along coasts, at river mouths, along riversides and at coastal lagoons and inland lakes. They also scavenge at seal carcasses, and sometimes kill birds such as ducks and gulls, while in forests they scavenge from deer carcasses.

With a wingspan of up to 2.5 metres, they are impressive, but what makes them so striking is the adults' boldly patterned plumage with white shoulders, rump, diamond-shaped tail and legs.

Several boat owners operate eagle-watching tours from Rausu Harbour and in doing so have created a local ecotourism opportunity. Nowhere else in the world can one approach so closely to these normally nervous birds, when they are hunting and feeding. Now, wherever one travels in Hokkaidō during winter, there is always the chance of seeing one of these magnificent eagles soaring overhead.

seeing all of the development and the abandoned buildings, vehicles and boats, you may wonder why this is a world heritage site. Many buildings are falling down or sealed up and there are innumerable abandoned boats, derelict vehicles, and piles of old fishing nets and floats, as if the area is not cared for at all. The debris of the past and present fishing industry and the old houses gives this area a general air of abandonment and disrepair. You will not find the attractive fishing communities that you might see in the British Isles, Scandinavia, Greenland, the Canadian Arctic or in the Mediterranean. Here the buildings are merely functional and haphazard with no unifying style or colour pattern. Furthermore, the road is lined with concrete poles and wires just as in the vast majority of Japan's urban areas.

However, if you visit Rausu in winter, and take a boat trip from the harbour into the Nemuro Strait to the ice, you will see the stunning inland scenery and understand why the peninsula was designated

Looking up Rusa River © Shiretoko Nature Foundation

a UNESCO World Natural Heritage Site in recognition of the dynamic web of life connecting the ocean, the ice and the land. In winter, there are eagles to be seen roosting in the trees, soaring over the harbour and foraging out to the sea ice and the whole scene is very different with everything white and covered with a masking layer of snow. The ice

Winter off the Shiretoko Peninsula, with drift ice and eagles

Birds of the Riverside

The topography of Eastern Hokkaidō is such that most roads in or close to the mountains cross streams and rivers with almost monotonous regularity. The many bridges provide opportunities to scan for wildlife beside the water. A readily visible creature associated with these flows is the Brown Dipper.

This short-tailed thrush-like bird with a prominently cocked tail resembles a large Eurasian Wren (also frequent in riverside vegetation). This chocolate-brown stream bird is resident in the region where it favours clear, fast-flowing streams that it

The wren-like Brown Dipper

may share with another resident, the large 'punk-crested' Crested Kingfisher *Megaceryle lugubris* and the flashy electric blue-and-orange Common Kingfisher *Alcedo atthis*, which is a summer visitor to the region. At 21–23 cm long, the Brown Dipper is the largest of the world's five dipper species.

Adults are more or less uniformly dark brown, whereas the plumage of young birds is mottled brown with pale spots. Rarely seen away from water, except when flying a straight line short-cut through forest where its home river meanders, the dipper finds its mostly invertebrate prey underwater by wading, swimming and diving. In flight it frequently gives a loud, hard *dzzeet* or buzzing *zzit* call. When the males are courting during the late winter and spring they produce a surprisingly loud song that contains extremely varied rich warbling notes with trills, rattles and buzzing — sounds that are easily audible over the loudest noise the fast-flowing water in the rushing mountain streams make.

Look for Crested and Common Kingfishers along streams and rivers

Looking towards Mt Rausu from the Kunashiri Observatory Tower above Rausu

is fickle and variable in extent, not only from year to year, but also from day to day as it is locally affected by currents and the wind. Even if ice is not present close to the harbour a boat excursion is well worthwhile to be able to see the scenery and the eagles from a very different perspective.

A kilometre southwest of town on Rt 335, a sign points uphill to the viewpoint overlooking Rausu Harbour. This narrow road winds uphill past the Rausu ski slope before reaching a large parking area. The panoramic view from the Rausu Kunashiri Observatory Tower[223] makes the detour well worthwhile. The immediate view is down over the town and the harbour; the view uphill is towards Mt Rausu, and the longe-range view is out over the Nemuro Strait to Kunashiri Island in the distance.

From here it is possible to see and judge the distribution of the winter drift-ice and sometimes to look down on eagles flying below the viewpoint and along the escarpment.

In summer the road between Utoro and Rausu makes for a pleasant way of seeing the peninsula's landscape but this road is closed for up to six months of the year, when a detour is required around the base of the peninsula. The way south along Rt 335 takes you steadily away from the Shiretoko Peninsula but always close to the Nemuro Strait coast. Just before the town of Shibetsu, Rt 335 joins Rt 244, which is main Shari–Utoro road, which is open year-round.

It is now time to explore more of Hokkaidō's east coast.

223 44.015573, 145.186389

6 Hokkaidō's Eastern Coast

Chapter Six

0 10 km 20 km
N
Shiretoko National Park
Shiretoko National Park Nature Center
Rusa Field House
Shiretoko Rausu Visitor Center
334
335
244
SHIBETSU
Nakashibetsu
Notsuke BH
272
244
NAKASHIBETSU
Nemuro Bay
On-ne-moto BH
BEKKAI
243
243
Meiji Park BH
Cape Nosappu BH
272
Lake Fūren
Tōbai BH
NEMURO
Shimin-no-mori BH
Shunkunitai Nature Center
Akkeshi Waterfowl Observation Center
44
Bettōga BH
HAMANAKA
Cape Ochiishi
Hanasaki Line
Kiritappu Wetland Center
AKKESHI
Okubiwase Wild bird Park
HOKKAIDŌ'S EASTERN COAST - SHIRETOKO TO NEMURO

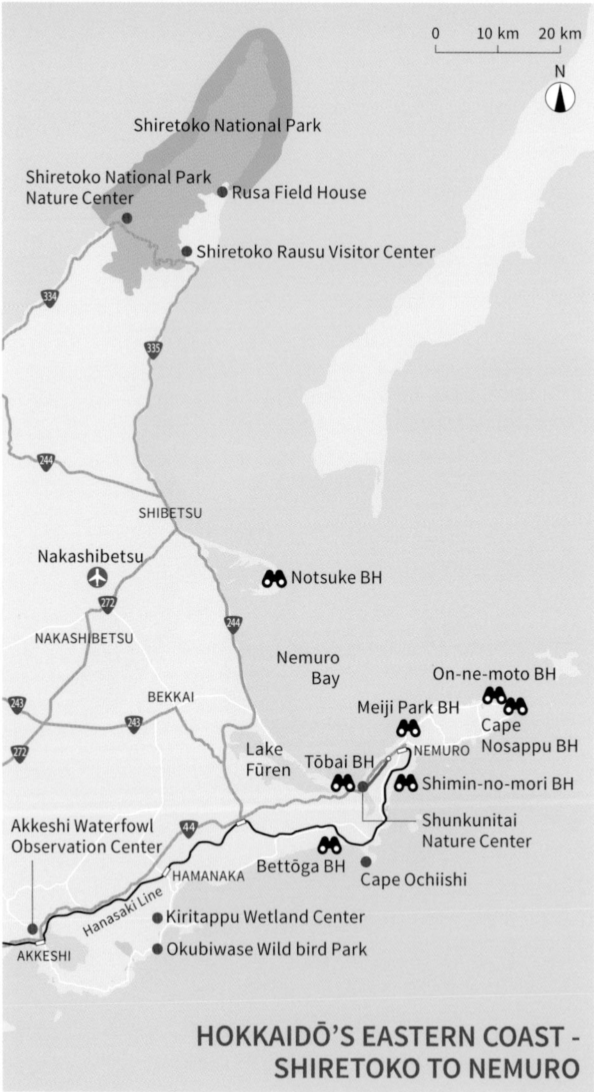

From the town of Rausu on the Shiretoko Peninsula to Nemuro City on the Nemuro Peninsula the distance is just 140 km. The drive is at first along coastal Rt 335 south towards Shibetsu, then on Rt 244 to Lake Fūren, and finally Rt 44 (the main route of southeast Hokkaidō from Kushiro) to Nemuro. The whole distance can be completed easily in less than three hours, but despite the proximity there is much to see and it is well-worth taking at least one whole day, even two, over the journey.

Almost the entire route from the Shiretoko NP to the Nemuro Peninsula is through lowlands and follows the coast. The views east are across the Nemuro Strait to the surprisingly close island of Kunashiri, while back to the north the mountains of the Shiretoko Peninsula make a wonderful backdrop. Ahead the low promontory beyond Nemuro fades into the distance.

Just inland from the mid-section of this coast lies the town of Nakashibetsu (population 24,000) and just northwest of the town is the first recommended stop — Kaiyō-dai[224]. From Rausu it is about 65 km (1 hr 15 mins via Rt 335, Rt 1145 and Rt 975) and from downtown Nakashibetsu it is a mere 13 km (about 20 mins). Along the way, just 15 km east of Kaiyō-dai, beside Rt 774, the Daisan Shibetsu parking area between Kamimusa and Kawakita offers a fine view of Mt Musa (1,005 m), which lies to the northwest. The route through this region is along what is known locally as the 'Milk Road'. You are most definitely in the dairy agriculture area of Eastern Hokkaidō here.

Although Kaiyō-dai is situated only 270 m above sea level, the open-to-the-sky top floor of

224 43.613911, 144.870235

Mt Musa from the Kaiyō-dai viewpoint

Summer scenery from the Kaiyō-dai viewpoint

the circular viewing building located on the hillside here gives wonderful panoramic views of Eastern Hokkaidō. Looking west from Kaiyō-dai you can see to the crater rim at Lake Mashū and, if you visit on a very clear day, to the Akan volcanoes beyond. Looking to the north-northeast, the closest mountain is Mt Musa, which itself makes for a very pleasant day hike. The view from the tower takes in dwarf bamboo in the foreground, plantations of Japanese Larch and spruce, intermixed with some farmland in the middle distance; then, on the more distant flanks of Mt Musa, natural mixed forest.

Looking eastwards you can see to the shore of the Nemuro Strait and across the channel to Kunashiri Island. With binoculars it is possible to make out the low-lying spit of Notsuke Peninsula

Holstein Friesians and Heavy Horses

Many of the various domesticated animals for agriculture known in other countries can be found somewhere in Japan, but in East Hokkaidō only two are commonly encountered: Holstein Friesian cattle and heavy horses known as Banba.

The black and white cattle found in considerable numbers in East Hokkaidō originated in the Dutch provinces of North Holland and Friesland, and Schleswig-Holstein in northern Germany — hence the breed's name of Holstein Friesian. This is the most widespread breed of cattle in the world, and they can be found in more than 150 countries, including Japan. Those raised in Europe were

Holstein heifers are hardy enough to weather Hokkaidō's cold winters

originally for both dairy and beef production, whereas those taken to the Americas were bred for milk production. Today, the term Holstein is used for American stock dairy cattle, whereas Friesian is used for those of dual purpose bred in Europe. The highly productive cattle, which serve as the mainstay of Hokkaidō's milk, cheese, butter and ice-cream industries, are called Holsteins here. They are kept inside barns for much of the year, but can be seen in pens or paddocks close to barns at times in winter, and they spend much of the summer grazing the lush grass of Hokkaidō's extensive pastureland.

Whereas southwestern Hokkaidō is renowned for breeding thoroughbred race horses, Eastern Hokkaidō

is where you will mostly see the large, heavyset draft horses known as *Banba* used in *Ban-ei* sled racing, and perhaps the smaller ponies known as *Dosanko*. The latter, an extremely hardy breed (one of eight surviving kinds of Japanese horse) originated in Hokkaidō where it was derived from horses brought in from northern Honshū in the 15th century by herring fishermen. They used the horses during the summer fishery for help in transporting their catches, then abandoned them to survive on their own over winter. The breed adapted well and survived and even thrived despite the very severe winter conditions. In the past the *Dosanko* horse's strength was depended upon wherever rough terrain made other transport difficult such as by the military, in agriculture, fisheries and the logging industry. Today, Hokkaidō-born Japanese are nicknamed *Dosanko*.

Banba Horses

on Hokkaidō's east coast. Looking to the southeast, over the two telecommunications antennae in the foreground, you can see all the way to the Nemuro Peninsula. If you face south, much of southeast Hokkaidō stretches away before you towards the Pacific Ocean coast. The views to the south-east

and south are across a broad plain with farmland interspersed with shelter belt forest (mostly larches), mixed woodland and dairy farms.

This is the most extensive and intensive dairy farming district of Hokkaidō. The cool summer weather of the region is conducive to the growth of lush grass ideal for the dairy industry, supporting some 400,000 beef cattle and 720,000 dairy cattle[225]. The region is best known for its high quality milk and butter, but towns like Nakashibetsu and the village of Tsurui are now making names for themselves as producers of excellent cheese. Hokkaidō's famous and delicious soft ice-cream is also renowned amongst residents and visitors alike.

Back in 1870–1871, when Hokkaidō was still in its early developmental phase, Horace Capron (1804–1885), an American hailing from Massachusetts, was invited to Hokkaidō as a foreign adviser to the Hokkaidō Development Commission. On seeing the region it was Capron who recommended large-scale farming using modern American implements, and it was he who suggested the idea of planting strips of forest between regularly laid out fields as windbreaks and wildlife corridors. The whole area was planned with roads, fields and forests laid out in a checkerboard pattern that is immediately noticeable from the Kaiyō-dai observatory. Capron is acknowledged on a monument set near the base of the viewing tower.

To reach the tower, climb the flight of steps up from the car park and follow the short trail up the hill to the observatory building. Beside the car park you will find the sign for the East Hokkaidō long trail, which once passed through this site, but which is, unfortunately, now closed. There is a toilet building, and near the top of the steps, the happiness bell — who can resist ringing it when happiness is promised? Just beyond the tower there is a campsite where water is available.

As the region is mostly rural, with no urban areas other than Nakashibetsu nearby, there is little light pollution, making the Kaiyō-dai viewing tower ideal for wonderful sky viewing and star gazing at night.

While touring Eastern Hokkaidō, you will find that Kaiyō-dai is not only easily visited, but it is

Snakes are uncommon, but present in Hokkaidō; here a non-venomous Japanese Ratsnake *Elaphe climacophora*

Venomous Japanese Mamushi *Gloydius blomhoffii* are scarce, but tempted out by summer sunshine

also well marked and easily accessible from Rt 150. Because it offers such an expansive view, it is not to be missed. It gives a tremendous feel for the landscape of eastern Hokkaidō.

Leaving Kaiyō-dai, you may opt to explore the landscape further, hike Mt Musa, visit the Jōmon site at Pōgawa Shiseki Shizen Kōen[226] (Pōgawa Historical Grassland) and Ichani Karikariusu Historical Site, or Shibetsu Salmon Science Museum[227]. For the fascinating Jōmon site, with the largest num-

225 According to: the official Eastern Hokkaidō website: http://en.visit-eastern-hokkaido.jp/discover/15380/   226 43.685490, 145.116212
227 43.659459, 145.115884

Hokkaidō's Salmonids

Pink Salmon heading to their breeding grounds © Kamada Sachiko

An annual miracle of death and re-birth takes place in Eastern Hokkaidō's rivers that I call 'the night of the swimming dead' — the running (and the dying) of the salmon.

These fish, though born in freshwater, adapt to lives spent mostly in the sea. Once mature they undergo an astonishing physiological transformation and return to the freshwater river of their birth, gathering off the river mouth before ascending in order to compete and breed. The females fight to scrape out an undisturbed shallow depression in the gravel stream bed in which to lay their eggs. The males fight to attract females and to fertilise their precious reddish-orange eggs. This pattern of fighting and fecundity is repeated until the female has laid several thousand eggs and exhausted her flesh and the battered and bruised male has no more fight left in him. Their powerful instincts to return 'home' to breed ultimately overtax their physical resources. They literally wear their bodies away as they batter against the current, rivals, and river rocks. They become strange, ugly, ghost-like creatures inhabiting the cold rivers of their birth. Stream beds become littered with pallid rotting corpses, the 'ghosts' of sleek marine past lives, but their sacrifice and suffering precede rebirth.

Chum Salmon © Kamada Sachiko

On the Shiretoko Peninsula, before they enter hibernation, bears feast on spawning salmon. More widely in Eastern Hokkaidō, later running salmon are still present in rivers when the first Steller's Eagles arrive in early winter. Then, certain river mouths attract congregations of eagles, gulls, and crows, all feeding on the salmon bounty. Salmon flesh is not wasted, any remains sink to the riverbed. There, in the cold water, they break down, slowly releasing nutrients and minerals back into the freshwater ecosystem. They provide food for riverine invertebrates, which in turn will form the food for the next generation of riverine fish.

Spent salmon litter the rivers of eastern Hokkaidō in autumn and winter © Kamada Sachiko

The salmon's pearl-like eggs, meanwhile, hatch into a new generation of tiny fingerling parr at home in the river where they feed on invertebrates that may have themselves benefited from the 'fertilising' nutrients of adult salmon bodies — part of nature's endless recycling system. Then, months or even years later as silvery smolt salmon they begin their journey to the sea where they will live and grow for several more years before they themselves are overcome with the urge to return 'home' and spawn.

Chum Salmon swarming up their natal river © Kamada Sachiko

Eastern Hokkaidō is generously supplied with freshwater in the form of springs, streams, rivers, lakes and brackish lagoons. As a consequence, it supports a wide range of fish including many prized by commercial fishermen and fly fishers, such as the native White-spotted Char and Dolly Varden Trout *Salvelinus malma*. In addition there are the introduced Brown Trout *Salmo trutta*[228], Rainbow Trout *Oncorhynchus mykiss* and Brook Trout *Salvelinus fontinalis*[229].

Various species of North Pacific salmon occur along Hokkaidō's east coast and in its associated rivers, including Masu or Cherry Salmon, Red Salmon[230] *Oncorhynchus nerka*, Pink Salmon and Chum Salmon.

Chum Salmon fighting for mating rights © Kamada Sachiko

The attractive, native White-spotted Char © Kamada Sachiko

The largest of all of Hokkaidō's salmonids is the Japanese Huchen, an essentially freshwater salmonid that is said to grow to an astonishing two metres in length © Kamada Sachiko

228 Introduced from Europe.   229 Introduced from eastern North America.   230 Also called Sockeye Salmon.

The trees that grow along Notsuke Peninsula are sculpted by the frequent winds from the sea

Snow Buntings visit Notsuke Peninsula in winter © Kurita Masateru

ber of pit-dwelling ruins in Japan, retrace your steps to Rt 244 north of Shibetsu and watch for the turn-off heading inland about 500 m south of the junction between Rt 335 and Rt 244.

Rt 244 runs down much of the east coast of Hokkaidō, so for the salmon museum, continue southwards. You will soon cross the large red bridge over the Shibetsu River. Within 2 km you will pass the Shibetsu Town Office. At the traffic lights turn right (inland) to the museum. Most signs here are in Japanese, but the lamp posts along the roadside are adorned with cut-out shapes of salmon riding waves, making for a unique and distinctive ap-

proach road. It is 2 km from town to the museum, easily recognised because of its tall grey tower on top of which there are three orange balls representing salmon eggs. The museum was opened in 1991 to showcase Hokkaidō's salmon in a global context.

For a complete change of scenery, leave the indoor attractions of the museum and return to the coast, rejoining Rt 244. As you drive south down Hokkaidō's east coast, look for the road sign to Notsuke-hantō (Notsuke Peninsula)[231]. Turn left here on to Rt 950. This dead-end road takes you down Japan's longest sand spit. The low-lying 26–28-km-long spit, or series of spits, has been formed by a process known as longshore drift. The bay it encloses provides a clear gradient from salt to brackish and freshwater, making it a very special area for coastal flora.

In winter the peninsula is a bleak place indeed, frigid, wind-blown and mostly deserted by humans, yet it is an excellent area in which to search for deer, foxes, both eagles and Snow Buntings *Plectrophenax nivalis*. In spring, early summer and autumn, migratory wildfowl and shorebirds visit and spend varying amounts of time here. During summer, there is a seasonal procession of wild-

231 43.5585769, 145.3261903

Irises are abundant along Notsuke Peninsula in summer

flowers in the meadows including Siberian Lupins, Japanese Irises, and Wild Roses, their relative concentrations changing as the weeks pass.

The strong current flowing through the Nemuro Strait carries a heavy load of silt, while the forceful seasonal winds and storm-related waves cause considerable erosion of this fragile coastline. Concrete tetrapods protect much of the Nemuro Strait shore from storm surges while on the inland side of the road along the Notsuke Peninsula windswept oak forest seems to hug the ground in a bid to avoid the cutting winter wind.

The mudflats and bays here are the haunts of herons, duck, shorebirds and sometimes cranes. Eelgrass[232] washes up in piles on the inner shore and any exposed expanses of mud are carpeted with Japanese Mudsnails[233] *Batillaria attramentaria*. In summer listen for Eurasian Skylarks singing overhead and watch for Stejneger's Stonechats calling from bush tops and roadside telephone wires. Look especially for the delightful red-gorgeted Siberian Rubythroat. The area with its small bird population supports a good number of Common Cuckoos, all eager to find bird nests in which to lay their eggs (the young cuckoos will be raised by a pair of unfortunate and hardworking

foster parents). If you notice any sudden flights of ducks or gulls, look quickly for a passing eagle or a Peregrine Falcon *Falco peregrinus* that may have spooked them.

Notsuke Peninsula Nature Center[234] is located just over 11 km from the turn onto Rt 950. This large and unmistakable wooden building, with a sign indicating the Todowara parking area, houses a café, shop and toilet facilities, all on the ground floor. An information desk, natural history displays and a photo gallery can be found on the floor above. From here it is possible to walk a short, level trail out to the drowned forest of Todowara or look out across the Nemuro Strait towards Kunashiri (here just 16 km away) and enjoy the view north to the Shiretoko Peninsula or visit inside the nature centre to see various interesting displays focusing on the area's natural history. The Todowara forest provides a sense of time travel, a feeling of the inexorability of time passing, of change, and the environment slowly unravelling season by season, year by year.

Three kilometres beyond the nature centre, the road ends at a car park from which it is a short walk along a gravel track to Notsuke Lighthouse[235] and just beyond it to the Notsuke birdwatching

232 A marine grass in the genus *Zostera*.   233 Also called Asian Hornsnail.   234 43.590644, 145.334865   235 43.563642, 145.347607

Longshore Currents, Longshore Drift, Coastal Spits and Coastal Protection

The north and east coasts of Eastern Hokkaidō exhibit some fine examples of rather special phenomena. Winds blowing at an oblique angle to the shore cause similarly oblique waves. Together the wind and waves push water forward parallel to the coastline forming a longshore current. This longshore current carries or pushes sediments (such as silt, sand and shingle) in what is called longshore drift.

The waves striking the shore at an oblique angle move the sediments ashore in the swash. That same water then drains back down the beach slope under gravity, so that the backwash is perpendicular to the shoreline. In this way, sediments are continuously being drifted along the beach in the direction of the current, forming a pattern like the teeth of a saw. That pattern is interrupted when the drift reaches a point where the shoreline changes direction, and especially where there are outflows of freshwater from streams and rivers towards the ocean that oppose the movement of the drift.

Spits build along the coast, their bases always attached and accessible, and often shelter a shallow inland lagoon. Further down the spit, which is in a constant state of deposition and erosion, there will be a point — perhaps several — sometimes curved or hooked depending on the currents from the river and from the sea. Notsuke Peninsula is a fine example of a spit with multiple hook-shaped tips, several of which are forested or have 'ghost forests' of dead trees.

The Nemuro Strait connects the Sea of Okhotsk to the Pacific Ocean between Eastern Hokkaidō and the southern end of Kunashiri Island. The strong current flowing through the strait is laden with sediment making much of the channel very shallow and providing an endless supply of material to be deposited ashore at places such as Notsuke-hantō and Fūren-ko. Notsuke Peninsula is in fact one of the most extensive coastal spits in the world where generation after generation of spits have developed with the recurved tips enclosing

The distinctive shape of Notsuke Peninsula is best seen from the air © The Hokkaido Shimbun Press

Coastal erosion control

the enormous Notsuke Bay and extensive areas of salt marsh.

Lake Saroma (see Chapter Four) also has spits, but offers a particularly fine example of a rather different system — involving short spits and a very long barrier island between them.

Much of Hokkaidō's coastline is protected by hard engineering. The aim of coastal engineering is to prevent damaging erosion that can result from extreme weather events and longshore drift.

Large interlocking tetrahedral blocks moulded from concrete are used to dissipate the force of incoming waves while allowing water and sediments to move between and around

Tetrapods along the shore of Notsuke Peninsula

them. The first blocks, known as tetrapods (meaning four footed), were developed in France in 1950 and were so successful that their use has spread worldwide. Many different tetrapod-inspired designs followed and were developed in various countries. They are very popular in Japan where they can be found in multiple shapes and forms. They are so useful that that it is estimated that at least half of the country's coastline is artificially protected with them, though this does spoil the natural beauty of the coast.

Although each design has its own name, for example Acropode, Akmon, Dolos, Hollow Cube, Modified Cube, Seabee, Stabit, and Stabilopod, in Japan the word tetrapod is not only an official trade mark but also used as a generic term for all such wave dissipating concrete blocks. They are especially noticeable down the east coast of Hokkaidō at Notsuke Peninsula and southwards along the shore of the Nemuro Strait.

Just one of many designs used for coastal protection

Birdwatching Hides in Eastern Hokkaidō

The popular hobby of birdwatching is being actively promoted in southeast Hokkaidō by the placement of birdwatching hides at various strategic locations around the coast. These are small, wooden, shed-like buildings containing benches and with slatted openings at the front and sides. They overlook suitable habitat for various kinds of birds from seabirds to marsh birds, allowing visitors to sit and wait in shelter and relative comfort as they look for birds in the immediate area.

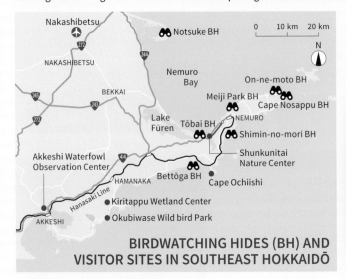

Tōbai Birdwatching Hide

BIRDWATCHING HIDES (BH) AND VISITOR SITES IN SOUTHEAST HOKKAIDŌ

hide (about 500 m in total). The freshwater pools in front of the hide are often visited by ducks, gulls and sometimes shorebirds while in summer the reed beds around the pool attract Common Reed Buntings *Emberiza schoeniclus* and Long-tailed Rosefinches. The panoramic view of the landscape from here is spectacular in any season and takes in the distant Mashū caldera rim, Mt Musa with the sharp peak of Mt Shari looking over its shoulder, then Mt Unabetsu between it and the Shiretoko range. Patience here is often rewarded, perhaps by a sighting of an eagle panicking a mixed flock of duck into the air.

As you return up the peninsula, continue watching for deer, foxes, cranes and other birds, then re-join Rt 244. There is a sign indicating that it is 87 km to Nemuro and 54 km to Attoko. Ten kilometres to the south, down Rt 244, you will reach Odaitō. Odaitō Harbour[236] is the base for a scallop

fishing fleet as well as the starting point for various nature cruises in search of seals and birds in Notsuke Bay. The whole area is a very good location for birdwatching, especially in winter. Wintering sea ducks, such as Greater Scaups, Black Scoters, Harlequin Ducks and Long-tailed Ducks, and various species of gulls can often be found sheltering in the harbour. The building in which to register for the boat rides is on the corner opposite a large red brick building. Short boat rides out into Notsuke Bay are excellent for viewing seals and larger birds. The longer course, which takes you into the shallow narrow Nemuro Strait[237], primarily to view the island of Kunashiri at relatively close range, also offers interesting birds in summer such as migratory Short-tailed Shearwaters (which come all the way from Australia) and Rhinoceros Auklets *Cerorhinca monocerata*, but with little time to stop and watch them.

236 43.568768, 145.222156   237 Only 9–10 m deep off the coast here, and narrowest off the Notsuke Peninsula when it is merely 16 km wide.

Latham's Snipe

Through its migratory birds, Eastern Hokkaidō is connected to places as far away as the Australian state of Tasmania and the vast Chukotka region in Russia's far northeast. One such international connector is a long-billed shorebird — Latham's Snipe. This snipe winters in Australasia and migrates all the way north to northern Japan, and beyond, to breed.

Following its arrival for its brief summer breeding season, especially during May and June, this shorebird engages in a highly distinctive display. High above its grassland or wooded wetland territory this bird makes dramatic swoops and dives, putting on an astonishing aerial show both during the day and night, that is combined with a peculiar clamorous display. It produces some of the most bizarre sounds in the bird world. As it climbs ever higher in the sky, it calls forcefully and repetitively: *tsupiyaku, tsupiyaku, tsupiyaku*. Then, after reaching the apex of its display flight, it drops like a stone, swooping earthwards and emitting bizarre thrumming sounds: *gwo-gwo-gwo-gwo*. These it makes by fanning out its stiff outer tail feathers which then vibrate in the wind during its rapid descent. At the bottom of its dive it swoops back skywards and repeats the process over and over again. As you travel around Hokkaidō in early summer, you may see these birds standing on roadside fences, atop telephone poles or snow arrows giving the vocal part of their display from a stationary platform.

By July they become quieter and more secretive as they raise their young, and then, in autumn, they migrate once more — all the way back to Australasia!

Latham's Snipe © Stuart Price

Atmospheric conditions on Hokkaidō's east coast are ideal for seeing the unusual phenomenon of a square sunrise! As the sun rises over the marine horizon, light from the bulging dome of the sun passes through a larger amount of the Earth's atmosphere than at any other time of day, and, in a kind of mirage, it briefly becomes square. Moments later, as it continues to rise, it elongates then eventually becomes the familiar solar disc.

Just south of Odaitō, Rt 244 crosses the Shunbetsu River[238]. Cranes breed nearby during the summer months, Black-browed Reed Warblers are noisy in the nearby reed beds, Latham's Snipe may display overhead and the fish-eating Common Merganser can often be found here or on other nearby rivers.

Continue on down the coast through low-lying

Large numbers of seals gather in Notsuke Bay © The Hokkaido Shimbun Press

coastal terrain and after 5 km you will reach Tokotan Bridge. Inland there are woods and reed beds, while out to sea you may notice long set nets.

After a further 6 km you will find a turning inland along a dirt track that after 2 km brings you

238 43.522645, 145.238509

Coastal Fisheries

The long lines of floats that stretch out perpendicular to the shore around Eastern Hokkaidō mark fishing nets that are put in place for set net fishing. Fishing vessels spend long periods at sea to catch fish with trawls or round-haul nets, while shore-based fishers commute daily to their fixed nets where fish will enter the nets during their natural movements. Where nets are set in deep water (more than 27 m) the process is called 'large-scale set net fishing' and in some places in Japan these may exceed 100 m deep.

Set nets are common around the coast

Marine fish have long been a crucial part of the Japanese diet of which more than 300 species are consumed around the country. Set net fishing is said to have been developed by the sixteenth century to help supply this basic need. Set nets may be of various designs, but those used in East Hokkaidō typically involve a long guide net that fish encounter and turn along so that they are led into the main body of the enclosing net. The buoys and floats mark the top of the various portions of the net.

to Barasan-tō[239]. There is a small parking area with a sign beside this attractive lake. From here it is a very pleasant walk along a gravel road around the south end of the lake. Listen for Common Cuckoos and other summer birds here such as Black-browed Reed Warblers, Middendorff's Grasshopper Warblers and Lanceolated Warblers. In spring and autumn look for migrating water birds at the lake, and in summer Red-necked Grebes sometimes

Barasan-numa

nest here.

Continuing south down Rt 244 you will see long lines of concrete tetrapods along the back of the beach and an artificial reef just offshore as witness to the severity of seasonal storms here. Just south of Hon-betsukai[240] you will cross the Betsukai[241] Bridge and then immediately turn left onto Rt 475 towards Hashirikotan in the Notsuke–Fūren Prefectural Natural Park.

The Ainu name, Hashirikotan[242], is used for the peninsula that encloses much of the north end of Lake Fūren. Like Notsuke-hantō, Hashirikotan is a long sandy spit formed by the action of longshore drift down the Nemuro Strait and the outflow to the sea from Lake Fūren. After 7 km the road forks: go straight on to the village and harbour of Hashirikotan, or keep left to continue down the peninsula. Three kilometres further on the road becomes a track and continues to the end of the long sandy spit. It may not be drivable the whole way as wind-blown sand often drifts in this area, and in winter it

---

239 Also known as Barasan-numa: 43.423483, 145.252304   240 Pronounced Honbekkai.   241 Pronounced Bekkai.   242 43.298352, 145.384959

A living legacy — Ainu place names

Ainu-moshiri is the name given to the traditional areas of Ainu settlement spanning southern Sakhalin, the Kuril Islands and Hokkaidō. The Ainu culture is a combination of elements derived from earlier cultures of the region known as Jōmon, Okhotsk and Satsumon and was certainly recognisable by the 12th century CE.

For most visitors to Hokkaidō, the strongest connection to Ainu will come through place names. Many, if not the majority, of the names of mountains, rivers, bays, capes and settlements in Eastern Hokkaidō are derived from the Japanised pronunciations of pre-existing Ainu names. A number of place names for example end in *-betsu* meaning river, such as Nakashibetsu, others end in *-kotan* meaning village or settlement, the largest of which is Akanko Ainu Kotan on the south shore of Lake Akan. Mountain names ending in *-nupuri* announce their Ainu significance, such as *Kamui-nupuri* (mountain of the gods) overlooking Lake Mashū. The northeastern tip of the region, Shiretoko, is derived from *sir etok* meaning a promontory, while the southeastern tip now known as Cape Nosappu is derived from *nosshamu* meaning 'a place where waves break'.

Distinctive embroidered patterns are a feature of Ainu clothing

may be blocked by snow.

The shoreward side of the Hashirikotan Peninsula is covered in wildflowers during the summer months of July and August. During that season, as at Notsuke-hantō, non-breeding cranes often frequent the area. In winter, watch for deer and foxes. This is a great place for getting away from it all. Should you make it all the way to the tip of the spit you will be facing the northern tip of Shunkuni-tai across the shallow exit channel from Lake Fūren. In winter, there are often Snow Buntings here and should you encounter a flock search carefully for a Lapland Longspur *Calcarius lapponicus* amongst them.

Hashirikotan Harbour is always worth visiting in winter when gull species here often include both Glaucous *Larus hyperboreus* and Glaucous-winged Gulls *Larus glaucescens*. In spring and autumn waterfowl include migrating Whooper Swans. Rare birds here and along the spit have included both Canvasback *Aythya valisineria* and Bufflehead *Bucephala albeola* — species that are more at home in North America.

After visiting Hashirikotan rejoin Rt 244 southbound; after a while it becomes Rt 243, then just over 30 km from Hashirikotan you will reach Rt 44 at Attoko in the southeastern region of Hokkaidō, the subject of the next chapter.

Notsuke–Fūren Prefectural Natural Park

In Japan it is quite common for non-contiguous areas to be included in a single protected area. In Eastern Hokkaidō this is clearly the case with both the Akan–Mashū NP and the Notsuke–Fūren Prefectural Natural Park. The latter was established in 1962 and consists of two main areas, Notsuke Peninsula, and Lake Fūren and it spans three municipalities. Notsuke Peninsula, a fine example of a coastal spit, encloses Notsuke Bay and is paired with the brackish lagoon near Nemuro known as Fūren-ko.

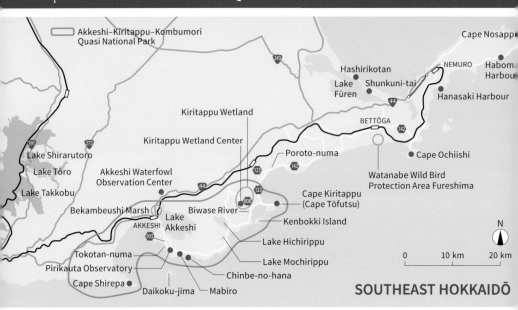

Akkeshi–Kiritappu–Kombumori
Quasi National Park

Cape Nosappu

NEMURO   Habom
Hashirikotan   Harbou
Lake   Shunkuni-tai
Fūren   Hanasaki Harbour

Kiritappu Wetland   BETTŌGA

Kiritappu Wetland Center

Lake Shirarutoro   Poroto-numa   Cape Ochiishi

Lake Tōro   Akkeshi Waterfowl   Watanabe Wild Bird
Observation Center   Protection Area Fureshima
Lake Takkobu

Bekambeushi Marsh   Biwase River   Cape Kiritappu
Lake   (Cape Tōfutsu)
AKKESHI Akkeshi
Kenbokki Island   N

Lake Hichirippu

Tokotan-numa   Lake Mochirippu   0   10 km   20 km
Pirikauta Observatory
Chinbe-no-hana
Cape Shirepa
Daikoku-jima   Mabiro   **SOUTHEAST HOKKAIDŌ**

Journeying along Hokkaidō's southeast coast, which includes the Nemuro Peninsula and the coastal area between Nemuro and Kushiro, will complete this circuit of the region and will take in some of the best birding and wildflower meadows Eastern Hokkaidō has to offer. Rt 44 is the obvious 'highway' through the area, but taking Rt 35 around the Nemuro Peninsula to Cape Nosappu and back from Nemuro, and Rt 142 ('the North Pacific Ocean Seaside Line') then Rt 123 between Nemuro and Akkeshi is far more interesting.

Having visited the northern part of Lake Fūren at Hashirikotan, continue south then eastwards around this large coastal lagoon. Stop first at the 'road station' or roadside rest area called Swan 44 Nemuro[243] overlooking the southern shore of the lake. The view from the outside terrace and the boardwalk below by the lakeshore is northwards across the shallow lagoon, to Shunkuni-tai — a long, low dune covered with mature forest.

In winter, when Lake Fūren is frozen over and the landscape white with snow and ice, the view is dramatic and brightened by the presence of magnificent Steller's Eagles. During spring and autumn, large flocks of waterfowl including Whooper Swans rest and refuel at Lake Fūren. Though they are more difficult to see than the waterfowl, flocks of migratory shorebirds gather here at these times. During summer, while you watch the behaviour

Lake Fūren is fed by a number of rivers and streams

243 43.261761, 145.437961

Shallow coastal wetlands, swamps and boreal forest at Shunkuni-tai

of the Grey Herons along the shore, look out for cranes and eagles, both of which are frequently in view.

Just over 2 km to the east, along Rt 44, you will see a geodesic dome structure, which is known as Lake Sunset[244]. Here, in winter, fish are put out on the ice for the eagles and for a small fee you can join the photographers who gather to snap both eagle species at close range. You can also visit on any day to enjoy the sunset across the lake. About 300 m further on you will pass the Tōbai Bird Hide which provides comfortable shelter from which to watch migratory birds and residents such as Grey Herons. Five hundred metres further on, the next left takes you downslope to sea level passing Minshuku Fūren on the way. Then turn left up and over a small bridge to the Shunkuni-tai parking area[245] and boardwalk entrance. The bridge crosses the narrow channel that is the southern outflow from brackish Lake Fūren to the sea.

It is possible to walk the length of Shunkuni-tai (about 8 km) from the car park watching for waterfowl, raptors, shorebirds and passerines each in their season. During summer the Eurasian Skylark is now the commonest small bird, but you may also find Stejneger's Stonechats and Middendorff's Grasshopper Warblers in the grasslands and Sand Martins flitting overhead chasing mosquitoes. Follow the boardwalk over a wooden bridge into the Shunkuni-tai forest and you can find a range of forest birds including Red-flanked Bluetails *Tarsiger cyanurus* and even a Black Woodpecker if you are lucky.

Considerable quantities of Eelgrass grow in Lake Fūren, which is one reason why it supports so many migratory waterfowl. Piles of eelgrass leaf blades wash up in the shallows, then are carried up in rolls to the back of the shore by the tide. Meanwhile, at low tide, the mudflats are covered with it and also the small spiral shells of Japanese Mudsnails.

Less than 1 km along Rt 44 from the Shunkuni-tai parking area you will find the Shunkunitai nature centre[246] This nature centre offers a sheltered view out to Nemuro Bay and across the bridge to Shunkuni-tai and a short nature trail for those

244 43.263495, 145.461704 245 43.272984, 145.471233 246 Its full title is a mouthful: the Nemuro City Shunkunitai Native Wild Bird Park Nature Center. 43.270486, 145.476450

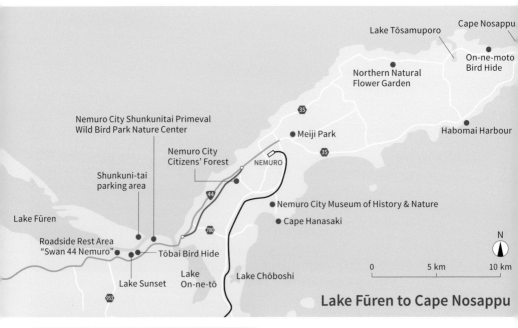

Lake Tōsamuporo

Cape Nosappu

On-ne-moto
Bird Hide

Northern Natural
Flower Garden

Nemuro City Shunkunitai Primeval
Wild Bird Park Nature Center

Meiji Park

Habomai Harbour

Nemuro City
Citizens' Forest

NEMURO

Shunkuni-tai
parking area

Lake Fūren

Nemuro City Museum of History & Nature

Cape Hanasaki

Roadside Rest Area
"Swan 44 Nemuro"

Tōbai Bird Hide

N

Lake Sunset

Lake
On-ne-tō

Lake Chōboshi

0   5 km   10 km

Lake Fūren to Cape Nosappu

Eelgrass is an important source of food for migratory waterfowl

Japanese Mudsnails are abundant in shallow coastal lagoons

looking for woodland birds and butterflies.

The next stop comes just 1 km further east where Rt 44 crosses the On-ne-tō Bridge[247]. There you will find a shallow bay to the left and Lake On-ne-tō to the right. A forest track (On-ne-tō Rindo) heads south into the forest just before the bridge and offers pleasant walking and forest birding. The bay is typically frequented by cranes and eagles are invariably in the area also.

The road along the coast into Nemuro City is through yet more dairy pastureland, past woodlands, small fishing harbours and boat-building businesses, and many places selling crabs in season. The land rises slightly and offers views northwards up Hokkaidō's east coast towards the Notsuke and Shiretoko peninsulas. In this area during the warm summer months Giant Knotweed, an exceedingly common megaherb in Eastern Hokkaidō, grows in profusion at the roadsides and some of the plants stand up to three metres tall.

Nearly 8 km further on, rather than turning onto the prominent section of highway, take a right that

247   Derived from Ainu the name *onne* means ancient, while *tō* means lake. 43.266242, 145.489590

after 700 m will take you past Nemuro City Citizens' Forest (Shimin-no-Mori)[248]. This park has numerous trails through pleasant woodland, and even has a bird hide about 700 m from the car park. It is an excellent area to enjoy local flowers, butterflies and woodland birds. After exploring the forest, return to Rt 44 and head east through Nemuro City (population 25,000 in September 2020). After about 4 km kilometres you will reach the far eastern end of town and see a sign above the road indicating Meiji Park lies straight ahead. From the final traffic lights it is just 600 m to the park's parking area[249]. This is a more open suburban park than Shimin-no-Mori but has a slightly hilly topography, plenty of trees and many plantings right on the edge of town abutting fern meadows with oaks and willows. Walk straight on across the playground area and after about a 10-minute walk you will reach the bird hide. Watch for Pacific Swifts in summer as they make their high speed passes overhead in search of insects and listen then too for Siberian Rubythroats singing nearby. About 200 metres from here you will reach a pond where Slaty-backed and Black-tailed Gulls visit to bathe in the freshwater and where a few ducks also gather. Many of the common woodland birds of Eastern Hokkaidō can be found in each of the parks. In winter pay special attention in case there are flocks of Bohemian Waxwings here or in the trees alongside the main road; sometimes a scarcer species, such as the Japanese Waxwing may be amongst them.

Leave urban Nemuro now, pass Nemuro Port and continue northeast on Rt 35 towards Cape Nosappu (Nosappu Misaki) along the north coast of the Nemuro Peninsula. This is an essential destination for Japanese tourists since it represents the easternmost point of mainland Japan and offers an opportunity to look wistfully out to the islands offshore that were inhabited by Japanese until the final days of World War II in 1945. On the way you will traverse a gently rolling landscape passing hay meadows, cattle ranches, windswept oak woods, and occasional wildflower meadows. Along the shore many Grey Herons forage in the shallows, Sand Martins are quite common along the low sandy cliffs in summer, and eagles are likely at any season.

Especially since the terrible disasters that hit Japan in March 2011[250], renewable energy sources are increasingly being tapped, so you will find many solar farms in this area, even though it is renowned for its cool and often foggy summers. Ten kilometres east of Meiji Park, and just before reaching the small Notsukamappu Wind Power Station, a narrow track leads left to the coast. It is less than 1 km kilometre from Rt 35 to the black-and-white lighthouse[251] that stands on the low headland here surrounded by wild irises, meadowsweet and other summer flowers. In contrast, in winter, drift-ice from the Sea of Okhotsk may be close inshore. Both Temminck's and Pelagic Cormorants frequent the rocks just offshore and the ubiquitous eagle is likely to cruise past.

Just over 3 km further east you will reach the 75 ha Hoppō Gensei-kaen (Northern Natural Flower Garden)[252]. There is a parking area here beside Rt 35, 12 km from Nemuro Station and 10 km from Cape Nosappu. A boardwalk provides access to the wildflower meadows in summer, which are best visited between early June and early August. More than 100 species can be found here but the summer carpet of purple irises is perhaps the most spectacular.

Five kilometres further on, Rt 35 descends and crosses the bridge at the north end of Lake Tōsamuporo[253]. The lake stretches well inland and the inner arms, where cranes sometimes breed, are hidden from the road; nevertheless look out for

248 43.309911, 145.553514 249 43.335516, 145.597397 250 The Great East Japan Earthquake triggered a deadly tsunami, caused destruction at nuclear power facilities and the subsequent collapse of tourism. 251 43.391371, 145.654973 252 43.384039, 145.690099 253 43.389520, 145.749837

There are numerous rocky headlands and offshore islets along the Nemuro Peninsula

them as they may be close to the road.

Two kilometres beyond the bridge you will see a narrow road forking off to the left near an installation of solar panels and wind turbines; this road loops out close to the coast and back again, rejoin-ing Rt 35 near On-ne-moto Harbour. At the road's nearest point to the coast you will see a sign to the left indicating the On-ne-moto Bird Hide and On-ne-moto Chashi-ato (ruins).

A short distance off the road is the small On-

The view from On-ne-moto to Cape Nosappu

ne-moto-chashi-ato parking area[254]. A short walk along the trail beyond takes you to the On-ne-moto Bird Hide (visible from Rt 35) which looks out to sea at a cluster of guano encrusted rocks. Slaty-backed and Black-tailed Gulls along with Temminck's and Pelagic Cormorants roost here and can be found year-round. Among birdwatchers this is a famous location from which to look for Rock Sandpipers[255] *Calidris ptilocnemis* between November and March. The Rock Sandpiper breeds in the Arctic and this is just about the only place in Japan where there is a chance of seeing it during the cold winter months. A small flock can sometimes be seen on these low offshore rocks — as long as there is no eagle nearby! A telescope is necessary to look for them as these shorebirds are small and hard to pick out among the rocks at a distance.

The trail continues, overlooking the sea, a further 100 m or so to the east beyond the hide to a hillock marking the location of an archeological site (nothing visible) overlooking On-ne-moto Harbour with views to the offshore rocks and set nets beyond. In summer, the air is filled with the somewhat plaintive cries of the gulls and the songs of Siberian Rubythroats and Middendorff's Grasshopper Warblers. Seen in the distance, at Cape Nosappu, the white tower with a bulbous top is the Aurora Tower with its views across the Nemuro Strait to the Russian-held Habomai group of islets.

Leaving the On-ne-moto Hide, continue eastwards about 2.5 km to reach Bōkyō-no Misaki Park at the cape with spacious parking and toilet facilities. A huge brown metal arch to the left of the road represents the occupied islands. The Aurora Tower stands on the inland side of the road and a little further on the cluster of small buildings includes restaurants, souvenir shops and a police station. Fog often shrouds the cape, especially on warmer summer days when warm air and cold water south and east of the cape meet, bringing slow-moving banks of fog to the south-facing coast.

Siberian Rubythroat

The Cape Nosappu birdwatching hide is hidden beyond the lighthouse

At Cape Nosappu[256] itself you will find an all-white lighthouse just beyond which is Eastern Hokkaidō's best birdwatching hide. Seawatching as it is known — when birdwatchers can sit for hours watching any seabirds passing by — takes patience, but several species of northern seabirds may be seen from here including Pacific Loon *Gavia pacifica*, Ancient Murrelet *Synthliboramphus antiquus* and Rhinoceros Auklet. Sometimes Northern Minke Whales are visible offshore in the distance and Sea Otters *Enhydra lutris* sometimes float by in the waves close to the tip or may be among the rocks and the kelp.

Continuing along Rt 35 from the cape you are now westbound, passing through Goyoumai to Habomai, about 7.5 km west of Cape Nosappu.

254 43.387150, 145.781289   255 A very scarce winter visitor to Japan usually only found on rocky shores.   256 43.385177, 145.816909

143

Sea Otter

The Sea Otter occurs widely around the coasts of the North Pacific and Bering Sea, but is at the very south-western limit of its range in northern Japan. Here in Eastern Hokkaidō, Sea Otters are scarce and only found around rocky headlands and offshore islands. This surprisingly large animal of the littoral zone weighs up to 45 kg and measures up to 110 cm long, with a 30 cm tail.

Whereas seals have a thick layer of insulating subcutaneous blubber, the Sea Otter has instead a thick fur coat for insulation against the cold northern waters. Its fur is considered the densest of any animal, with as many as 140,000 hairs per square centimetre.

It is closely associated with coastal areas of kelp and considered a keystone species in the kelp beds of the nearshore ecosystem. It feeds on a range of marine organisms including shellfish, fish, and especially sea urchins, which it obtains by diving as deep as 90 m in coastal waters. When it is not foraging it spends

Sea Otters frequently float on their backs when feeding and grooming © Wakasa Masanobu

much of its time grooming its dense fur to maintain its insulation.

Hunting and trade in the Sea Otter's luxuriously dense fur led to the species' near extinction during the latter half of the 19th century and it has taken a century for even partial recovery. Though still rare, it is now regularly sighted around the rocky headlands of southeast Hokkaidō, such as at the capes at Nosappu, Hanasaki, Ochi-ishi and Kiritappu, and around offshore islands such as Moyururi and Yururi.

From here you can take the Habomai Nature Cruise from which you will see the small offshore islands of Habomai-moshiri and Iso-moshiri, the rocky coastline to Cape Nosappu, along with various seabirds and perhaps even a Sea Otter.

As you continue westwards, especially if you are visiting during July, you may see kelp harvesting and drying. Nemuro is renowned in Japan for the quality of its kelp. You could, if you have time,

Hanasaki Wheel Rocks

explore Cape Hikiusu or Cape Tomoshiri, stopping to look at two ponds (On-ne-tō then Tan-ne-numa) with meadows of sedges, umbellifers and lilies in summer just before you reach Nemuro again. If time is limited do not miss Cape Hanasaki[257], perhaps most famous for the local delicacy — Hanasaki Crab. Hanasaki is about 20 km west of Habomai and is reached by turning left as soon as you reach Nemuro and then paralleling the railway (Hanasaki Line) following the signs for the cape. It is approximately 7.5 km from the Rt 35 turn-off to the cape. You will pass Nemuro City Museum of History and Nature on your left and 1 km further on you will reach the parking area (with toilets) for the red-and-white Hanasaki Misaki lighthouse and the 'Wheel Rocks'.

A weathered boardwalk leads from the parking area to various viewpoints from which it is possi-

257 43.278214, 145.589085

Edible Kelp

In coastal areas of Eastern Hokkaidō, especially in the southeast around Nemuro and westwards along the Pacific coast, it is common to see large patches of gravel — which resemble temporary car parks — beside houses and farms. These are special areas for drying the marine product known here as konbu[258] — edible kelp. Various kinds of kelp are harvested commercially for use in Japanese cuisine, but in this region two species predominate. Japanese Kelp *Saccharina japonica*[259] is harvested from the coast of the Shiretoko Peninsula, but is best known commercially as *Rausu Konbu*. Long-blade Kelp *Saccharina longissima*, known officially as *Saomae Konbu*, but locally also as *Naga Konbu* or *Hamanaka Konbu*, is from the Nemuro and Kushiro area and is the second of the two commonest species harvested. *Konbu* is used in broth making, especially for miso soup, hot pot dishes known as *oden*, and is rich in minerals and *umami*; it may also be used to make pickles and even powdered tea.

Kelp provides important habitat for many marine species © Kamada Sachiko

During summer, kelp is harvested from shallow inshore waters, brought ashore and laid out across the gravel beds to dry in the sun and wind. Families gather at this time with multiple generations helping to spread out the harvest. The kelp is commonly cut and packaged locally and sold as an edible souvenir to tourists as well as being much sought after commercially throughout the country.

Kelp is preserved by drying it in the sun and wind

Although many Japanese dishes rely on *konbu* in one form or another, steadily rising ocean temperatures around Eastern Hokkaidō threaten the future of Japan's edible kelp industry, which has been in decline since 1990. The kelp beds of Hokkaidō also support important Ezobafun Sea Urchin *Strongylocentrotus intermedius* and Northern Purple Sea Urchin *Strongylocentrotus nudus* populations — much sought after delicacies in Japan — and provide nursery grounds for many marine organisms, especially fish, but also Sea Otters. As harvests have fallen, so *konbu* prices have increased with some having doubled in price over the last five years. By 2040, several varieties are predicted to become locally extinct or their availability will be greatly reduced because the local sea water will be too warm for them.

Sea urchins graze on kelp © Kamada Sachiko

258 You may see this spelled *kombu* in some publications.   259 *Saccharina japonica* variant *diabolica*; formerly called *Laminaria japonica*.

ble to see not only the locally famous Kuruma-ishi or 'Wheel Rocks' in the low cliffs but also cliffside flowers. The cliffs are of basalt and the famous rocks consist of radially fractured basalt with columns spreading out from apparent central hubs as if they are large stone wheels. The largest and most easily seen example is said to measure six metres in diameter and, because of its rarity, has been designated a natural monument. Rocks and artificial reefs of tetrapods offshore serve as roosting sites for various gull and cormorant species. Sea Otters may sometimes be seen lazing amongst the kelp or swimming just offshore, and very occasionally they haul out and rest on the rocks.

Continuing along Rt 780 from Hanasaki you will soon join Rt 142. After 7 km there is a turning towards the coast and Lake Chōboshi[260]. It is 2 km to the lake from Rt 142. The lake itself is surrounded by woodland and lush vegetation including megaherbs. There is a pilgrim trail with statuary around the lake, but the trail is in varying states of disrepair and requires caution. Watch for gulls bathing at the lake and for summer birds in the meadows near the north end.

One of southeast Hokkaidō's two most prominent capes along this stretch of coast is at Ochi-

ishi. Continue along Rt 142 for about 15 km until you reach Ochiishi Village. The way up to the cape involves passing the harbour, taking a right at the end of the road then a left that winds uphill onto the plateau of the Ochiishi headland. The road becomes a gravel track that ends at a small solar farm and wind turbine and is blocked by a gate. Park here[261] and walk 1.2 km (about 25 mins) to the lighthouse.

After 200 m or so the trail passes a single story concrete structure. After the same distance again, you will reach the start of a rather uneven and rickety boardwalk from where it is about a 20-minute walk to the cape. The cape is often shrouded in fog, and the climate here is particularly cool year-round encouraging a rather special botanical complex of forest, cotton sedge, moss and peat-related plants. In summer you may hear and even see Oriental Turtle Doves Streptopelia orientalis, Red-flanked Bluetails, Eurasian Wrens and Coal Tits Periparus ater in the forest. Beyond the trees the cape is covered with low dwarf bamboo and, from the far edge of the forest, it is now only a short distance to the red-and-white lighthouse. From here you will hear the dramatic sound of waves crashing onto the rocks far below the cliffs and the breeze rustling the dwarf bamboo.

On sunny days the views are very attractive and if you explore the eastern part of the cape you will see the important seabird breeding islands of Yururi and Moyururi offshore to the northeast. During summer White Wagtails Motacilla alba frequent the cliffs here as they do elsewhere in Eastern Hokkaidō, and you are also likely to encounter Stejneger's Stonechats, Middendorff's Grasshopper Warblers and Eurasian Skylarks in the bamboo grasslands at the cape and near the car park.

A few kilometres west of Ochiishi is Bettōga Station, and about 700 m to the west of the station on Rt 142, beside a snow gate, you will find a nar-

Cape Ochiishi is reached via a long raised board walk

260 43.247900, 145.552035 Officially called Chōboshi, but frequently, and especially in the past locally, pronounced and spelled Chōbushi.   261 43.172690, 145.506461

row gravel road turning off to the south. This track leads down towards the Pacific coast and after 3 km reaches an area of wet meadows and marshland pools that will give you a delightful feeling of remoteness. In summer the area can truly be called a wildflower lover's paradise. The bird sanctuary here, called Watanabe Wild Bird Protection Area Fureshima[262], attracts cranes and many other bird species in summer, including Siberian Rubythroat, Middendorff's Grasshopper Warbler, Black-browed Reed Warbler, Stejneger's Stonechat, and Common Reed Bunting; even more species drop in to these wetlands on migration. The area is especially attractive in summer when the Wild Roses are in bloom, but it also possesses a bleak beauty at other times of year.

The second of the two most prominent capes along Hokkaidō's southeast coast is at Kiritappu[263]. This headland can be reached from Chanai on Rt 44 by following the signs, but can also be reached by

Southeast coast scenery

following Rt 142, the North Pacific Ocean Seaside Line, westwards from Ochiishi. The road rises and falls, sometimes almost to sea level, sometimes passing through pasture land along the top of low cliffs overlooking the North Pacific Ocean. Along the way it passes several shallow lagoons including Esahito-numa at which cranes, as well as various waterfowl, may be found. You may also find heavy

Wild flowers enhance summer walks at Cape Kiritappu

262 43.195178, 145.415400   263 43.076257, 145.171477

Coastal Currents and Coastal Fog

Two major currents flow past Japan's Pacific Ocean coast. These western boundary currents, the warm Kuroshio and the cold Oyashio, greatly affect the climate and ecosystems of the western North Pacific and especially Japan. The Kuroshio flows northwards past Kyūshū, Shikoku and Honshū before veering out into the Pacific Ocean. Conversely, the Oyashio flows southwards from the Bering Sea past the Kuril Islands, Hokkaidō, then northern Honshū, before encountering the Kuroshio and also veering east and further out into the North Pacific. The region in which the two currents meet and mix varies northwards or southwards depending on the season and a wide range of more complex factors.

The Oyashio strongly influences the climate of Eastern Hokkaidō and affects the distributions of many species from oceanic plankton and fish to terrestrial plants and animals. The impact of this cold current is witnessed most notably by visitors during summer. The weather news and the weather maps regularly show the temperature in Kushiro (and other coastal towns to the east) to be several degrees cooler than elsewhere in Hokkaidō. Explore this area during the months of May, June or July and it is highly likely that you will experience coastal fog at some point, most likely in the mornings.

Sometimes known as a haar, or a fret, the coastal fog is a consequence of warming moist spring and summer air passing over the cool surface above the cold current. As the warm air cools it is less able to carry its moisture, which condenses forming tiny droplets of water. Visible fog, essentially a low-lying cloud, is an aerosol the nuclei of which are salt particles raised into the atmosphere by breaking waves. Water vapour condenses and forms into tiny droplets around these particles, the whole fog cloud being affected by the local topography, wind and water bodies.

Coastal fog reduces visibility, the extent depending on the concentration of water droplets in the air, and can make driving difficult and landing and take-off difficult for aircraft at regional airports near the coast — one reason why Kushiro Airport is situated inland and atop an escarpment.

Summer fog may linger only at the coast or spread far inland

White Bows, Halos and Green Flashes

Where water occurs in the atmosphere as water droplets (such as during rain or fog), or as spray (from waves or waterfalls), you may find unusual meteorological optical phenomena. The most familiar of these are colourful rainbows. Rainbows are multicoloured arcs that appear in the sky as a result of reflection, refraction and dispersion of light through water droplets. The resulting spectrum of light appears in the sky directly opposite the sun.

A fog bow at Cape Kiritappu

Solar rainbows are typically seen as arcs, but they can be fully circular, with red as the outer colour and violet as the inner colour and between them bands of orange, yellow, green, blue, and indigo. The colours actually span a continuous spectrum; we see them as bands only because of an artefact of our colour perception. Sometimes double rainbows occur. The second occurs as an outer arc, but its hues are seen in reversed order, with red as the inner colour and indigo as the outer.

Less familiar are moonbows[264] though they form in exactly the same way as solar rainbows — refraction of light in water droplets in the sky opposite the moon. As their name suggests they are produced by moonlight and are best seen when the moon is low in the sky, at or near full and two or three hours after sunset or before sunrise. Moonbows are much rarer than solar rainbows. The small amount of light reflected by the moon is not sufficient to stimulate the cone (colour) receptors in our eyes making it difficult, if not impossible, for us to discern any colours. Moonbows appear fainter, and whiter, than any solar rainbow.

Another form of white rainbow is the fog bow, formed during daylight but in fog. Fog bows have very weak colours because of the very small size of the droplets through which light is refracted.

Sometimes, high in the atmosphere, sunlight may be refracted through ice crystals rather than water droplets, leading to another meteorological optical phenomenon known as parhelion. Sun dogs, or mock suns, as they are also known, are a form of halo. They appear as bright spots on either side of the sun at about 22° to left and right of the solar disc. Occasionally you might witness a sun pillar, a vertical beam of light, in the east just before dawn and before or as the sun rises, when light reflects off tiny ice crystals that are suspended in the atmosphere or in high-altitude clouds

An additional, and strangely exciting, phenomenon is the green flash. Seen only at sunset and sunrise on clear days, the green flash consists of a green spot or band seen momentarily (literally for just one or two seconds) immediately above the upper rim of the sun just after it has disappeared from view at sunset or

A halo around the sun

just before it appears at the horizon before sunrise. When the sun is close to the horizon, the thickness of the Earth's atmosphere causes the sunlight to be refracted into its component colours. The other colours appear as in a rainbow, but are very much more difficult to observe, leaving the green flash as the predominant one noticed. I have seen a blue flash following a green flash, though not yet in Japan.

Keeping watch for these various meteorological optical phenomena will enhance your time spent in nature.

---

264 Moonbows are also known as lunar rainbows or white rainbows.

horses in the meadows near the lagoons. Eight to 10 km further west a pullout on the seaward side of the road leads to the Urayakotan Viewpoint[265] and 3 km further on you will reach Poroto Bridge[266] and Poroto-numa (Poroto Lagoon). This is another reed-fringed lagoon close to the sea, with woodland nearby on higher ground. Sometimes gulls visit the lagoon to bathe in the freshwater, and occasionally there are cranes. In summer Sand Martins breed nearby in the coastal sand cliffs and forage here in good numbers. Typical summer birds include Common Cuckoos, Stejneger's Stonechats, Siberian Rubythroats, Middendorff's Grasshopper Warblers, Black-browed Reed Warblers, White Wagtails, and Eurasian Skylarks.

Four kilometres further on you will pass through the Sakaki-machi Tunnel, then reach the junction of Rt 142 and Rt 123. The road to the right heads north to Betsukai, while Rt 123 straight ahead hugs the coastline and leads to Kiritappu. Continue on through Kiritappu, taking the road up to the headland there and turn left at the crossroads at the top; the road then continues and ends at a spacious parking area[267] (just past the campsite). A trail leads from here past the lighthouse to the cape itself. In spring, the cape is carpeted with colourful flowers, white trilliums, yellow dandelions,

purple orchids, and then in summer irises and other wildflowers come into bloom. The cape itself is actually called Tōfutsu-misaki[268], though it is commonly known as Kiritappu-misaki (Cape Kiritappu). This name is derived from a much earlier Ainu name *ki-ta-p*, meaning a place to cut *kaya* (Maiden Silvergrass *Miscanthus sinensis*). This later morphed into Japanese as *ki-i-tappu* before becoming Kiritappu, typically interpreted as foggy cape (it is often foggy here in summer). The soundscape here is wonderful — the air is filled with the deep sounds of crashing waves, the wind, and, in summer, bird song (Siberian Rubythroat, Eurasian Skylark, and White Wagtail are all here) and buzzing bumblebees — and especially atmospheric on foggy days. Watch out too for fog bows!

There is a very clear and easily followed path to Cape Kiritappu bounded by a post-and-rail fence. Just offshore from the cape's tip is a small island with a breeding colony of Temminck's Cormorants and Slaty-backed Gulls in summer[269]. In winter, cormorants roost on the rocks, and before dusk, small rafts of Pelagic Cormorants gather on the sea before they fly to their overnight roosting area. The sea around the rocks and cape is a good place to watch for pretty Harlequin Ducks and other seabirds as well as seals, and even Sea Otters.

Kiritappu is also renowned for its enormous wetland, stretching 4 km from north to south and up to 9 km from east to west. This wetland offers important habitat to birds such as cranes and for vast quantities of wildflowers and other wetland-loving plants. After visiting the cape return to Rt 123 and turn inland on Rt 808. Ten kilometres from the parking area at the cape you will find the Kiritappu Wetland Center[270] This large building offers a panoramic view out across the marshes from the second floor, but unfortunately there is no outside access onto the roof. There are however a few reasonable exhibits and specimens inside, as well

Cape Kiritappu

265 43.149461, 145.176249   266 43.146824, 145.146507   267 43.078531, 145.164257   268 Also Tōbutsu-misaki.   269 And some rather faded old puffin decoys — this little island was once a breeding site of the Tufted Puffin.   270 43.086736, 145.060791

150

Extensive wetlands in southeast Hokkaidō are home to cranes and a host of marshland plant species

as toilet facilities. From below the visitor centre it is possible to take a short walk along a boardwalk into the marsh amongst the Common Reeds, Japanese Alders and low bushes.

Part of Kiritappu Wetland, located in Hamanaka Town, has been registered as a wetland of international importance[271]. This area consists mostly of sphagnum peat bog, but is traversed by several rivers, has over 30 ponds, and areas of swamp forest. As the lower sections of the various rivers are tidal, the wetland is brackish at high tide. The whole area is renowned for its attractive scenery and seasonal wildflowers. It has very recently been designated as the 41,487 ha Akkeshi–Kiritappu–Kombumori Quasi National Park, the central portion of which has been designated a National Wildlife Protection Area Special Protection Zone and a Natural Monument specifically because of its peat bog plant communities.

Various boardwalks allow access to the wetland terrain without disturbing it and permit visitors to enjoy close proximity to the flora including to the delightful 30–60 cm high tussocks of the sedge known as Hare's-tail Cottongrass Eriophorum vagi-

natum and bright yellow Dumortier's Daylilies.

Return to Rt 123 and continue southwards around Biwase Bay with Kenbokki Island[272] just offshore. This island, easiest of the nearshore islands of southeast Hokkaidō to access, can be visited by local fishing boat and is best seen from June to August when the wildflowers there are wonderful.

There are more wildflower meadows near the road along the way and during July they are filled with irises and daylilies. The road then crosses the Biwase River after which it climbs up onto the coastal terrace. Here, Biwase viewpoint[273], with a raised viewing platform situated south of the road, provides the very best panoramic view across Kiritappu Wetland to the north, revealing the extent of water and its flow through this enormous wetland. With binoculars it may be possible to pick out several pairs of cranes from here.

Six kilometres beyond the Biwase Viewpoint you will reach Hichirippu[274], the first of two more lagoons inland of the road. The second, a kilometre further ahead is the smaller Mochirippu[275]. Three kilometres beyond Mochirippu you will see a parking area on the left for Cape Namida and Tate-

271 An area of 2,504 ha was registered as a Ramsar site in 1993. 272 Contact Kiritappu Wetland Trust for access. 273 43.045212, 145.069696 274 43.031204, 145.025025 275 43.021386, 145.019829

Wetland Conservation in Eastern Hokkaidō

Since October 1980, Japan has been a party to the Convention on Wetlands of International Importance especially as Waterfowl Habitat. This international treaty, known widely as the Ramsar Convention, was adopted in 1971 with the aim of combining the conservation and sustainable use of wetlands. As of July 2020, Japan has designated 52 Ramsar sites. Of these 52, 13 are in Hokkaidō seven of which are in the east. They are: Kushiro Shitsugen (Japan's first Ramsar Site), Tōfutsu-ko, Notsuke-hanto and Notsuke-wan, Akan-ko, Furen-ko and Shunkuni-tai, Kiritappu-shitsugen, and Akkeshi-ko and Bekambeushi-shitsugen. These sites also protect a wide range of wetland plants, insects, amphibians, fish and birds in addition to migratory waterfowl.

iwa[276]. The easy walk to this impressively craggy cape is only about 500 metres on a broad path. The view of the cliffs to the west is spectacular. When walking back, follow the trail a little further east taking the turning to Tate-iwa for more wonderful views not only of this rock pillar but also along the cliffs to the east. The cliffs are the summer haunts of Pacific Swifts which dash overhead at breakneck speed and add their screams to the sounds of the waves and wind. Peregrine Falcons may also be found in the area.

In the district of Mabiro, look for the sign pointing south to Ayame-ga-hara[277]. There is a small parking area with toilets near the main road, but if you turn southwards and continue a further 800 m through pleasant shady woodland, you will reach another parking area (also with toilets) at the trail entrance. This approximately 100 ha wildflower meadowland is part of Akkeshi–Kiritappu–Kom-

bumori Quasi National Park. It takes only about five minutes to walk to Chinbe viewpoint (the first viewpoint to the left of the main trail), offering a view eastwards along the coast towards Tateiwa. A further five minutes through more open flower meadows takes you to Chinbe-no-hana (Chinbe Tip) viewpoint[278] in total only about 600–700 m from the car park. Another 3–4 minutes to the west is the Daikoku-jima and Kojima Viewpoint.

The Ayame-ga-hara area offers lovely short walks with a wide range of summer flowers, such as Wild Flag or Beachhead Irises *Iris setosa* and Keyflowers *Dactylorhiza aristata* amongst many others. There are likely to be Pacific Swifts tearing overhead — they probably nest in the cliffs here — and in the lush vegetation watch and listen for Middendorff's Grasshopper Warblers and Siberian Rubythroats. The flower season begins in late May and continues into August with species changing steadily as the weeks pass. In summer the coastal fog may obscure the offshore islands, but the meadows are attractive regardless, and you may find photogenic heavy horses are present in the area.

Continuing westwards there is another viewpoint situated in Mabiro. To reach it, continue along Rt 123 and then turn off following the signs to Tokotan on Rt 955. Pass the pretty lake (Tokotan-numa) where gulls bathe, then turn left towards Mabiro and after about 1.5 km turn uphill to

Cape Namida and Tate-iwa

276 42.998134, 145.007887 Tate-iwa literally means standing rock.   277 42.989037, 144.923094   278 42.982375, 144.922704

The trail entrance to Chinbe-no-hana viewpoint

Wild flowers are abundant at Cape Chinbe

the Pirikauta viewpoint car park[279] and the nearby viewing tower. Pirikauta Viewpoint lies a little further uphill (5 mins walk) along the broad track to the tower platform, which gives views across the bay to Cape Shirepa to the west and to Daikoku Island to the south.

Our route now continues for approximately 7 km to Akkeshi. Eventually the municipality's landmark red main bridge will appear and to the east you will see Lake Akkeshi (a mostly enclosed brackish lagoon) and to the west a broad bay. Classified as a town, with a population of just over 9,000, like most Japanese communities Akkeshi sprawls in a somewhat linear fashion along the coast and along the main road and like most communities in east Hokkaidō its population is declining steadily. It is historically famous for its delicious oysters and clams and, much more recently, for its Akkeshi single malt whiskies. A few drops on a raw oyster on the shell is recommended! Aquaculture for oysters and short-necked clams in the lagoon relies on high water quality, partly achieved by forest stewardship inland.

From Akkeshi either detour east a short distance to visit the Akkeshi Waterfowl Observation Center[280] which lies just east of the Ōbetsu River, or continue westwards for Cape Shirepa. The former is located beside Rt 44 and here you can learn about the migratory waterfowl that use the area. From the upper floor you can look out across Rt 44 and the railway tracks to the river and marsh beyond, scanning for swans and other waterfowl during the winter.

The wetlands of Lake Akkeshi and Bekambeushi Marsh (5,277 ha) combining high and low moor, salt marsh, river and brackish lagoon, are part of Akkeshi–Kiritappu–Kombumori Quasi National Park. They have been designated as a National Wildlife Protection Area and a wetland of international significance[281]. The 43-km-long Bekambeushi River system traversing the 8,300 ha of Bekambeushi Wetland has been so little affected by human activity that it is considered to be the most pristine major river in all of Hokkaidō. It supports cranes and Japanese Huchen and flows out into the 3,230 ha brackish Lake Akkeshi. Lo-

279 42.988976, 144.878156   280 43.096838, 144.863366   281 A Ramsar Site since 1993.

cal operators run tightly regulated canoe tours of the river and wetlands. The partly saline waters of the lake do not completely freeze over, thus both White-tailed and Steller's Eagles can be found here in winter. It is also an important resting area for the more than 10,000 Whooper Swans that pass through on migration. The area also provides breeding habitat for cranes.

Cape Shirepa[282] is located south-southwest of Akkeshi and partly encloses Akkeshi Bay. The cape is shaped like a plough-share, and can be reached by travelling west at first along Rt 44 in the direction of Kushiro. Then in Oboro, turn south onto Rt 142 following the signs for Shirepa Misaki for about 11 km. The final turn east is onto a dirt road that ends after about 4 km at the Shirepa Misaki parking area[283]. A pleasant walk of about 1.5 km over undulating open terrain from the car park to the cape takes 20 minutes one way. The coastline here consists of very steep grassy slopes, rather than cliffs, topped with open meadows and, in the hollows, wind-blasted woodland. The road may be closed

The Falcated Duck is a scarce winter visitor to wetlands in Eastern Hokkaidō

The Eastern Spotbilled Duck is a common breeder and scarce winter visitor in Eastern Hokkaidō

The Grey-tailed Tattler migrates through Hokkaidō in spring and autumn

Cape Shirepa

282 42.936976, 144.784833   283 42.936822, 144.770911

Seasons and weather in Eastern Hokkaidō

Kushiro, the largest city in Eastern Hokkaidō, is located at latitude 42.9849° N, just south of the latitude of Marseille, France, and just north of the latitude of Boston, USA, but its climate hardly resembles either place. Hokkaidō, generally, experiences distinct seasons dominated by long cold winters, cool to warm springs, brief hot and even humid summers, and cool to cold autumns.

Strong seasonal contrasts include colourful autumns

It is widely said that Hokkaidō has no rainy season (a very dominating season in the main islands of Japan to the south overlapping late spring and early summer); yet as the annual rainy season fades further south during June or July, Hokkaidō then experiences prolonged periods of rain. Rain in Eastern Hokkaidō can be heavy too during the late summer and early autumn typhoon season. Although few typhoons directly impact the region, the outer portions of their extensive weather systems certainly do bring heavy rain and even flooding in some years. Autumn brings increasingly hard frosts and eventually the ground freezes, and finally, in winter, some of the lakes freeze over. Snow cover in Eastern Hokkaidō is far less than in the west of the island, but nevertheless snow may

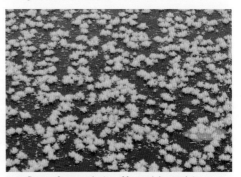

Frost flowers form on the ice of frozen lakes and rivers

drift making driving hazardous in the lowlands. The mountains begin to turn white during October and remain covered with snow into early June. Summer temperatures may reach 30°C or above, and winter temperatures can fall to minus 30°C or even below, although temperatures are generally less extreme. The proximity of the sea ameliorates the climate year-round, although summer fogs along the Pacific coast make many summer days feel very cool.

Hard ground frosts form ice needles

in late winter because of snow. In summer there are meadow flowers and the common birds of such open grassland and woodland edge habitats, with eagles and Pacific Swifts overhead, White Wagtails on the shore, Slaty-backed and Black-tailed Gulls along with Pelagic and Temminck's Cormorants just offshore, and Middendorff's Grasshopper Warblers, Eurasian Skylarks, and Stejneger's Stonechats in the grasslands.

Concluding this journey around Eastern Hokkaidō, it is now about 40 km (one hour's drive) from the cape to downtown Kushiro, or about 60 km (bypassing the city) back to Tancho Kushiro Airport.

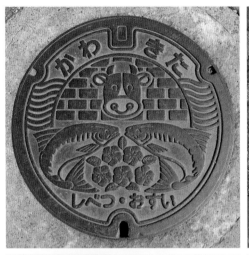

Many Ways to Enjoy Eastern Hokkaidō

Varied, dramatic and even spectacular scenery is a major attraction of touring Eastern Hokkaidō

The beautiful mountain ranges, spectacular volcanoes, extensive forests, rivers, lakes, and the many natural parks all contribute to making nature a very conspicuous element of Eastern Hokkaidō. A

The author hiking the Akan Volcanoes © Ministry of the Environment

wide range of outdoor opportunities and activities is possible, from camping and hiking to hot spring bathing, and this is Japan's premier region for wildlife watching. The route around Eastern Hokkaidō that I have introduced is only one of many approaches to the national parks and other wild places of the region. Multiple driving routes are possible by car or motorcycle. Cycling is increasingly popular and there are local companies ready to assist you in your journey by bicycle with a variety of equipment including road bikes, e-bikes, mountain bikes and fat bikes that can be hired locally.

There are many mountain trails in the Akan–Mashū and Shiretoko national parks, and outside those areas Mt Musa and Mt Shari and various other peaks have their own trails. There is even a long trail, the c 44 km Mashū–Kussharo Trail which extends from Nishibetsu mountain hut via Mt Nishibetsu, Mt Mashū and the Lake Mashū viewpoint to Kawayu Onsen and the southern shore of Lake Kussharo. Unfortunately the longest trail, the Kitanemuro Ranchway or Kiraway which stretched 71.4 km from Nakashibetsu to Biruwa Station by way of Lake Mashū, though still marked on signs and maps was closed in October 2020. There are six shorter trails maintained as part of the footpaths associated with Nemuro City. Several sections of these are suitable for half- or full-day hikes. Their presence makes walking, hiking and trekking through the region another attractive proposition. If you wish to try walking of a different kind, then consider a winter wander through the drift-ice on the Sea of Okhotsk shore!

Kushiro River offers year-round canoeing opportunities

The rivers and lakes of the Akan–Mashū NP and Kushiro Shitsugen NP provide fine canoeing opportunities and many local operators exist to help you enjoy seeing the region from the water. Open Canadian-style canoes are stable, roomy, and great whether travelling alone, as a couple, or as a family, making it possible to experience the wetlands close-up, enjoying the special sounds and relaxing atmosphere of the water world here. The rocky coasts of the Shiretoko and Nemuro peninsulas lend themselves to sea-kayaking, though weather conditions can change quickly and make this a risky activity at certain times of year.

Canoeing is a marvellous way of experiencing the lakes and rivers of Eastern Hokkaidō © Ministry of the Environment

In addition to the many inns, lodges and hotels in East Hokkaidō, there are also numerous widely scattered campsites making it possible to support almost any kind of activity from a nearby location. The availability of rental camper vans is increasing in Hokkaidō, but as yet there are few fully serviced campsites for them. Surprisingly, many Japanese travelers who tour the area in camper vans seem content to spend their nights in the rather sterile conditions of car parks and at road stations rath-

The quiet rural roads of Hokkaidō offer fun for cyclists, riders and drivers

Wildlife photographers find numerous subjects amid the spectacular scenery of eastern Hokkaidō

Cycling, whether on a road bike, a mountain bike or a fat bike is an excellent way of exploring rural Hokkaidō

er than demanding attractive out-of-town sites such as the ones offered in various countries such as Australia, Canada, New Zealand, USA and the UK. However, this situation is likely to change and evolve in the coming years as demand grows.

Hokkaidō's main downhill skiing and snowboarding areas are all situated much further west, in places such as Niseko, Furano, and Sōunkyo; however backcountry skiing and snowshoeing are certainly possible on many of the mountains served with summer hiking trails in the Akan–Mashū and Shiretoko national parks, and on many more where there are no trails. Backcountry activities are not

without risk, so do take sensible precautions, such as going with a companion, telling others where you are going, and carrying safety equipment. As yet there are no established cross-country skiing courses in Eastern Hokkaidō; but using narrow forest roads closed by winter snow make it possible to head off for classical style cross-country skiing to enjoy a magical winter landscape.

Whichever way you approach it, as an adventure traveller, as a naturalist, a birdwatcher, photographer or as a tourist, East Hokkaidō has a tremendous variety of activities to offer. Have a great time here!

Iramkarapte! — Irasshaimase! — Welcome!

Recommended Hiking Routes

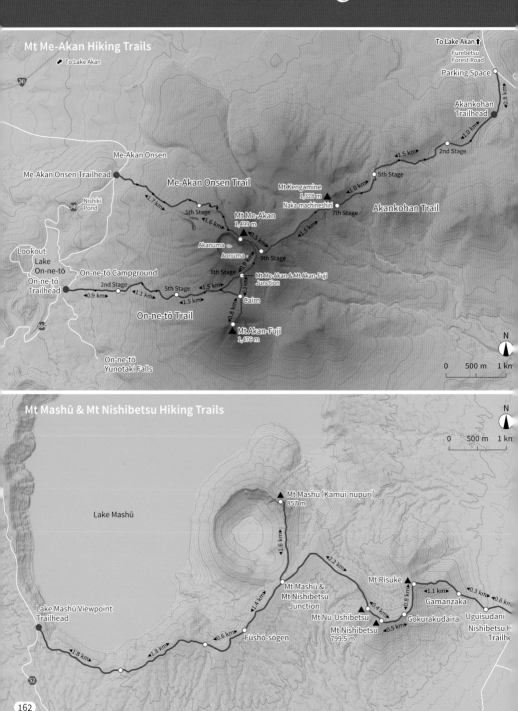

Mt Me-Akan Hiking Trails

▶ To Lake Akan

To Lake Akan ↑
Furebetsu Forest Road

241

Parking Space

◀0.8 km▶

Akankohan Trailhead

◀1.0 km▶

Me-Akan Onsen

Me-Akan Onsen Trailhead

Me-Akan Onsen Trail

Nishiki Pond

949

◀1.7 km▶

5th Stage

◀1.6 km▶

Mt Kengamine
1,328 m

◀1.5 km▶   2nd Stage

5th Stage

◀1.0 km▶

Naka-machineshiri

7th Stage

Akankohan Trail

Mt Me-Akan
1,499 m

◀0.5 km▶

◀1.5 km▶

Akanuma

Aonuma

9th Stage

Lookout
Lake
On-ne-tō

On-ne-tō
Trailhead

On-ne-tō Campground

8th Stage

◀0.9 km▶

Mt Me-Akan & Mt Akan-Fuji Junction

2nd Stage

◀0.9 km▶   ◀1.1 km▶   5th Stage   ◀1.5 km▶

◀2.1 km▶

Cairn

664

On-ne-tō Trail

◀0.8 km▶

Mt Akan-Fuji
1,476 m

On-ne-tō
Yunotaki Falls

N

0   500 m   1 km

Mt Mashū & Mt Nishibetsu Hiking Trails

N

0   500 m   1 km

Lake Mashū

Mt Mashū (Kamui-nupuri)
857 m

◀1.6 km▶

◀2.2 km▶

Mt Risuke

◀1.4 km▶

Mt Mashū &
Mt Nishibetsu
Junction

◀0.8 km▶   ◀1.1 km▶   ◀0.3 km▶   ◀0.6 km▶

Gamanzaka

Uguisudani

Lake Mashū Viewpoint
Trailhead

◀0.4 km▶

Mt Nu-Ushibetsu

Gokurakudaira

Nishibetsu
Trailhe

◀1.8 km▶   ◀1.8 km▶   ◀0.6 km▶   Fūshō-sōgen

Mt Nishibetsu
799.5 m

◀0.5 km▶

52

Mt O-Akan Hiking Trail

Mt O-Akan
1,370 m

9th Stage

8th Stage

7th Stage

6th Stage

5th Stage

4th Stage

3rd Stage

2nd Stage

1st Stage

Lake Jirō

Lake Tarō

Lake Akan

Trailhead
(Takiguchi Waterfall)

240 241

nko Onsen
nkohan
-museum Center)

Takimi Bridge

KUSHIRO

0.4 km

0.2 km

0.5 km

0.3 km

0.5 km

0.9 km

0.7 km

0.9 km

0.9 km

0.5 km

0.3 km

0.6 km

N

0   500 m   1 km

Bibliography and Recommended Reading

Abe H, Ishii N, Itō T, Kaneko Y, Maeda K, Miura S & Yoneda M 2008 *A Guide to the Mammals of Japan* 2nd Revised Edition. Tōkai University Press; Japan.

Benedict R 1989 *The Chrysanthemum and the Sword. Patterns of Japanese Culture.* Houghton Mifflin Company; Boston.

Brazil MA 1987 *A Birdwatcher's Guide to Japan.* Kodansha International; Tōkyō.

Brazil MA 1991 *The Birds of Japan.* Helm, A & C Black; London.

Brazil MA 2018a *The Nature of Japan 2nd Edition.* Japan Nature Guides; Sapporo.

Brazil MA 2018b *Helm Field Guides Birds of Japan.* Bloomsbury; London.

Brazil MA 2021 *Japan: The Natural History of an Asian Archipelago.* Princeton University Press; Princeton.

Chamberlain BH & Mason WB 1891 *A Handbook for Travellers in Japan. Third Edition.* Murray; London.

Davies RJ & Ikeno O (Eds) 2002 *The Japanese Mind. Understanding Contemporary Japanese Culture.* Tuttle Publishing; Tōkyō.

Department of Agriculture Hokkaidō Government 2020 Agriculture in Hokkaidō Japan. http://www.pref.hokkaido.lg.jp/ns/nsi/genjyou_english_0206.pdf.

Gakuhari T, Nakagome S, Rasmussen S *et al.* 2020 Ancient Jomon genome sequence analysis sheds light on migration patterns of early East Asian populations. *Communication Biol* 3: 437. https://doi.org/10.1038/s42003-020-01162-2.

Goris RC & Maeda N 2004 *Guide to the Amphibians and Reptiles of Japan.* Krieger Publishing; Malabar.

Hashimoto M (Ed.) 1991 *The geology of Japan.* Terra Scientific Publishing; Tokyo.

Higashi S, Osawa A & Kanagawa K (Eds) 1993 *Biodiversity and Ecology in the Northernmost Japan.* Hokkaidō University Press; Sapporo.

Ito Y, Nakamura K & Kanasaka K 2011 *Discovering Japan. A New Regional Geography.* Teikoku-shoin; Tōkyō.

Japan Butterfly Conservation Society (Suda S, Nagahata Y, Nakamura Y, Hasegawa T & Yago M) 2017 *Field Guide to the Butterflies of Japan.* Seibundo-Shinkosha; Tōkyō.

Japan Crops 2020 Japanese agriculture — Japanese agricultural products promotion. https://japancrops.com/en/

Japan Wildlife Research Center 2002 Threatened Wildlife of Japan — Red Data Book 2nd ed. Japan Wildlife Research Center; Tōkyō.

Kanzawa-Kiriyama H, Jinam TA, Kawai Y, Sato T, Hosomichi K, Tajima A, Adachi N, Matsumura H, Kryukov K, Saitou N & Shinoda K 2019 Late Jomon male and female genome sequences from the Funadomari site in Hokkaidō, Japan. *Anthropological Science* 127(2): 83–108.

Kasuya T 2017 *Small Cetaceans of Japan: Exploitation and Biology.* CRC Press; Boca Raton.

Meteorological Agency 2019 List of Active Volcanoes in Japan. https://www.data.jma.go.jp/svd/vois/data/tokyo/STOCK/souran_eng/intro/volcano_list.pdf Accessed 21 December 2019.

Ministry of the Environment 2008 *Beautiful Nature of Four Seasons. National Parks of Japan & Japan's Strategy for a Sustainable Society.* Yama-Kei; Tōkyō.

Ministry of the Environment 2016 *Natural Beauty of the Four Seasons. National Parks of Japan.* Yama-Kei; Tōkyō.

Miura H, Wada K & Katsui Y 2004 Tephrochronology and diagenesis of the manganese wad deposit at the Akan Yunotaki hotspring, Hokkaidō, Japan. Journal of Mineralogical and Petrological Sciences 99: 368–374.

Miyaki M, Takashima Y & Sukeno M 2006 The influence of sika deer on the vegetation in Hashirikotan, Notsuke–Furen Prefectural National Park. Agris 30: 49–55.

Nakada S, Yamamoto T & F Maeno 2016 Miocene–Holocene volcanism. *In*: Moreno T, Wallis S, Kojima T & W Gibbons (eds) *The Geology of Japan*. Geological Society; London.

Nakashima T 1993 *Kushiro Shitsugen Nature Guide. Onnenai Trail Nature Guide.* Japanese Society for Preservation of Birds; Kushiro.

National Agriculture and Food Research Organization 2020 Hokkaidō Agricultural Research Center, NARO (HARC/NARO) http://www.naro.affrc.go.jp/publicity_report/publication/files/2017NARO_english_1.pdf

Natural Parks Foundation 2004 *Shiretoko National Park Park Guide. World Natural Heritage Site Shiretoko.* Natural Parks Foundation; Tōkyō.

Nihei T 2018 *The Regional Geography of Japan.* Hokkaidō University Press; Sapporo.

Ohashi H, Yoshikawa M, Oono K, Tanaka N, Hatase Y & Murakami Y 2014 The Impact of Sika Deer on Vegetation in Japan: Setting Management Priorities on a National Scale. Environmental Management 54 (3): 631–640.

Ohdachi SD, Ishibashi Y, Iwasa MA, Fukui D & Saitoh T 2015 *The Wild Mammals of Japan Second Edition.* Shoukadoh Book Sellers and the Mammal Society of Japan; Kyoto.

Ono Y 1990 The Northern Landbridge of Japan. The Quaternary Research 29(3): 183–192.

Ozono A, Kawashima I & Futahashi R 2017 *Nihon no Tombo* [*Dragonflies of Japan*]. Bun-ichi Shuppan; Tōkyō.

Satō K, Hino S, Wada K & Wakana I (Eds) 2017 *Akan no Daishizen-shi. Saishin Kenkyu ga Tokiakasu: Kazan, Mori, Mizuumi to Ainu Minzoku no Monogatari.* [*The Great Nature of Akan: Volcanoes, Forests, Lakes and Ainu*]. Kushiro-shi Kyōiku Iinkai; Kushiro.

Sato T 1990 *Trees and Shrubs of Hokkaidō.* Alicesha; Sapporo.

Sato T 1993 *Kushiro Shitsugen Nature Guide. Siberian Salamander.* Japanese Society for Preservation of Birds; Kushiro.

Snow HJ 1910 *In forbidden seas: Recollections of sea-otter hunting in the Kurils.* E. Arnold; London.

Sutherland M & Britton D 1980 *National Parks of Japan.* Kodansha International; Tōkyō.

Teikoku-shoin (Ed) 2009 *Discovering Japan A New Regional Geography.* Teikoku-shoin; Tōkyō.

Togashi T, Sasaki H & Yoshimura J 2014 A geometrical approach explains Lake Ball (Marimo) formations in the green alga, *Aegagropila linnaei. Sci Rep* 4: 3761. https://doi.org/10.1038/srep03761

Ubukata H 1993 *Kushiro Shitsugen Nature Guide. Dragonflies of Kushiro Shitsugen.* Japanese Society for Preservation of Birds; Kushiro.

Uchiyama R, Maeda N, Numata K & Seki S 2002 *A Photographic Guide: Amphibians and Reptiles in Japan.* Heibonsha; Tōkyō.

Umezawa S 2007 *Wild Flowers of Hokkaidō.* Hokkaidō University Press; Sapporo.

Umezawa S 2018 *Wild Flowers of Hokkaidō.* Hokkaido Shimbunsha; Sapporo.

Varley P 2000 *Japanese Culture.* Fourth Edition. University of Hawai'i Press; Honolulu.

Directory

Chapter One

Ainu
www.ainu-assn.or.jp/english/begin.html
www.pref.hokkaido.lg.jp/ks/ass/new_timeilist.htm
www.kantei.go.jp/jp/singi/ainusuishin/index_e.html
www.ff-ainu.or.jp/web/english/
https://ich.unesco.org/en/RL/traditional-ainu-dance-00278
https://en.unesco.org/courier/numero-especial-octubre-2009/saga-ainu-language

Ministry of the Environment National and Natural Parks
www.env.go.jp/en/nature/nps/park/
www.env.go.jp/en/nature/nps/park/parks/index.html
https://www.env.go.jp/en/nature/nps/park/guide/index.html

Abashiri Quasi-National Park
www.env.go.jp/en/nature/nps/parks_list.html

Akan–Mashū National Park
http://www.env.go.jp/en/nature/nps/park/akan/index.html
https://www.japan.travel/national-parks/parks/akan-mashu/

Akkeshi–Kiritappu–Kombumori Quasi National Park
http://www.gov-base.info/en/2020/12/03/132525

Kushiro Shitsugen National Park
www.env.go.jp/en/nature/nps/park/kushiro/point/index.html
www.env.go.jp/en/nature/nps/park/kushiro/guide/view.html
www.env.go.jp/park/common/data/04_kushiro_map_e.pdf
www.env.go.jp/en/nature/nps/park/kushiro/access/index.html
https://noctive.jp/spot/02301-1500738

Shiretoko National Park
www.env.go.jp/en/nature/nps/park/shiretoko/index.html
http://www.yichuans.github.io/datasheet/output/site/shiretoko/
http://whc.unesco.org/en/list/1193/
http://dc.shiretoko-whc.com/data/process/200401/english_02/Appendix1.pdf
https://world-natural-heritage.jp/en/shiretoko
www.env.go.jp/en/nature/nps/park/shiretoko/guide/view.html
www.shiretoko.asia/world/shiretoko_goko.html
www.shiretoko.asia/world/shiretoko_trip_guide.html
www.shiretoko.asia/world/shiretoko_access.html
https://center.shiretoko.or.jp/i-box/english.html

Japanese Geoparks Network
https://geopark.jp/en/

Japan Nature Guide
www.japannatureguides.com

Ramsar Convention and Sites in Eastern Hokkaidō
www.ramsar.org/wetland/japan
www.env.go.jp/en/nature/npr/ramsar_wetland/pamph/index.html
www.kiwc.net/english/wetlands/index.html

Regulations for flying drones
www.mlit.go.jp/en/koku/uas.html
https://naka4.com/drone/english/

Tourism in Eastern Hokkaidō
https://en.visit-hokkaido.jp
https://en.visit-eastern-hokkaido.jp
https://en.kushiro-lakeakan.com/overview/2363/
https://en.kushiro-lakeakan.com
www.masyuko.or.jp/pc/english/index.html
www.kiyosatokankou.com/multilingual_eng/index.html
https://en.tsurui-kanko.com
www.abakanko.jp/en/
http://nemuro-hokkaido.com
www.kiritappu.jp/en/home/nn/taiken/taiken291214old.html
www.dotoinfo.com/naturecenter/tours-e.htm
http://dosanko-farm.com (Japanese only)
https://rausu-shiretoko.net
http://hokkaido-okhotsk-cycle.com/topics
http://hokkaido-okhotsk-cycle.com/cycling-route/

Weather, Sea Ice, Travel and Roads
www.jma.go.jp/jma/indexe.html
www1.kaiho.mlit.go.jp/KAN1/drift_ice/ice_chart/ice_calendar.html
https://info-road.hdb.hkd.mlit.go.jp/en/

Wild Bird Society of Japan
www.wbsj.org

Chapter Two
Nature Centres & Visitor Centres
Onnenai Visitor Center
Onnenai, Tsurui, Akan-gun, 085-1145
T: 0154-65-2323
Closed Tuesdays, New Year's holidays

https://www.japan.travel/national-parks/parks/
kushiroshitsugen/see-and-do/onnenai-visitor-
center/

Kushiro Shitsugen Wildlife Center
2-2101 Hokuto, Kushiro, 084-0922
T: 0154-56-2345
https://www.env.go.jp/nature/kisho/wildlifecenter/
kushiro-shitsugen.html

Lake Tōro Eco-museum Center
Tōrogenya, Shibecha, Kawakami-gun, 088-2261
T: 0154-87-3003
Open Summer 10:00-17:00 Winter 10:00-16:00
Closed Wednesdays, New Year's holiday
https://www.japan.travel/national-parks/parks/
kushiroshitsugen/see-and-do/lake-toro-eco-
museum-center-arukotto/

Shirarutoro Nature Center
127 Kottarogenya, Shibecha, Kawakami-gun, 088-2266
T: 0154-87-2121
Open 09:00-17:00 May to October
https://www.japan.travel/national-parks/parks/
kushiroshitsugen/see-and-do/shirarutoro-nature-
center/

Tourist Information
Kushiro Station Tourist Information
14 Kitaōdōri, Kushiro, 085-0015
T: 0154-22-8294
Open 09:00-17:30
http://ja.kushiro-lakeakan.com/overview/370/

Kushiro Tourist Concierge
Kushiro Tourism and Convention Center 1F, 3-3,
Saiwai-cho, Kushiro, 085-0017
T: 0154-31-1996
Open 09:00-19:00
http://ja.kushiro-lakeakan.com/overview/375/

Kushiro Airport Tourist Information
2 Tsuruoka, Kushiro, 084-0926
T: 0154-57-8304
Open 09:00-20:00
http://ja.kushiro-lakeakan.com/overview/368/

Michi-no-eki (Road Station with 24 hr toilets)
Akan Tancho-no-Sato
On Rt 240, 23-36-1, Kamiakan, Akan, Kushiro, 085-0245
T: 0154-66-2969
Open 09:00-18:00
http://www.hokkaido-michinoeki.jp/michinoeki/810/

Accommodation
Kushiro
Hotel WBF Kushiro
4-1 Kawakami, Kushiro, 085-0012
T: 0154-23-3311
https://www.hotelwbf.com/kushiro/

La Vista Kushirogawa
2-1 Kitaōdōri, Kushiro, 085-0015
T: 0154-31-5489
https://www.hotespa.net

ANA Crowne Plaza Hotel Kushiro
3-7 Nishiki-chō, Kushiro, 085-0016
T: 0154-31-4111
https://www.anaihghotels.co.jp/search/hkd/cp-kuhja/

Kushiro Century Castle Hotel
2-5 Ōkawa-chō, Kushiro, 085-0837
T: 0154-43-2111
http://www.castlehotel.jp

Kushiro Prince Hotel
7-1 Saiwai-chō, Kushiro, 085-8581
T: 0154-31-1111
www.princehotels.co.jp/kushiro/

Tsurui
Hotel Taito
1-5 Tsuruinishi, Tsurui, Akan-gun, 085-1203
T: 0154-64-3111
www.hotel-taito.co.jp

Wilderness Lodge Hickory Wind
14-kita, Setsurigennya, Tsurui, Akan-gun, 085-1200
T: 0154-64-2956
http://hickorywind.jp/

Woody Hotel & Restaurant Yume Kōbō
37-20 Minami 4, Hororogenya, Tsurui, Akan-gun,
085-1144
T: 0154-65-2181
http://yumekobo96.sub.jp/

Campsites
Yamahana Kōen Auto Campsite
11-37 Ninishibetsu, Akan, Kushiro, 085-0201
T: 0154-56-3020
Open June to October
http://www.kushiro-park.com/publics/index/60/

Takkobu-numa Auto Campsite
6-5 Takkobu, Kushiro Kushiro-gun, 088-2141
T: 0154-40-4448
Open May to October

http://www.town.kushiro.lg.jp/kankou/html/camp/
takkobu.html

Restaurants and Cafés
Kushiro
Robata Izakaya Hatagoya
Utaya Suehiro 2F, 4-2 Sakae-machi, Kushiro, 085-0013
T: 0154-22-1717
http://www.946hatagoya.com/en/

Ganpeki Robata
2-4 Nishiki-chō, Kushiro, 085-0016
T: 0154-23-0600
http://www.moo946.com

Kushiro Aburiya
5-6 Suehiro-chō, Kushiro, 085-0014
T: 0154-22-7777
http://aburiya946.com

Restaurant & Community Iomante
2-23 Suehiro-chō, Kushiro, 085-0014
T: 0154-65-1802
www.i-omante.com

Tsurui
Doremifasora
17-18 Higashi, Kita 4, Setsurigenya, Tsurui, Akan-gun,
085-1200
T: 0154-64-3987
http://doremifasora.jp/

Wada Masahiro Art Square Café & Bar
Next to Hotel Taito, 1-5 Tsuruinishi, Tsurui, Akan-gun,
085-1203
T: 0154-64-3111
www.hotel-taito.co.jp

Heartn Tree
496-4 Seturi, Tsurui, Akan-gun, 085-1200
T: 0154-64-2542
https://heartntree.jimdo.com/

Restaurant Tsuru
Akai Beret 1F, 23-36-1, Kamiakan, Akan-chō, Kushiro,
085-0245
T: 0154-66-2330
http://www.akan.jp

Museums & Art Galleries
Kushiro City Museum
1-7 Shunkodai, Kushiro, 085-0822
T: 0154-41-5809
Open 09:30-17:00 Closed Mondays, National Holidays
https://www.city.kushiro.lg.jp/museum/

Kushiro Tancho Nature Park
112 Tsuoka, Kushiro, 084-0926
T: 0154-56-2219
Open 09:00-16:00
http://www.kushiro-park.com/publics/index/72/

Tsurui
Wada Masahiro Art Square Café & Bar
Next to Hotel Taito, 1-5 Tsuruinishi, Tsurui, Akan-gun,
085-1203
T: 0154-64-3111
www.hotel-taito.co.jp

Activities
Cycling (Hotel Taito)
1-5 Tsuruinishi, Tsurui, Akan-gun, 085-1203
T: 0154-64-3111
http://www.hotel-taito.co.jp/cyclist/

Chapter Three
Nature Centres & Visitor Centres
Lake Akan
Akankohan Eco-museum Center
1-1-1 Akanko Onsen, Akan, Kushiro, 085-0467
T: 0154-67-4100
Open 09:00-17:00
Closed Tuesdays, 29 December to 3 January
http://business4.plala.or.jp/akan-eco/about.html

Akanko Marimukan Tourist Information Center
2-6-20 Akanko-onsen, Akan, Kushiro, 085-0467
T: 0154-67-3200
Open 09:00-18:00
https://ja.kushiro-lakeakan.com/overview/378

Teshikaga
Kawayu Eco-museum Center
2-2-6 Kawayu Onsen, Teshikaga, Kawakami-gun,
088-3465
T: 015-483-4100
Open 09:00-16:00
Closed Wednesdays, 29 December to 3 January
http://www.kawayu-eco-museum.com/english/

Wakoto Field House
Kussharo Wakoto, Teshikaga, Kawakami-gun,
088-3465
T: 015-484-2835
Open 08:00-17:00 7 days a week May to October
http://hokkaido.env.go.jp/kushiro/wakoto.pdf

JR Mashū Station Tourist Information
1-7-26, Asahi, Teshikaga, Kawakami-gun, 088-3204
T: 015-482-2642
Open 10:00-16:00

https://www.masyuko.or.jp/introduce/m_kankou/

Kawayu Onsen Tourist Information
Kawayu Furusato-kan, 2-3-40, Kawayuonsen,
    Teshikaga, Kawakami-gun, 088-3465
T: 015-483-2670
Open 09:00-17:00
https://www.masyuko.or.jp/introduce/kawayu_
kankou/

Michi-no-eki Mashū Onsen Tourist Information
3-3-5, Yunoshima, Teshikaga, Kawakami-gun,
    088-3203
T: 015-482-2500
Open 09:00-17:00 Closed 30 December to 3 January
https://www.masyuko.or.jp/introduce/michinoeki/

Michi-no-eki (Road Station with 24 hr toilets)
Mashū Onsen
On Rt 241, 3-5-5, Yunoshima, Teshikaga, Kawakami-
gun, 088-3203
T: 015-482-2500
Open 09:00-17:00 Closed 30 December to 3 January
http://www.hokkaido-michinoeki.jp/michinoeki/440/

Accommodation
Lake Akan
Akan Yuku no Sato Tsuruga
4-6-10 Akanko-onsen, Akan, Kushiro, 085-0467
T: 0154-67-2531
https://www.tsuruga.com/

Akan-no-mori Hotel Hanayūka
1-6-1 Akanko-onsen, Akan, Kushiro, 085-0467
T: 0154-67-2311
https://www.hanayuuka.com

La Vista Akangawa
3-1 Okurushube, Akan, Kushiro, 085-0468
T: 0154-67-5600
https://www.hotespa.net/hotels/akangawa

Lake Akan Tsuruga Wings
4-6-10 Akanko-onsen, Akan, Kushiro, 085-0467
T: 0154-67-2531
https://www.tsurugagroup.com/

Teshikaga
Forest Lodge Subaru
286-41 Biruwagenya, Teshikaga, Kawakami-gun,
    088-3331
T: 015-482-2224
http://www.forestlodge-subaru.jp/

Gasthof Papilio
Kussharokohan, Teshikaga, Kawakami-gun, 088-3395

T: 015-484-2201
https://lakeside-papilio.com

Kawayu Kanko Hotel
1-2-30 Kawayu-onsen, Teshikaga, Kawakami-gun,
    088-3465
T: 015-483-2121
http://www.iionsen.com

Oyado Kinkiyu
1-5-10 Kawayu-onsen, Teshikaga, Kawakami-gun,
    088-3465
T: 015-483-2211
https://www.kinkiyu.com/english/

Kussharo Prince Hotel
Kussharo-onsen, Teshikaga, Kawakami-gun, 088-3395
T: 015-484-2111
Open April to October
www.princehotels.co.jp/kussharo/

Kinkiyu Hotel Bettei Suikazura
1-2-3 Kawayuonsen Teshikaga, Kawakami-gun,
    088-3465
T: 015-483-2211
http://suikzura.jp/en/

Campsites
Akan Lakeside Campsite
Akanko Onsen, Akan, Kushiro, 085-0467
T: 0154-67-3263
Open June to September
http://en.kushiro-lakeakan.com/news/12387/

RECAMP Wakoto
Wakoto, Kussharo, Teshikaga, Kawakami-gun,
    088-3341
Open April to October
https://www.recamp.co.jp/wakoto

RECAMP Sunayu
Sunayu, Biruwa, Teshikaga, Kawakami-gun, 088-3331
Open June to October
https://www.recamp.co.jp/sunayu

RECAMP Mashū
2-6-1, Sakuraoka, Teshikaga, Kawakami-gun, 088-3213
Open April to January
https://www.recamp.co.jp/mashu

Restaurants and Cafés
Lake Akan
Oshokujidokoro Ajishin
1-3-20, Akankoonsen, Akanchō, Kushiro, 085-0467
T: 0154-67-2848
http://ajishin2848.parallel.jp

Senkaku
2-3-18, Akankoonsen, Akanchō, Kushiro, 085-0467
T: 0154-67-2272
https://senkaku-akanko.crayonsite.net

Teshikaga
Teshikaga Ramen
1-1-18 Mashū, Teshikaga, Kawakami-gun, 088-3201
T: 015-482-5511
http://www.teshikaga-ramen.com/shop/teshikaga/

Restaurant The Great Bear
883 Teshikagagenya, Teshikaga, Kawakami-gun, 088-3222
T: 015-482-3830
http://greatbear.sakura.ne.jp

Marukibune (Ainu cuisine)
Kotan, Kussharo, Teshikaga, Kawakami-gun, 088-3351
T: 015-484-2644
https://marukibune.jimdofree.com/

Restaurant & Café Poppo-tei
1-7-18, Asahi, Teshikaga, Kawakami-gun, 088-3204
T: 015-482-2412
https://poppotei.wixsite.com/home/en

Miraku Sushi
5-36, Kawayuonsen 1, Teshikaga, Kawakami-gun, 088-3465
T: 015-483-2036
http://mirakusushi.com

Inakaya Genpei
1-5-30 Kawayuonsen, Teshikaga, Kawakami-gun, 088-3465
T: 015-483-3338
https://www.masyuko.or.jp/introduce/genpei/

Coffee & Sweets Kanon
5-8 Sawanchisappu, Teshikaga, Kawakami-gun, 088-3464
T: 015-486-7890
http://www.sweets-kanon.com/

Museums & Art Galleries
Teshikaga
Ainu Folklore Museum
11 Kussharo, Teshikaga, 088-3341
T: 015-484-2128
Open 09:00-17:00 April to November
http://www.masyuko.or.jp/pc/english/sightseeing.html

Taihō Sumo Museum
2-1-20, Kawayu-onsen, Teshikaga, 088-3465
T: 015-483-2924

Open 09:00-17:00
http://www.masyuko.or.jp/sumo/

Akan
Marimo Museum
1-5-20, Akanko-onsen, Akan, Kushiro, 085-0467
http://www.akankisen.com/exMarimo.html

Activities
Akan Sightseeing Cruise
1-5-20, Akanko-onsen, Akan, Kushiro, 085-0467
T: 0154-67-2511
Open 08:00-16:00
http://www.akankisen.com/index.html

Teshikaga Navigation
For various areas and activities including Canoeing and Horseback Riding
http://www.masyuko.or.jp/pc/english/activity.html

Chapter Four
Nature Centres & Visitor Centres
Abashiri
Tōfutsu-ko Waterfowl and Wetland Center
203-3, Kitahama, Abashiri, 099-3112
T: 0152-46-2400
Open 09:00-17:00
Closed Mondays, Year End & New Year
https://www.abakanko.jp/en/seen/facility/tofutsu-ko.html

Lake Saroma
Lake Saroma Wakka Nature Center
242-1, Sakaeura, Tokoro, Kitami, 093-0216
T: 0152-54-3434
Open 08:00-17:00 April to October
http://www.city.kitami.lg.jp.e.fu.hp.transer.com/docs/2011042100243/

Abashiri
Michi-no-eki Ryūhyōkaidō Abashiri Tourist Information
5 Higashi 4, Minami 3, Abashiri, 093-0003
T: 0152-67-5007
Open 09:00-18:00
http://en.visit-eastern-hokkaido.jp/plan_your_trip/7285/

Abashiri Station Tourist Information
2 Shinmachi, Abashiri, 093-0046
T: 0152-44-5849
Open 09:00-17:30

Koshimizu

Koshimizu Tourism Association Visitor Center
Mont-bell, 474-7 Hamakoshimizu, Koshimizu,
 Shari-gun, 099-3452
T: 0152-67-5120
https://koshimizu-kanko.com/visitor/

Memanbetsu

Memanbetsu Airport Tourist Information
201-3, Memanbetsuchūō, Ōzora, Abashiri-gun, 099-237
T: 0152-74-4182

Michi-no-eki (Road Station; 24 hr toilets)

Lake Saroma
On Rt 238, 121-3, Naniwa, Saroma, Tokoro-gun,
 093-0421
T: 01587-5-2828
Open 09:00-17:00 Closed 31 December to 3 January
http://www.hokkaido-michinoeki.jp/michinoeki/1787/

Hanayaka Koshimizu
On Rt 244, 474-7, hamakoshimizu, Koshimizu,
 Shari-gun, 099-3452
T: 0152-67-7752
Open 09:00-17:30 Closed 1 January
http://www.hokkaido-michinoeki.jp/michinoeki/2375/

Bihoro Path
On Rt 243, Furuume, Bihoro, Abashiri-gun, 092-0022
T: 0152-75-0700
Open 09:00-17:00 Closed 31 December to 3 January
http://www.hokkaido-michinoeki.jp/michinoeki/2502/

Märchen-no-oka Memanbetsu
On Rt 39, 96-1, Memanbetsushōwa, Ōzora,
 Abashiri-gun, 088-3201
T: 0152-75-6160
Open 09:00-18:00 Closed 30 December to 5 January
http://www.hokkaido-michinoeki.jp/michinoeki/2548/

Ryūhyōkaidō Abashiri
5-1, Higashi 4, Minami 3, Abashiri, 093-0003
T: 0152-67-5007
Open 09:00-18:00 Closed 31 December and 1 January
http://www.hokkaido-michinoeki.jp/michinoeki/2986/

Accommodation

Abashiri

Dormy Inn Abashiri
1-1, Minami 2, Nishi 3, Abashiri, 093-0012
T: 0152-45-5489
https://www.hotespa.net/hotels/abashiri/

Abashiri Royal Hotel
Kita 6, Nishi 7, Abashiri, 093-0076

T: 0152-43-1888
http://abashiri-royal.jp

Hokuten-no-oka Lake Abashiri Tsuruga Resort
159 Yobito, Abashiri, 099-2421
T: 0152-48-3211
https://www.hokutennooka.com/en/

Hotel Abashiriko-sō
78 Yobito, Abashiri, 099-2421
T: 0152-48-2311
https://www.abashirikoso.com/english/index.html

Sea Side Stay (Guesthouse)
4-1, Daimachi, Abashiri, 093-0031
Tel: 090-7511-5314
https://seasidestay2.jimdofree.com

Campsites

Auto camp site Tent Land
1 Yasaka, Abashiri, 099-2422
T: 0152-45-2277
Open April to October
https://www.tentland.or.jp/english.html

Yobitoura Camping Ground
Yobito, Abashiri, 099-2424
T: 0152-44-6111
Open April to October
https://www.abakanko.jp/en/play/playinfo.html

Lakeside Park Notoro
5-1 Notorominato-machi, Abashiri, 093-0131
T: 0152-47-1255
Open June to September
https://www.city.abashiri.hokkaido.jp/
 040shisetsu/050sports/410lakesidepark_
 notoro/040camp.html

Restaurants and Cafés

Abashiri

Yakiniku Abashiri Beer Kan
4-1-2 Nishi, Minami 2-jo, Abashiri, 093-0012
T: 0152-41-0008
Open 17:00-22:00 Closed 31 December
http://www.takahasi.co.jp/beer/yakiniku/

Restaurant White House
2-5 Minami 4-jo Nishi, Abashiri, 093-0014
T: 0152-44-9552
Open 11:30-16:00 & 17:00-20:00 Closed Thursdays
https://whitehouse-abashiri.gorp.jp

Shusai-tei Kihachi
3 Minami 4 jonishi, Abashiri, 093-0014
T: 0152-43-8108

171

Open 16:30-23:00
http://www.theearth1990.co.jp/kihachi

Sushi-Dining Kiyomasa
Nishi 2, Minami 3, Abashiri, 093-0013
T: 0152-61-0003
Open 11:00-14:00 & 17:00-23:00 Closed Tuesdays
https://seiwa-dining.com/kiyomasa/

Shikishunsai Izakaya Sawa
Higashi 1, Minami 3, Abashiri, 093-0003
T: 0152-43-2645
Open 17:30-01:00 Closed Sundays
http://abashiri-sawa.com

Museums & Art Galleries

Hokkaidō Museum of Northern Peoples
309-1 Shiomi, Abashiri, 093-0042
T: 0152-45-3888
Open 09:30-16:30 Closed Mondays
http://hoppohm.org/english/index.htm

Okhotsk Ryūhyō Museum
244-3 Tentozan, Abashiri, 093-0044
T: 0152-43-5951
Open 09:00-16:30
https://www.ryuhyokan.com

Activities

Abashiri Nature Cruise
Inside Michi-no-Eki, 5-1, Higashi 4, Minami 3, Abashiri, 093-0003
T: 0152-44-5849
Open April to October (booking 09:00-18:00)
https://www.abakanko.jp/naturecruise/nature-cruise-e.html

Abashiri Drift Ice Sightseeing & Icebreaker
Inside Michi-no-Eki, 5-1, Higashi 4, Minami 3, Abashiri, 093-0003
T: 0152-43-6000
Open January to March
https://www.ms-aurora.com/abashiri/en/

Chapter Five

Nature Centres & Visitor Centres

Shiretoko World Heritage Conservation Center
186-10 Utoronishi, Shari, Shari-gun, 099-4354
T: 0152-24-3255
Open Summer 08:30-17:30 Winter 09:00-16:30
Closed Tuesdays
http://en.visit-eastern-hokkaido.jp/things_to_do/8416/

Shiretoko World Heritage Rusa Field House
8 Kitahama, Rausu, Menashi-gun, 086-1813

T: 0153-89-2722
Open May to October 09:00-17:00 November to April 10:00-16:00
http://shiretoko-whc.jp/rfh/_index.php

Shiretoko Rausu Visitor Center
6-27 Yunosawa, Rausu, Menashi-gun, 086-1822
T: 0153-87-2828
Open Summer 09:00-17:00 Winter 10:00-16:00
Closed Mondays, Year End & New Year
http://rausu-vc.jp/lake/

Shiretoko Goko Field House
549 Iwaobetsu, Onnnebetsu, Shari, Shari-gun, 099-4356
T: 0152-24-3323
Open 08:00-17:00
https://www.japan.travel/national-parks/parks/shiretoko/see-and-do/shiretoko-goko-lakes-field-house/

Utoro Tourist Information
Michi-no-eki Shirietoku, 186-8 Utoronishi Shari, Shari-gun, 099-4354
T: 0152-24-2639
https://www.shiretoko.asia/world/index.html

Shiretoko Rausu Tourism Association
Michi no eki Shiretoko Rausu, 361-1, Honchō, Rausu, Menashi-gun, 086-1833
T: 0153-87-3330
www.rausu-shiretoko.com/index.html

Michi-no-eki (Road Station; 24 hr toilets)

Shiretoko Rausu
On Rt 335, 361-1, Honchō, Rausu, Menashi-gun, 086-1833
T: 0153-87-3330
Open 10:00-16:00 Closed 28 December to 5 January
http://www.hokkaido-michinoeki.jp/michinoeki/2217/

Utoro Shirietoku
186-8 Utoronishi Shari, Shari-gun, 099-4354
T: 0152-22-5000
Open 09:00-17:00 Closed 29 December to 3 January
http://www.hokkaido-michinoeki.jp/michinoeki/2884/

Shari
37, Honchō, Shari, Shari-gun, 099-4113
T: 0152-26-8888
Open 09:00-19:00 Closed 31 December to 5 January
http://www.hokkaido-michinoeki.jp/michinoeki/2905/

Accommodation

Utoro
Hotel Shiretoko
37 Utorokagawa Shari, Shari-gun, 099-4351

T: 0152-24-2131
www.hotel-shiretoko.com

Iruka Hotel
5 Utoronishi, Shari, Shari-gun, 099-4354
T: 0152-24-2888
http://www.iruka-hotel.com

Kitakobushi Shiretoko Hotel & Resort
172 Utorohigashi, Shari, Shari-gun, 099-4355
T: 0152-24-2021
www.shiretoko.co.jp

Shiretoko Daiichi Hotel
306 Utorokawa Shari, Shari-gun, 099-4351
T: 0152-24-2334
https://shiretoko-1.com/

Shiretoko Yūhi-no-ataru-ie Onsen Hostel
189 Utorokawa Shari, Shari-gun, 099-4351
T: 0152-24-2764
https://www.yuuhinoataruie.com/

Rausu
Pension Rausukuru
74 Kaigan-chō, Rausu, Menashi-gun, 086-0815
T: 0153-89-2036
https://kamuiwakka.jp/rausu_kuru/

Shiretoko Serai
41-5 Rebun-chō Rausu, Menashi-gun, 086-1834
T: 0153-85-8800
https://www.shiretokoserai.com/

Campsites
Shiretoko National Park Rausu Onsen Yaeijō
Yunosawa, Rausu, Menashi-gun, 086-1822
T: 0153-87-2126
Open 10 June to 30 September
https://kanko.rausu-town.jp/spots/view/29

Kokusetu Shiretoko Yaeijō
Kagawa, Utoro, Shari, Shari-gun, 099-4112
T: 0152-24-2722
Open Mid June to 30 September
https://www.shiretoko.asia/hotel/camp_utoro.html

Restaurants and Cafés
Coffee Albireo
Familyshop Sasaki 2F, 14 Utorohigashi Shari-cho, Shari-gun, 099-4355
T: 0152-26-8101
http://110albireo.com/

Cafe & Bar 334
Kitakobushi Shiretoko Hotel 1F,

172 Utorohigashi, Shari, Shari-gun, 099-4355
T: 0152-24-2021
www.shiretoko.co.jp

Michi-no-Eki Utoro, Shirietoku Restaurant
Utoronishi, Shari, Shari-gun, 099-4354
T: 0152-22-5000
Open 09:00-15:00
http://www.hokkaido-michinoeki.jp/en/michi-no-eki/332/

Activities
Utoro
Gojiraiwa Kankō: Shiretoko Cruising
51 Utorohigashi, Shari, Shari-gun, 099-4355
T: 0152-24-3060
Open April to October
https://kamuiwakka.jp/cruising/index-en.php

Shiretoko Sightseeing Boat
53 Utorohigashi, Shari, Shari-gun, 099-4355
T: 0152-24-3777
Open April to October
https://www.shiretoko-kazu.com

Shiretoko Sightseeing Cruiser Dolphin
52 Utorohigashi, Shari, Shari-gun, 099-4355
T: 0152-22-5018
Open April to October
http://www.shiretoko-kankosen.com/2T: 015/index.html

Shiretoko Sightseeing Boat Aurora
Utorohigashi, Shari, Shari-gun, 099-4355
T: 0152-24-2146
Open April to October
https://www.ms-aurora.com/shiretoko/

Shiretoko Cycling Support
96 Utorohigashi, Shari, Shari-gun, 099-4355
T: 0152-24-2380
Open January to November
http://shiretokocycling.com/en/

Rausu
Gojiraiwa Kankō: Whale, Dolphin, Birdwatching Cruise
30-2, Hon-chō, Rausu, Menashi-gun, 086-1833
T: 0153-85-7575
https://kamuiwakka.jp/whale/index-en.php

Shiretoko Nature Cruise
27-1, Hon-chō, Rausu, Menashi-un, 086-1833
T: 0153-87-4001
https://www.e-shiretoko.com/en/

Shiretoko Rausu Lincle
13 Fujimi, Rausu, Menashi-gun, 086-1831
T: 0153-85-7604
https://shiretoko-rausu-lincle.com/en/

Museums & Art Galleries

Shari
Shiretoko Museum
49-2 Hon-machi, Shari-cho, Shari-gun, 099-4113
T: 0152-23-1256
Closed Mondays & National Holidays
http://shiretoko-museum.mydns.jp/english/english

Chapter Six

Nature Centres & Visitor Centres

Notsuke Peninsula Nature Center
63 Notsuke, Betsukai, Notsuke-gun, 086-1645
T: 0153-82-1270
Open Summer 09:00-17:00 Winter 09:00-16:00
Closed 30 December to 5 January
http://notsuke.jp

Nakashibetsu
Nemuro Nakashibetsu Airport Information Center
16-9 Kitanaka, Nakashibetsu, Nakashibetsu-gun, 086-1145
T: 0153-73-5651
Open 9:00-17:00
https://nakashibetsu-airport.jp/

Michi-no-eki (Road Station with 24 hr toilets)

Odaitō Michi-no-eki
On Rt 244, 5-24, Odaitō, Betsukai, Notsuke-gun, 086-1641
T: 0153-86-2449
Open 09:00-17:00
http://www.hokkaido-michinoeki.jp/michinoeki/3099/

Swan 44 Nemuro
On Rt 44, 1 Rakuyō, Nemuro, 086-0073
T: 0153-25-3055
Open 09:00-17:00
http://www.hokkaido-michinoeki.jp/michinoeki/2143/

Accommodation

Yōrōushi Onsen
Yuyado Daiichi
518 Yōrōushi, Nakashibetsu, Shibetsu-gun, 088-268
T: 0153-78-2131
http://www.yoroushi.jp/en/

Nemuro
East Harbor Hotel
26-1 Kōwa, Nemuro, 087-0027
T: 0153-24-1515
https://eastharborhotel.com

Field Inn Fūro-sō
249-1 Tōbai Nemuro, 086-0075
T: 0153-25-3905
http://www.nemuro.pref.hokkaido.lg.jp/ss/srk/kanko/nmrgsdb/5stay/5snm-fuurosou.htm

Lake Sunset
218-5 Tōbai, Nemuro, 086-0074
T: 0153-25-3510
http://www.lakesunset.jp

Minshuku Fūren
213-17 Tōbai, Nemuro, 086-0074
T: 0153-25-3919
http://www.nemuro.pref.hokkaido.lg.jp/ss/srk/kanko/nmrgsdb/5stay/5snm-fuuren.htm

Campsites

Chikutaku Campsite
101 Akesato, Nemuro, 086-0061
T: 0153-26-2798
Open April to October
https://chikutakucampsite.jimdofree.com

Odaitō Fureai Campsite
66 Odaitōmisaki, Betsukai, Notsuke-gun, 086-1642
T: 0153-86-2208
Open April to October
http://www.aurens.or.jp/~odaitoufureai/english.html

Restaurants and Cafés

Nemuro
Dorian
2-9 Tokiwa, Nemuro, 087-0041
T: 0153-24-3403
Open 10:00-20:45
https://www.tripadvisor.com/Restaurant_Review-g1122366-d1657316-Reviews-Dorian-Nemuro_Hokkaido.html

Nemuro Hanamaru Kaitenzushi
9-35 Hanazono, Nemuro, 087-0045
T: 0153-24-1444
Open 11:00-21:00
https://www.sushi-hanamaru.com/store/details/s01.html?#store

Bird Pal
1 Rakuyo, Michi no Eki Swan 44 Nemuro 1F, Nemuro,

086-0073
T: 0153-25-3055
Open Summer 11:00-15:00 Winter 11:00-14:00
https://www.swan44nemuro.com/restaurant/

Café & Restaurant Lake Sunset
218-5 Tōbai, Nemuro, 086-0074
T: 0153-25-3510
Open 10:00-21:00 Closed Wednesdays
http://www.lakesunset.jp

Activities

Betsukai
Bekkai Nature Cruise
Kankō-sen information Center 1F, 232 Minato, Odaitō,
    Notsuke-gun, 086-1643
T: 0153-86-2533
Open 08:30-16:30 June to October
http://www.aurens.or.jp/~kankousen/

Nemuro
Ochiishi Nature Cruise (Birdwatching)
Etopirikan, 112 Ochiishinishi, Nemuro, 088-1781
T: 0153-27-2772
Open 08:30-16:00 Closed 28 July to 4 August
http://www.ochiishi-cruising.com/reservation.html

Habomai Pleasure Cruise
Habomai Fishermen's Cooperative Association
    Building 2F, 120-1, Habomai 4, Nemuro, 087-0192
T: 0153-28-2124
Open 09:00-17:00 November to April
https://www.jf-habomai.jp/pleasure-cruises.html

Nemuro Footpath
http://www.nemuro-foottourism.com

Chapter Seven

Nature Centres & Visitor Centres

Akkeshi Waterfowl Observation Center
66 Sannushi, Akkeshi, Akkeshi-gun, 088-1140
T: 0153-52-5988
Open 08:45-17:00 Closed Mondays
http://www.akkeshi-bekanbeushi.com

Kiritappu Wetland Center
20 Yobansawa, Hamanaka, Akkeshi-gun, 088-1304
T: 0153-65-2779
Open 09:00-17:00 Closed Tuesdays
http://www.kiritappu.or.jp/center/en/

Akkeshi Tourist Information
Conchiglie, 2-2 Suinoe Akkeshi, Akkeshi-gun,
    088-1119
T: 0153-52-4139

Open 10:00-19:00 Closed Tuesdays
https://www.nihon-kankou.or.jp/hokkaido/016624/
    detail/01662aa1030000274

Accommodation

Hamanaka
Poroto Guide Lodge (B&B)
126 Poroto, Hamanaka, Akkeshi-gun, 088-1403
T: 0153-64-2528
http://poroto.la.coocan.jp/NewEnglish.html

Campsites

Kiritappu Misaki Campsite
Tōfutsu, Hamanaka, Akkeshi-gun, 088-1522
T: 0153-62-2111
Open June to October
https://calymagazine.com/blog/g-kiritappu/

Restaurants and Cafés

Akkeshi
Escale
Conchiglie 2F, 2-2 Suminoe, Akkeshi, Akkeshi-gun,
    088-1119
T: 0153-52-4139
Open 11:00-19:00
https://www.conchiglie.net

Oyster Bar Pittoresque
Conchiglie 2F, 2-2 Suminoe, Akkeshi, Akkeshi-gun,
    088-1119
T: 0153-52-4139
Open 11:00-19:00
https://www.conchiglie.net

Oyster Bar Kakiba
Kakikin 2F, 137 Ponto, Akkeshi, Akkeshi-gun, 088-1111
T: 0153-52-5277
Open 18:00-22:00
https://kakikin.com

Michi-no-eki (Road Station with 24 hr toilets)

Akkeshi
Conchiglie
2-2 Suminoe Akkeshi, Akkeshi-gun, 088-1119
T: 0153-52-4139
Open 10:00-19:00
https://www.conchiglie.net/

INDEX

A

Abashiri 25, 31, 80, 81, 86, 88, 91, 102, 105, 170–172
Abashiri Quasi National Park 7, 9, 12, 16, 80–83, 96, 103, 166
Accentor, Japanese 86
Accommodation 167, 169, 171–172, 174–175
Activities 168, 170, 172–173, 175
Agriculture 30, 84, 122, 124
Aidomari 96, 114
Ainu 4, 6–7, 10–12, 22, 25, 32, 61, 63, 66, 69, 71, 96–97, 99, 107–108, 134–135, 140, 150, 170
Ainu Moshiri 25, 135
Akan Tancho no Sato 32, 167
Akanko Ainu Kotan 63, 135
Akankohan Eco-museum Center 7, 54, 62, 168
Akkeshi 12, 101, 138, 151–154
Akkeshi–Kiritappu–Kombumori Quasi National Park 9, 16, 151–153, 166
Akkeshi Waterfowl Observation Center 122, 132, 153, 175
Alder 30–31, 34, 38, 41, 43
Alder, Japanese & Montane 36, 39, 41, 47, 98, 151
Apple, Siberian Crab 45
Ash, Manchurian & Späth's 23
Auklet, Rhinoceros 132, 143
Avens, Aleutian 98
Azalea, Daurian 61

B

Bamboo, Dwarf 22–23, 35, 37, 44, 49, 59, 86, 89, 115, 123, 146
Bay, Akkeshi 74, 154
Bay, Biwase 151
Bay, Nemuro 122, 132, 139
Bay, Notsuke 12, 131–133
Bear 5, 10, 13, 24, 62, 75–76, 83, 97, 99, 104, 106–107, 109, 114–115, 126
Beech, Siebold's 23
Bekambeushi Marsh 152–153
Biomineralization 65
Birch 7, 73, 85–86
Birch, Erman's, Japanese White & Stone 21, 23, 45, 59, 86, 98, 111
Bittersweet, Oriental 23
Blueberry, Oval-leaved 23
Bokke 18–19, 60, 62, 66
Bōkyō-no Misaki Park 143
Bluetail, Red-flanked 139, 146
Bugbane 51
Bulbul, Brown-eared 57
Bunting, Chestnut-eared 84, 104
Bunting, Common Reed 132, 147
Bunting, Masked 43
Bunting, Snow 128, 135
Butterbur, Japanese 35, 51, 76–77
Butterfly, Black-veined White 21

C

Cabbage, Asian Skunk 20, 22, 38, 64, 76–77
Café 56, 129, 168, 170–171, 173–175

Caldera, Akan 62
Caldera, Mashū 11, 18, 71–72, 132
Caldera, Kussharo 18, 55, 68–69, 85–86
Campsite 48, 56, 65, 69, 82–83, 93, 112, 125, 150, 159, 167–169, 171, 173–175
Cape Hanasaki 144
Cape Kimuaneppu 80, 82–83
Cape Kiritappu 11, 16, 147, 149–150
Cape Namida 151–152
Cape Nosappu 122, 135, 138, 140–144, 148
Cape Notoro 80–81, 83, 85, 88, 91
Cape Ochiishi 122, 132, 138, 146
Cape Puyuni 109
Cape Shirepa 16, 88, 138, 153–154
Cape Shiretoko 96–97, 99, 105, 111
Capron, Horace 125
Cave, Makkausu 112
Cattle 56, 84, 124–125, 141
Char, White-spotted 62, 127
Cherry 20, 35, 51
Chipmunk, Siberian 66
Chōko Bridge 69
Cicada 21, 65, 69
Cinquefoil, Meakan 98
Clione 23, 99, 102
Coastal Spit 81–84, 123, 128, 130–131, 134–135
Cormorant, Pelagic & Temminck's 84, 90, 104, 141, 143, 146, 150, 155
Corydalis, Blue 38
Cottongrass, Hare's-tail 151
Crane 4–5, 10, 24, 31–33, 35–37, 39, 41–43, 47, 51, 56, 91, 93, 99, 103, 129, 132–133, 135, 139, 140–141, 147, 150–151, 153–154
Cricket 19, 21, 93
Crow 36, 46, 56, 58, 126
Crowberry 45
Cuckoo 35–36, 43, 58, 83, 129, 134, 150
Current 34, 61, 80, 98, 100, 102, 126, 130, 148
Current, Oyashio 100

D

Damselfly, Red-eyed 21
Daphne, Kamchatka 20
Darner, Subarctic 21
Daylily 83, 92
Deer 13, 24, 37, 43–47, 50, 56, 67, 104, 106–107, 115–116, 128, 132, 135
Dipper, Brown 73, 109, 112, 115, 118
Dolphin 102, 105
Dove, Oriental Turtle 146
Dragonfly, Boreal 21
Duck 37, 49, 58, 83, 89–93, 104, 115–116, 129, 132, 141, 150, 154

E

Eagle 5, 8, 10, 19, 37, 43, 47–49, 51, 58, 83, 89, 91–92, 98–99, 102, 104, 112, 115–117, 119, 126, 128–129, 132, 138–141, 143, 154–155
Eco-museum 7, 54, 62, 163, 167–168
Ecological Succession 34, 40
Eelgrass 129, 139, 140
Elephant, Naumann's 11

Elm, Father David 23, 37

F

Falcon, Peregrine 129, 152
Fir, Sakhalin 23, 98
Flycatcher, Narcissus 58, 83
Flycatcher, Blue-and-white 58, 109
Fog 34–35, 71, 73, 111, 141, 143, 146, 148–150, 152, 155
Fog bow 149–150
Fox 13, 24, 35–36, 50, 56, 66, 75, 87, 115, 128, 132, 135
Fritillary, Kamchatka 92–93
Frog, Hokkaidō Brown 31, 34
Frog, Japanese Tree 34
Fumarole 18, 113

G

Gadwall 93
Gentian, Japanese 51
Geyser 18, 25, 112–113
Glasswort, Common 85
Grebe 51, 90, 93, 134
Greenfinch, Oriental 83
Green Flash 149
Grosbeak, Japanese 83
Grosbeak, Pine 111
Grouse, Hazel 67
Goldcrest 83
Guillemot, Spectacled 105, 108–109
Gull 37, 90, 92, 104, 108, 114, 116, 126, 129, 132, 135, 141, 143, 146, 150, 152, 155

H

Halo 149
Harbour 90, 105, 108, 112, 114, 116–117, 119, 132, 134–135, 138, 140, 142, 146
Hare, Mountain 50, 56, 67
Harrier, Eastern Marsh 92
Hashirikotan 45, 134–135, 138
Hawfinch 83
Hellebore, White 38, 51, 76–77
Hepburn romanisation system 6
Heron, Grey 43, 49, 139, 141
Higashi Mokoto Shibazakura Park 86
Hokuto 31, 36–37
Hoppō Gensei-kaen 141
Hornet, Asian Giant 13
Horse 34, 42–43, 84, 124, 150, 152
Hoso-oka 28, 31, 43, 46–47
Hot springs 17–19, 39, 51, 54, 60, 64–65, 69, 74, 105, 109, 113, 115, 158
Huchen, Japanese 34, 40, 48, 62, 127, 153
Hydrangea, Climbing 23

I

Ichani Karikariusu Historical Site 125
Ike-no-yu Rindō 69
Iris 21, 83, 85, 93, 129, 141, 150–152
Island, Chūrui 62
Island, Kenbokki 138, 151
Island, Kunashiri 23, 96, 111, 114, 119, 122–123, 129–130, 132, 148
Iwao-betsu 108–110

J

Jōmon 10–12, 125, 135

K
Kaiyō-dai   56, 122–123, 125
Kami-no-ko Pond   73
Katsura   23, 64
Kawayu Onsen   23, 25, 69, 71–72, 85–86, 159, 169
Kelp   102, 114–115, 143–146
Keyflower   152
Kite, Black-eared   43, 46, 51
Kingfisher, Crested   118
Kingfisher, Common   118
Kinmu-tō   54, 69
Kiritappu Wetland Center   122, 132, 138, 150
Knotweed, Giant   76–77, 140
Komakusa   98
Koshiabura   23
Koshimizu Gensei-kaen   92
Kottaro   42–43, 46, 51
Kushiro City   25, 28, 34–36, 38, 43, 47
Kushiro Shitsugen Wildlife Center   37, 167

L
Lacquer, Climbing   23
Lake Akan   11, 16, 18, 54–55, 60–64, 67–69, 135, 163
Lake Akkeshi   138, 153
Lake Chōboshi   146
Lake Fūren   12, 45, 116, 122, 130, 132, 134–135, 138–140
Lake Kussharo   18–19, 23, 25, 31, 34, 48, 54, 61, 68–72, 74, 80–81, 86, 159
Lake Mashū   16, 18–19, 34, 54, 56, 69, 71–73, 86, 123, 135, 159, 162
Lake Notoro   16, 80, 84–85
Lake On-ne-tō   54–55, 64–65, 140, 162
Lake Penke (Penke-tō)   16, 54–55, 60, 62
Lake Panke (Panke-tō)   16, 54–55, 60, 62
Lake Rausu   111
Lake Saroma   80–83, 85, 131, 170
Lake Saroma Wakka Nature Center   80, 83, 84, 170
Lake Shirarutoro   29, 48, 51, 167
Lake Takkobu (Takkobu-numa)   29, 43, 48–49, 168
Lake Tōfutsu (Tōfutsu-ko)   12, 74, 80, 85, 91–93, 103, 152, 170
Lake Tōro   16, 29, 46, 48–49, 51, 138, 167
Lake Tōsamuporo   141
Larch, Japanese   42, 47, 56, 123–124
Law, Japan's Natural Parks   9
Lighthouse, Hanasaki Misaki   144
Lighthouse, Kiritappu   150
Lighthouse, Notoro   88
Lighthouse, Notsuke   129
Lighthouse, Ochiishi   146
Lily, Heartleaf   22, 76–77
Lily, Siberian   83
Lily, Small Yellow Pond   110
Lime, Japanese   23, 37, 86
Linden, Japanese   37
Longshore Current   130
Longshore Drift   128, 130–131, 134
Longspur, Lapland   135
Loon, Pacific   143
Lupin, Siberian   20–21, 83, 93, 129

M
Magnolia   20, 23, 36, 51, 85, 87
Mammoth, Woolly   11
Manganese oxide   64–66
Maple   23, 61, 98
Maps   16, 28, 54, 80, 96, 122, 132, 138, 140, 162–163
Marimo   61–62, 68, 170
Martin, Sand   43, 56, 58, 139, 141, 150
Megaherb   76–77, 106–107, 140, 146
Meiji Period   10
Meiji Park   122, 132, 141
Merganser, Common   93, 133
Merganser, Red-breasted   89–90
Mink, American   46, 67
Mistletoe, Japanese   56–57
Monkshood, Hokkaidō   51
Moonbow   149
Mt Akan-Fuji   16–18, 39, 54–55, 64, 162
Mt Birao   51
Mt Hakutō   54–55, 64, 66, 68
Mt Horo-iwa   80–83
Mt Iwō   18, 68–69, 71, 86, 97, 110–111
Mt Mashū (Kamui-nupuri)   16, 19, 54, 71, 73, 159, 162
Mt Me-Akan   16–18, 39, 47, 54–55, 60–62, 64–65, 162
Mt Mokoto (Mokoto-yama)   55, 80–81, 85–86, 92
Mt Musa   16, 122–123, 125, 132, 159
Mt Nishibetsu   71, 159
Mt O-Akan   16, 39, 42, 47, 51, 54–55, 60–62, 64, 68, 86, 163
Mt Rausu   16, 80, 97–98, 108–112, 119
Mt Shari   12, 16, 71, 80, 84, 86, 92–93, 103, 132, 159
Mt Shiretoko   16, 96–97, 111
Mt Unabetsu   16, 103, 132
Mudsnail, Japanese   129, 139–140
Murrelet, Ancient   143
Museums & Art Galleries   25, 36, 60, 62–63, 69, 91, 125, 128, 144, 168, 170, 172, 174
Museum, Drift Ice (Okhotsk Ryūhyō Museum)   25, 172
Museum, Hokkaidō Museum of Northern Peoples   25, 91, 172
Museum, Hokuto Archaeological   36–37
Museum, Kushiro City   25, 168
Museum, Kussharo Kotan Ainu   25, 69
Museum, Moyoro Shell Mound Historic Site   91
Museum, Taihō Sumo   25, 170
Museum, Shibetsu Salmon Science   25, 125, 128
Museum, Shiretoko   25, 174

N
Nakashibetsu   122, 125, 135, 159
National Park, Akan–Mashū   9, 12–13, 16, 18–19, 21–22, 24–25, 34, 51, **54–77**, 81, 135, 159–163, 166
National Park, Kushiro Shitsugen   5, 7, 9, 12, 24, **28–51**, 55, 61, 152, 159, 166
National Park, Shiretoko   7, 9, 12, 18, **96–119**, 122, 158, 160
National Park System   8–9
Nature Centre   25, 31, 37, 51, 63, 83–84, 91, 105, 109–110, 115, 122, 129, 132, 138–139, 150, 153, 166, 168, 170, 172, 174–175

Nemuro City   98, 122, 132, 135, 138–139, 140–141, 144–145, 159, 174
Nemuro City Citizen's Forest   141
Nemuro Peninsula   101, 108, 116, 122, 124, 138, 141–142, 159
Nemuro Strait   23, 80, 96–98, 102, 111, 114, 116–117, 119, 122–123, 129–132, 134, 143, 148
Notoro Gensei-kaen   84
Notsuke Peninsula   12, 123, 128–129, 130–132, 134–135, 152
Notsuke Peninsula Nature Center   129, 174
Notsuke Lighthouse   129
Notsuke–Fūren Prefectural Natural Park   12, 134–135
Nutcracker, Spotted   86

O
Oak   23, 37, 69, 73, 86, 98, 103, 106, 110–112, 129, 141
Observatory, Furetoi   93
Observatory, Kushiro Marsh   38–39, 47
Observatory, Ura-mashū   73
On-ne-moto Harbour   142–143
On-ne-moto Bird Hide   122, 132, 140, 142–143
On-ne-moto Chashi-ato   142–143
On-ne-nai Visitor Center   39, 166
On-ne-tō Hot Falls   54, 64–65
On-ne-tō Rindō   140
Onsen   16, 23, 25, 54, 56, 60, 62, 64, 67–69, 71–72, 74, 85–86, 96, 110, 112, 114, 159, 162–163, 168–170, 173–174
Orca (Killer Whale)   10, 102, 114
Otter, River   46
Otter, Sea   143–146, 150
Owl, Blakiston's Fish   10–11, 20, 62, 99
Owl, Short-eared   92
Owl, Ural   49, 87
Oyster   81, 91, 153, 175

P
Park, Kujira-no-mieru-oka   96, 114
Park, Meiji   122, 132, 141
Pass, Bihoro   54, 68–69, 81
Pass, Koshimizu   54, 69, 81
Pass, Nagayama   54, 60, 62
Pass, Nogami   54, 103
Pass, Senpoku   54, 67
Pass, Shiretoko   96, 109–111
Peat   28, 30–31, 34, 39–41, 48, 146, 151
Phlox, Moss   86–87
Pine, Japanese Stone   21–23, 56, 69, 86, 98, 111
Plantain, Branched Indian   76–77
Pōgawa Shiseki Shizen Kōen   125
Pollock, Walleye   102, 112, 115
Porpoise, Dall's   102
Primrose, Wedge-leaf   98
Puffin, Tufted   108, 150

R
Ragwort, Alpine   51
Rainbow   149
Ramsar   30, 62, 151–153, 166
Rausu   8, 16, 18–19, 25, 80, 96, 98–99, 102, 105, 108–117, 119, 122, 173
Rausu Geyser   112–113
Rausu Kunashiri Observatory Tower   96, 119

Rausu Onsen campsite   112
Reed   31–32, 34–35, 37–38, 40–41, 43, 47–49, 92–93, 132–133, 147, 150–151
Restaurant   51, 56, 143, 167–168, 170–175
Rhododendron   23, 61, 69
River, Abashiri   67, 88
River, Bekambeushi   153
River, Iwao-betsu   109
River, Kushiro   28–31, 34, 43, 46–48, 51, 56, 69–70, 159
River, On-ne-betsu   104
River, Rusa   96, 115, 117
River, Rusha   96, 105, 108–109
River, Setsuri   42
Robin, Japanese   73
Rock, Oronko   105, 108
Rock, Wheel   144, 146
Rose, Wild   21, 45, 83, 92–93, 104, 129, 147
Rosefinch, Long-tailed   83, 132
Rowan, Japanese   21–22, 57, 73, 98
Rubythroat, Siberian   5, 83–84, 86, 129, 141, 143, 147, 150, 152
Rusa Field House   111, 115, 117, 172

S

Sable   5, 6, 24, 67
Salamander, Siberian   34
Salmon | Salmonid   10, 22, 104, 106, 126–128
Salmon, Cherry   11, 73, 75, 127
Salmon, Chum   102, 106, 126–127
Salmon, Masu   127
Salmon, Pink   102, 106, 108, 115, 126–127
Salmon, Red   127
Sanrihama Camping Ground   82
Saroma Michi-no-eki   80–82
Scaup, Greater   90, 132
Scoter, Black   58, 89–90, 132
Scoter, Siberian   58
Sea Angel   23, 99
Sea Lion   10, 23, 100–102, 115
Sea of Okhotsk   19, 23–24, 72, 74, 80–82, 86, 88, 89, 91, 93, 96–97, 100, 102–104, 108–109, 116, 130, 141, 148, 159
Sea Urchin   102, 115, 144–145
Seal   23, 37, 89, 91, 99–102, 106, 115–116, 132–133, 144, 150
Sedge   30–31, 38–39, 43, 144, 146, 151
Seseki Onsen   96, 114–115
Shearwater, Short-tailed   91, 132
Sheep, Suffolk   56
Shibetsu   16, 25, 119, 122, 128
Shintō   33, 86, 88
Shiretoko Five Lakes   96, 109–110
Shiretoko National Park Nature Center   96, 109
Shiretoko Peninsula   19, 23, 25, 71, 80–81, 83, 91, 96–100, 102–103, 105–106, 108–112, 114–117, 119, 122, 126, 129, 140, 145, 159
Shiretoko World Heritage Conservation Center   25, 96, 105
Shiretoko World Heritage Rusa Field House   96, 111, 115, 117, 172
Shiretoko World Natural Heritage Site   **96–119**
Shrimp, Lake   91
Shunkuni-tai   45, 135, 138–140, 152

Skylark, Eurasian   83–84, 91, 129, 139, 146, 150, 155
Smelt   64, 91
Snipe, Latham's   34, 58, 133
Sphagnum   40, 151
Spindle, Siebold's   23
Spindletree, Hamilton's   23
Spruce   23, 59, 64, 73, 85–86, 98, 103, 111, 123
Squirrel, Eurasian Red   65–66
Squirrel, Siberian Flying   63, 66, 87, 99
Stargazing   56
Steller, Georg Wilhelm   116
Stonechat, Stejneger's   36, 58, 83, 129, 139, 146, 147, 150, 155
Stubtail, Asian   83
Sumac, Climbing   23
Sun dog   149
Sun pillar   149
Suna-yu   69, 74
Sundew, Round-leaved   110–111
Swallow, Bank   43
Swallow, Barn   43
Swallowtail, Yellow or Old World   38
Swallowtail, Alpine Black   21
Swan, Whooper   19, 24, 36, 58, 70–71, 74, 91, 135, 138, 154
Swan 44 Nemuro   138, 174
Swift, Pacific   43, 58, 73, 108–109, 141, 152, 155

T

Takkobu Auto Campground   31, 48, 168
Tanuki   5, 24, 75
Temple, Namikiri-fudō   96, 112
Teshikaga   6, 37, 43, 51, 54–56, 60, 62, 68–72, 81, 85, 103, 169–170
Tetrapod   114, 129, 131, 134, 146
Theatre, Ikor   63
Thrush, Dusky   5, 57
Tit, Coal   144
Tōbai Bird Hide   122, 132, 139
Tōfutsu-ko Waterfowl and Wetland Center   80, 91, 170
Tree, Amur Cork   23
Tree, Prickly Castor Oil   23, 98
Treecreeper, Eurasian   38
Trillium, White   43, 51, 150
Trout, Brook   127
Trout, Brown   127
Trout, Dolly Varden   127
Trout, Rainbow   127
Tsurui Ito Tancho Sanctuary   32
Tsurui Village   4–5, 16, 28, 31–32, 36–37, 39, 42, 125, 167
Tsurumi-dai   28, 32
Tsutsuji-ga-hara Nature Trail   69

U

Ubaranai   80, 85
UNESCO World Natural Heritage Site   97, 117
Uratōfutsu   93
Utoro   25, 80, 96–97, 99, 104–105, 108–111, 114–115, 119, 172

V

Viburnum, Forked   23
Viewpoint, Biwase   151
Viewpoint, Chinbe-no-hana   153

Viewpoint, Hoso-oka   28, 31, 43, 46–47
Viewpoint, Kaiyō-dai   56, 122–123, 125
Viewpoint, Kottaro   28, 42–43
Viewpoint, Mt Mokoto   55, 85
Viewpoint, Pirikauta   153
Viewpoint, Ryūgū-dai   82
Viewpoint, Saroma   82–83
Viewpoint, Sarubo   28
Viewpoint, Sarurun   28, 49, 51
Viewpoint, Sōgaku-dai   60
Viewpoint, Sōkodai   60
Viewpoint, Tawa-daira   56
Viewpoint, Yume-ga-oka   31, 49
Vine, Crimson Glory   22
Vine, Hardy Kiwi   21
Vine, Silver   21
Vine, Variegated Kiwi   21, 61
Violet, Shiretoko   98
Visitor Centre   25, 39, 73, 112–113, 115, 122, 151, 166, 168, 170, 172, 174–175
Vole   35, 49–50, 56, 66, 75, 87, 99

W

Wagtail   109, 146, 150, 155
Wakka Primeval Flower Garden   83
Wakoto Peninsula   54, 69, 168
Walnut   23, 65
Warbler, Black-browed Reed   35, 40, 43, 83–84, 133–134, 147, 150
Warbler, Eastern Crowned   38
Warbler, Japanese Bush   73, 84
Warbler, Lanceolated   84, 134
Warbler, Middendorff's Grasshopper   83, 134, 139, 143, 146–147, 150, 152, 155
Warbler, Sakhalin Grasshopper   84
Warbler, Sakhalin Leaf   38
Watanabe Wild Bird Protection Area Fureshima   138, 147
Waterfall, Furepe   96, 109
Waterfall, Kamuiwakka   96–97, 105, 109
Waterfall, Kumagoe   96, 111–112
Waterfall, Oshinkoshin   96, 104
Waterfall, Sandan   96, 105
Waterfall, Seseki   96, 114
Waterfall, Shirafuji   96
Waxwing, Bohemian   57, 141
Waxwing, Japanese   57, 141
Weather   42, 43, 71–72, 74, 90, 106, 108, 110–111, 115, 124, 131, 145, 159, 166
Whale, Killer (Orca)   10, 102, 114
Whale, Northern Minke   5, 91, 102, 143
Whale, Sperm   102
Whale watching   91, 105, 112, 114, 173
Wingnut, Japanese   23
Woodpecker, Black   62–63, 66–67, 83, 139
Woodpecker, Great Spotted   38, 63
Woodpecker, Grey-headed   63
Woodpecker, Japanese Pygmy   63, 66
Woodpecker, Lesser Spotted   63
Woodpecker, White-backed   63
Wren, Eurasian   73, 118, 146

Y

Yew, Japanese   98

Mark Brazil PhD
Author, Expedition Leader and Lecturer

Mark Brazil was born in the UK (1955) and educated in England and Scotland. He has degrees in Biology, English Literature and Psychology, and has had careers in conservation biology, in natural history television, as a university lecturer, and as a freelance wildlife-expedition leader.

Mark combines his scientific interests with writing about the natural world. He began writing for magazines and newspapers while a student and is now a widely published author with several hundred articles and more than 10 books to his name.

Mark is a frequent expedition leader of small land-based, wildlife-focused expeditions worldwide, and also works in the expedition cruise industry from the Arctic to Antarctica. He is the founder of Japan Nature Guides.

Between international assignments, Mark, a long-term resident of Hokkaidō, works as a consultant, and as a writer and editor. His experience in nature tourism and adventure travel ranges from itinerary designer and developer to leader, consumer and most recently as an adventure travel evaluator.